EXPERIMENTS WITH TRUTH AND NON-VIOLENCE

China Challenged

About the Authors

Dr. Bhaskar Vyas (1937) and **Dr. Rajni Vyas** (1937) are medical specialists, hypnotherapists and stem cell scientists. They are visiting professors at the M.S. University, Department of Psychology, Baroda, India. Both have been Past Presidents, Indian Society for Clinical and Experimental Research in Hypnosis. They are examiners for M.Sc. and Ph.D. at Swami Vivekanand Yoga Anu Sansthan. They are convincing protagonists of mind-body continuum.

They are philosophers studying consciousness. Their bifurcation to hypnotherapy was to explore the States of Consciousness. They have studied esoteric meditation practices of Hindu and Buddhist traditions as well as teachings of J. Krishnamurty, Zen practices, Kashmir Shavism, Vajrayana and varieties of trans-cultural religious experiences.

That led them to the Dalai Lama in 1987 and, in Service of Tibet. Rooted in Gandhian thought, Tibetan political tragedy was eloquently evident to their sensibilities. A quantum jump in compassionate consciousness was embodied in the personage of His Holiness. A cry in the wilderness in the innocent naïve smiling faces of the orphans in Tibetan Children Village provided a glimpse of what catastrophic damage can be caused through crooked clutches of convoluted communist ideology. This is the genesis of the book.

The explorations in regeneration and rejuvenation processes led them to the study of genomics and stem cells. Their present commitment is to decipher genomics of States of Consciousness and the healing potentials of stem cells.

While their devotion to the Dalai Lama will devolve for lives to come, they now continuously interact with Tibetan youths and sing Rangzen songs with them. They profoundly believe, "We shall overcome some day."

Experiments with Truth and Non-Violence

China Challenged

(Revised and Enlarged Edition)

By
Bhaskar Vyas
Rajni Vyas

CONCEPT PUBLISHING COMPANY PVT. LTD.,
NEW DELHI-110059

ISBN-13: 978-81-8069-900-9

First Published 2007
Revised & Enlarged Edition 2013

Published and Printed by

Concept Since 1974

Concept Publishing Company Pvt. Ltd.
A/15-16, Commercial Block, Mohan Garden
New Delhi-110059 (India)
T: 25351460, 25351794, *F*: 091-11-25357109
E: publishing@conceptpub.com, W: www.conceptpub.com
Editorial Office: H-13, Bali Nagar, New Delhi-110 015, India.

Cataloging in Publication Data--Courtesy: D.K. Agencies (P) Ltd. <docinfo@dkagencies.com>

Vyas, Bhaskar.
Experiments with truth and non-violence : China challenged / by Bhaskar Vyas, Rajni Vyas. — Rev. & enl. ed.
p. cm.
Includes bibliographical references and index.
ISBN 9788180699009

1. Bstan-'dzin-rgya-mtsho, Dalai Lama XIV, 1935- —Exile—India. 2. Tibet Autonomous Region (China) —History—1951- I. Vyas, Rajni, joint author. II. Title.

DDC 294.3923 23

DEDICATED
to
THE TORCHBEARERS OF RANGZEN

Never give up
No matter what is going on
Never give up
Develop the heart
Too much in your country is spent developing the mind
Instead of that,
Be compassionate
Work for peace in your heart and, in the world
Work for peace.
And, I say again,
Never give up
No matter what is going on around you
Never give up.
And we say, never give up independence!

Foreword to the Second Edition

China's treatment of Tibet is an indelible stain on its conscience. Tibet is not just a piece of land or a territorial unit to which China can make proprietary claims. It is a people, and no people can be said to belong to another without being regarded as slaves with no will and liberty of their own.

Even if China's initial annexation of Tibet were accepted as justified in ethics, history and international law, its subsequent systematic destruction of Tibetan civilisation is nothing short of scandalous. It eroded Tibet's identity and cultural heritage, rendered its people anchorless, caused deep divisions among them, and destroyed the integrity of their way of life by transplanting alien ethnic groups. This was done in the name of integrating Tibet into China and developing among its people a common sense of belonging with the rest of the Chinese people. The results have been opposite. The Chinese policy deeply alienated the Tibetans, created a measure of moral unease among its own enlightened groups, sullied the good name of the country, and created a festering sore that weakens its stability. China is a strong, thoughtful and powerful country and can certainly afford to be generous in its treatment of its regional, religious, ethnic and other minorities.

The Tibetans have a genuine grievance, but mass violence is not the answer because it will not work against such a determined opponent and is also counterproductive. The Tibetans have only two options: to mount a quiet and sustained moral and political pressure on the Chinese government from within and outside the country, and to urge the international community to keep the issue alive in relevant global forums and exert diplomatic and political pressure on China.

In their struggle, the Tibetans could not have had a better leader than His Holiness the Dalai Lama. A man of great natural dignity and nobility, he is firmly committed to the principle of non-violence. Free of duplicity and full of goodwill to his opponents, he is nevertheless shrewd enough to know what is possible to achieve and how to retain the loyalty of his rightly impatient followers. He is highly articulate, at ease with both Western and Tibetan idioms of thought, and provides an authoritative and dignified voice to his people's aspirations.

Drs. Bhaskar Vyas and Rajni Vyas' well written book tells the story of the Dalai Lama's life in the context of his country's struggle for cultural autonomy. Sensitive to both the personal and political dimensions of the story, it locates the Dalai Lama's life in its political context even as it sees the latter through the prism of how he thinks and feels about it. Drs. Vyas trace the history of Tibet, explain the complexity of Buddhism, and examine the origins and dynamics of its struggle. They show their sympathy for the struggle without becoming its naïve propagandist. I learnt much from it and recommend it to all with interest in the subject.

Bhikhu Parekh
University of Westminster and House of Lords

Preface to the Second Edition

Following the watershed event of disintegration of Soviet Russia, the world has become a unipolar world. With the advent of New Millennium, pragmatism so prevails that all isms are "wasms" now. Fundamental human values are solidly enshrined in 21st Century civilization. And yet, interactions between the nations and civilizations are basically entwined to the trade and commerce. Machiavelli appears to be the currency of the political class now.

Lofty communist ideals have remained in Des Capital. Instead of withering of the State following the dictatorship of the proletariat, The New Class has emerged in China that is stifling the fundamental values of freedom, equality and fraternity for maintaining its stranglehold. In contrast, peoples' movements have toppled several dictatorial regimes in Africa and Middle East. Karl Marx considered Class Consciousness as fundamental to the conflicts for revolutionary change. That is a far cry: today, the world maps are changing because of hunger for fundamental freedom. There is enough evidence in contemporary history to deduce this as a prime motivation for the upheavals.

The evolution of the motives cannot be traced as a straight line while interpreting historical data through the statements of formal logic or of political science. What rationalists decry as poetical, emotive, pictorial or motivational has a tremendous relevance to life processes and happenings at the societal-political-cultural- religious-spiritual panorama. They are the gigantic forces that demolish demonic dictatorial regimes. This consciousness mode is an attribute of all and, is experientially known to the most. When the skeptics will dismiss it as romantic, they are denying the Forces of History; they are refuting the Evolution of Consciousness. They simply need to regress to the state of pristine innocence of a childlike consciousness to realize that ideas are the first reality.

The holistic view of interdependence and interconnectedness for our civilization prevails today. There are no isolated facts/events in the world; even a subatomic entangled particle, automatically changes its axis of rotation no sooner the axis of rotation of the corresponding one is changed through a manipulation. Yet paradoxes abound: they are being perpetrated through fear of tyranny by military might – spectre of Tiananmen Square horror – and, sustained by the greed arising out of spreading virus of conspicuous consumerism – "imagine the collapse of economy that can occur if one party system collapses". As a counter-point, hermeneutic approach to history provides a clear perspective of the process of change; it provides hope to find a solution too.

In the discursive, dialectical, didactic cycle of thesis – antithesis – synthesis, it is time that a new synthesis emerges in China. Rooted in great philosophers, Confucius and Lao-tse, the Chinese Genius must flower out. In the orchestration of a symphony being played out through the Collective Consciousness of a huge mass of humanity that calls itself Chinese, a new order will have to be born. A vital key has gone astray in the composition of the orchestra: there must be a built-in cybernetic formula that is bound to correct itself.

This is a process in History and, is provided succor through the geniuses of a few. They have the memories without hang over; they are intelligent with great wisdom; and, they are patient since they know that God knows the Truth but waits. How such a person comes to be selected may be arbitrary and mystical; yet, the Dalai Lama is one such person.

Following his immaculate and articulate commitment to the means of Truth and Non-violence, Tibet has made huge sacrifices and endured great suffering. However, when everything seems to be going to pieces, a huge wave of awakening comes and on the topmost crest of the wave is a shining soul. He is the impetus that makes the nation rise. The Dalai Lama has engraved a lasting imprint on the collective consciousness of the present day civilization. In so doing, the Chinese main stream will change as surely as the Changing Course of Brahmaputra. Moreover, entire Tibetan tragedy will have further humanized the humanity to a higher level of consciousness.

We gratefully acknowledge our gratitude to several Tibetan workers, activists and officials as well as organizations. Their names are not mentioned simply to spare the embarrassment to them. We have interacted and derived inspiration from Presidents and members of Tibetan Youth Congress. They are, we repeat, the Torchbearers of Rangzen. First Edition was released by George Fernandes and Jaya Jaitly. For the release of Hindi translation, they travelled to Baroda. Sudershan Aiyengar, Vice-Chancellor of Gujarat Vidyapith introduced the book to his students as well as at the inaugural function at New Delhi. Suresh Parikh has an invisible contribution. Dr. D.V. Nene has made several suggestions.

Introduction by Lord Bhikhu Parekh, an internationally renowned scholar of Gandhian thought, has added further significance to the book.

Mr. Ashok Mittal, Concept Publishing Company has made dedicated efforts. Without their perseverance, second edition may not have been possible.

Preface to the First Edition

We present this book with great humility and devotion to His Holiness the Dalai Lama on the occasion of his 72nd birthday. We have embarked upon this task with no little trepidation. Our only asset is the privilege that we have had of sitting with him for numerous audiences over last twenty years. We had little understanding of the Tibetan situation when we first approached him in 1987 to understand the Buddhist concept of consciousness. Yet our bearings are in the Indian freedom struggle. After spending a few days at Dharmashala then, we have been repeatedly drawn over there, always to look for the news of any break through that has not occurred thus far. In the year 2000, we read out a few pages from our book, *The Collision of Cultures.* There the Dalai Lama was quoted as saying that what happens to Tibet is now a mandate of heaven. He asked us to revise and revisit the entire situation because, though rooted in *karmic connection,* he has not left the matters to drift. That was a command that we had to follow and so this book.

Rooted as we are in the Buddhist postulate that we have to use our reason, the book has turned out to be way away from hagiography. We have come to a bifurcation point with him. We were devastated to hear the Dalai Lama announce on March 10, 2005 that Tibet is willing to remain as a part of China. With profound reverence to him, we believe not even the Dalai Lama has the right to give away Tibet. And, he is following Mahatma Gandhi once again, so as to commit a Himalayan blunder.

Considering the increasing might of China, our book may be thought as a cry in wilderness. We believe that youth is the very salt of the Nation and Tibetan youths will not fail their motherland in carrying the torch of Rangzen. Rohit Mehta, a freedom fighter and our mentor in philosophy, has taught us to believe in fundamental truths. When he wrote in 1935 that USSR cannot survive, that may have been said to be idle talk. We have faith in values that lie deeply ingrained in human heart so that Tibet will be a free nation someday.

It was imperative that the permission to use the letters from various dignitaries should be sought. We have written numerous letters to them. The response was encouraging since none of them denied permission; nobody has answered our repeated requests. Should the publication hurt them in anyway, we apologize. International support is the mainstay of Tibet policy and the correspondence is self-evident to demonstrate the results of experiments with truth and non-violence.

Several Tibetans have helped us throughout the period of six years that have gone in writing this book and before that. We wish not to embarrass them by mentioning their names. We are grateful to the Department of Information and International Relations for the photographs that we have taken from their album. Photograph of Tenzin Tsundue is taken from the *Hindu* and we are indebted to them. The book would not have seen the light of the day but for the support of Damodar Nene, Suresh Parikh, Sudarshan Iyengar, Ravindra Varma. Tsering Shakya spent time, on a Sunday morning in London sharing inside view of his Chinese visit. Anthony Copley was with us then. Prof. Dava Norbu provided data about the proceedings at United Nations. Prof Devvrat Pathak did a prepublication review.

We are obliged for the support we have received from Tibetan Youth Congress and its maverick President, Kalsung. Finally, we remain indebted to Shri Ashok Kumar Mittal of Concept Publishing Company. They have worked over time to get the book printed for release on 6th July, 2006. In the process they have been proactive so as to involve themselves for the Tibetan cause. That makes their work a mission.

Baroda

Bhaskar Vyas
Rajni Vyas

Contents

List of Colour Photographs

Introduction to the First Edition

It gave me immense pleasure to meet three medical doctors when they called at my residence. I mistook them to be old comrades since they told me that they have worked on a book on His Holiness the Dalai Lama and are exploring the relevance of ends and means.

Historical facts may be fudged, but the freedom is the fundamental appetite of the soul. The book harps on this basic tenet in the history of human civilization. While His Holiness is experimenting very patiently with the tool of non-violence following the footsteps of Mahatma Gandhi, the forces of history are experimenting with Tibet. Whether this tiny feeble nation without much of wherewithal will survive in the face of multifarious forces of consumerism, globalization and, in contrast, increasing yearning of the newer generation for the spiritual values, is a test case for the believers in value based action. It is said that God sees the Truth but waits. Whatever God that it may be, whether God in the form of Marxist philosophy or, God in the form of a reincarnated Dalai Lama, it has waited enough. Tibetans, inside and outside of Tibet, have a tryst with destiny. That tryst is in the form of independence, call it by whatever name, be it genuine autonomy, suzerainty or *Rangzen.* Tibet as a nationality and Tibetans as people have proved themselves so, through the acid test of innumerable critiques by political pundits as well as international jurists and, through the sacrifice with blood. And their just aspirations must prevail.

The sacrifice and sufferings of Tibetans are unparalleled in the history of freedom struggles. The Dalai Lama has indeed walked more than half way through his middle way proposals. Marxist ideology envisaged the welfare of the humanity. Let our comrades in China administer that with a human face. The world has taken over to many of the capitalistic ways and, even when the new generation remembers Marx, does so as the God that failed. If Marx was face to face with the distortions of the Chinese ideological implications, he also would not want to be a Marxist of that brand.

Having gone through various vicissitudes in implementation of Marxist ideology and its dealing with fundamental values, I have come to believe, Freedom first and freedom till the last. Only Tibetans will decide their destiny and in that assertion of their birth right, not even His Holiness can deter the torchbearers of Rangzen.

I consider that Drs. Bhaskar and Rajni Vyas have done a valuable service to the cause of Tibetan independence through elaborate efforts to discover history and expound political philosophy. Aldous Huxley will feel gratified: means are the ends.

2nd October, 2005 **Rajni Kothari**
Sahvikas Society
Delhi-110 092

1
The Issue

In a contest between two parties with conflict of interest there could be several ways that the concerned parties engage in conflict resolution. When views differ it is elemêntary that each party may view its own stand and position as correct but is open to listening and carefully considering the opponent's views. This leads to a process of dialogue. Classically speaking this is an interaction between thesis and anti-thesis and it may result in a synthesis that might be satisfying to both parties. This is a win-win situation. It involves the least expenditure of energies of different kinds and probably yields a kind of growth that surpasses the input. In this synergetic interaction, summation of the parts build up a whole that is larger than the total.

However, there are contentious issues where motivation of different kinds is behind the actions. Often people say things they do not mean. Promises are made and not kept. And in such situation both the parties may use the process of dialogue as a means of tossing the issue and procrastination so as to while away the time. The process is either neutral as evident by stagnation. More often than not, it is a lose-lose situation.

It may also happen that in the process of such game playing one of the parties, (self righteous and aggrieved as it may see itself), perceives procrastination in the process as a simple waste of time. It may lose patience. The means at its disposal may not be of the kind to afford the waste of time. Often, in such a situation, the other party is stepping on the toes. This may bring about an abreaction so that the inconvenienced party gets provoked and hits back physically. This is the genesis of terrorism.

But it has now tilted the balance in the game instead of a 'lose-lose' game. It has turned into a 'win-and-lose' game. If the power of the terrorists' attack is strong, that party may win. This was the case in the revolutions of nineteenth and twentieth century. On the other hand, violence has been decried as un-civil and the present civilization has come to abhor its use in conflict resolution. In conflicts with the establishment, it is the established authority which is more powerful when the contest turns out to be a contest of might. More powerful wins. Obviously it will be the State when it is the case of State *versus* People in a straight combat with the use of repressive measures by the State.

Probably the greatest contribution of the twentieth century in the field of dynamics of human interaction was to evolve a method where Right may engage in a fight with the Might; however weak the Right be against however mighty the powerful opponent be. Mahatma Gandhi described this as a fight between the Right and the Might. This noble crusade is based on non-violent, non-cooperation, inviting any amount of toil, suffering, incarceration, even death.

According to Mahatma Gandhi every human being is endowed with conscience. What is fundamentally right and true does not need to be argued out through any process of logic or law but is intrinsically in the minds of all people. People refuse to see their own wrong doing because they are blinded by their so-called self-interest which may be just greed. According to Mahatma Gandhi, when the party that has been wronged continues to assert the values that are time-cherished and universal, the other side is bound to realize, sooner or later, the true ground realities and come to even terms.

The independence struggle led by Mahatma Gandhi provides a road-map of non-violent actions. He called off the nation-wide agitation in 1921 because of a single violent action at Chauri-Chaura. This is unique. When people courted death for a few grains of salt in 1930, it resulted in the Salt Satyagraha. This turned out to be soul-stirring for the universal world-consciousness. It made the British search their souls. The method has come to be a legacy for mankind, so that for generations to come this may be cultivated, refined and enriched so as to become a universal model for conflict resolution[1].

The minds of the mighty are not always open to dialogue. Those who are powerful are prone to believe that with strokes of power, they may wipe out a weak enemy. An enemy he is; so he must be wrong! And what the world history has seen during the period following Gandhi's assassination is a definite assertion of the anti-thesis. There has not been even a single year in post-Gandhi era when some kind of war was not going on somewhere in the world. Concurrently, it is of paramount importance to note that all the wars that have been waged during this period have failed to sort out any of the issues.

In the struggle between the weak and the mighty, lets suppose that truth was to be on the side of the weak. Then, is there any natural design that protects the weak? Can the weak survive the onslaught of the powerful? Is there a phenomenon like 'survival of the weakest?' If the weak were to survive, its methodology has to be different. Non-violence and truth are the values that philosophers preach because of their intrinsic worth. They may also be perceived as strategic tools of the weak. They would be powerful tools for use by the weak. They were able to so engage the mighty so as to disturb, perturb, vacillate and yield.

Let us paraphrase the Tibetan struggle. The United Nations debates label it "Tibet question". At one point of time the Dalai Lama called it, issue of Tibetan independence. Then he called it, issue of Tibetan autonomy. The Chinese have used phrases like rebellion, subversion and division of the motherland. Their references to the Dalai Lama are derogatory.

The purpose of the book is not to catalogue or review the facts. Political scientists would frown at there being no question of trying to counterbalance the arguments. Dialectics, discourse, discursive logic and discussion are the basics for political science. This is not a book of political science. We reflect on the actions of· the Dalai Lama and juxtapose them with repercussions such as the conclusions arrived at by the international jurists as well as lawyers. In 1956, the International Commission of Jurists confirmed the genocide in Tibet. Thereafter there are several such reports which castigate the Chinese. Several international conferences of lawyers have concluded that Tibet is an occupied nation.

We have, therefore, not considered it worthwhile to engage into a discussion of the righteousness of the Tibetan struggle. Our objective is directed to:

1. Explore the efficacy of the tools, namely truth and non-violence as strategically powerful, or otherwise.
2. Illustrate this exploration through the actions of the Dalai Lama; most important being the latest in renouncing his sovereign role.
3. Reflect on the ends aimed at and incidentally accrued in terms of values.

REFERENCE

1. Gene Sharp, *The Dynamics of Nonviolent Action*, Vols. I-III, Boston, 1984.

2

The Escape: Diplomacy of Only Choice

Historical Perspective

The Thirteenth Dalai Lama dies, 1933; Tibet is governed by the rule of regents – 1933-50; The Fourteenth Dalai Lama, Tenzin Gyatso is born in Amdo province – 1935; Following the Long March, Mao-tse-Tung comes to rule mainland China-1949; Amdo and Kham provinces overrun by PLA – 1950; the Dalai Lama crowned as the Sovereign – 17th November, 1950; the Dalai Lama moves to south – December 1950; Tibetan delegation arrives in Beijing – April 1951; Seventeen Point agreement is signed – May 1951; Panchsheel treaty signed between India and China – 1954; The Dalai Lama's visit and stay in China – 1954; Visit to India by the Dalai Lama, for Buddha Jayanti Celebration – 1956; Refused asylum by Nehru; People's unrest, the Dalai Lama flees Tibet – 1959; revokes Seventeen Point Agreement – 1959; Sets up Government in Exile – 1959.

Diplomacy is evolving to a better and finer mode from time immemorial: survival strategies remain more or less same. In a challenging situation, most individuals would take recourse to either fight or flight. Some people have innate ability to manage to suvive; however, it is an art that can be enhanced and cultivated too. While diplomacy is exercised for betterment of national prospects in strategic arenas, and so requires sophistication, facility to ensure survival is a natural attribute of entire mankind. Diplomatic exercise for the Dalai Lama, then a boy of barely 16, had begun when he was crowned a sovereign.

Tibetan culture identifies the individual as an inseparable part of Nature. The individual and the environment are seen to reflect (w)holistically. So, when there was an earthquake in the summer of 1950 in Lhasa, Tibet and way up to Kolkata simultaneously, it meant to convey portentous ill-meanings to the Tibetans. About the same time, there was an extraordinary celestial event. There was a red glow in the sky with a very loud bang. Heinrich Harrer, (author of *Seven Years in Tibet*), tried to explain to the Dalai Lama the scientific basis behind such happenings. However, the Dalai Lama, true to his tradition, believed this to be something truly mysterious and metaphysical.

Let us just overview the backdrop before the coronation. Seventeen years (1934-1950) had gone since the demise of the last (13th) Dalai Lama. The rule by the Regency during these years was a nefarious rule by corruption, nepotism, feuds and exploitation. That the Dalai Lama had to be a King is not his choice. It is also anticipated that he will be able to restore proper governance. The people of Tibet have unshakable faith in their God-King. He may be just a young child and so, immature. But that is only according to his physical body; he is, in fact, the embodiment of wisdom accumulated over his previous thirteen incarnations.

Amongst all the factors that influence outcome of any action, howsoever considerate and wise. Tibetan tradition considers the mandate of heaven as the most important. This mandate is not arbitrary. It is ordained through a chain of events of *karmic connection*. Through the best of wisdom, the choice of any person is bound to be in accordance with his *karma* of the past, including his previous birth[1]. So the Dalai Lama, though a boy of sixteen, was supposed to have the accumulated merit and wisdom of all his predecessors when he was discovered as a young boy of three. Tibetans had no doubt that he will lead them wisely.

The respect for the mandate in Tibetan tradition is reflected in the institution of the oracle. An oracle is a person who has almost magical powers. There is supposed to be a spirit named Dorje Drakden. This spirit is the protector divinity of the Dalai Lama and it manifests in a magical trance through the Nechung oracle. No decision of any consequence can be taken without consultation to this spirit. It is this oracle that has given a clear mandate that though minor in age, the Dalai Lama should assume temporal powers.

The Dalai Lama was crowned to the Lion Throne as sovereign of Tibet at a tender age under impelling circumstances of Chinese threat. He will go down in history as the youngest sovereign. The period of indecision and mal-administration following the death of 13th Dalai Lama had left Tibet standstill while the world underwent a metamorphosis during the same period. The Second World War, emergence of Cold War between the two power blocs – communism *versus* capitalistic free enterprise, independence of India and the communist take over of China through the Long March of People's Liberation Army led by Mao. Even such cataclysmic events did not wake up Tibet from its self-absorption till the Chinese knocked at their door.

The monarch in the form of the boy Dalai Lama could hardly have been expected to understand the magnitude of events as well as the stature of two giant personalities that were to influence his life. Mao so overshadowed the Chinese scene, that people almost came to believe that he was almost the sole arbiter of Chinese destiny. Even when the Dalai Lama was thought to have realized that there was no escape from the jaws of the Chinese Dragon, he is said to have penned a poem in praise of Chairman Mao. The poem describes Mao as one who gives "timely rain".[2] The poem reads as,

> "Your will is like the gathering of clouds, your call like a thunder;
> From these comes timely rain to nourish selflessly the Earth!"

The poem now adores a decoration at the Buddhist Temple of Broad Charity at Beijing as 'Hymn to Mao.'

Yet, historical enmity with China was taught to him right from his infant age. So the forbidding of the Chinese invasion, though it may not be explicit in detail in the mind of the boy-king Dalai Lama, was not lost to him. However, good people see no evil. This could be particularly evident in the naivety of an innocent adolescent mind. This becomes clear with the Dalai Lama's first meeting with his elder brother after assuming office. In fact, this is his first encounter with realities of treachery and subterfuge.

An obviously shattered elder brother, Taktser Rimpoche, told him what the practice of communism involves. He had been able to get out of the clutches of the Chinese on the promise that either he will convert the Dalai Lama to communism, or failing which he will kill him! His immediate advice to the Dalai Lama is to go to India in Exile and seek US support to counter China.

The actions of the Dalai Lama during 1950-1959 have to be viewed in this perspective. He is a helpless prisoner within his own homeland. The poem that he wrote, the subsequent statements and events culminating in three letters that he wrote to General Tan before his escape, reflect an attitude of learnt helplessness. Winston Churchill would want defiance in the face of defeat and magnanimity in victory. There is no possibility for the Dalai Lama to show magnanimity in victory even 50 years after. There can be tragic consequences to defiance in a hopeless situation. There is no value in inviting incalculable suffering or even death just for the sake of defiance. Confucius and Lao tse preached the bending of the bamboo in the face of storm. The young Dalai Lama may not have had any brush with the Chinese philosophers but to bend rather than break is common wisdom.

The first official action by the Dalai Lama after his coronation was the appointment of two prime ministers – Lobsang Tashi and Lukhangwa. Along with his newly appointed ministers one of the most important decisions by the juvenile sovereign was to dispatch emissaries to USA, UK, India and Nepal. The delegations that he sent abroad soon after his coronation were turned away except from the Chinese. Meanwhile, the Peoples Liberation Army has already marched into Eastern Tibet and Amdo and Khan Provinces fell. Against the strength of 80,000 PLA, the Tibetan strength was a meagre 8,500, and that too with antiquated weapons.

The desperation of the Dalai Lama was clear when he moved to the South soon after his coronation. The intentions of the Kashag were also evident when they moved a part of Potala treasures along with him to South. Obviously, the prisoner had been exploring the escape routes.

A ray of hope emerged when the Dalai Lama was invited to India on the eve of the celebrations of 2500 years of Buddha Jayanti. But there was overpowering despair when Prime Minister Nehru turned down the request for the Dalai Lama to stay on in India. His desperation to stay in India is best seen from a not so known anecdote. When he was in Kolkata, he was indisposed and needed a doctor. He chose Dr. B.C. Roy, the then Chief Minister of West Bengal! Roy was hardly a medical doctor by then but the choice was dictated by his closeness to Nehru. The Dalai Lama is said to have asked for Roy's good offices to persuade Nehru. Whether he obliged or not, this too did not work. Torn in the dilemma of returning to his people and finding a safer haven to resist the Chinese from somewhere else. The Dalai Lama was guided by the oracle to return to an unsafe and insecure future in the homeland. Lukhangwa, the then Prime Minister of Tibet, had exclaimed in desperation that when men become desperate they consult gods and when gods become desperate they tell lies!

The subsequent visit of the Dalai Lama to China is a clear indication that he accepted the 17-Point Agreement, though this was signed without his knowledge and consent, using treacherous means. However, the Dalai Lama saw no other options but to try to see that the Agreement was implemented in letter and spirit. On his way to communist China when they had to travel through certain Himalayan tracks, there were clear signals as to who was in command. The Tibetans could not exercise their own choice of safer routes. The Chinese generals though apparently showing courtesy were ready to bully at the slightest provocation.

Chinese obduracy was glaringly obvious when much against his own will, the Dalai Lama was forced to sack his Prime Ministers. The prime ministers were doing what they were supposed to do: protect Tibetan interests and Tibetan people. But there was overwhelming PLA might in the visible distance. And there was charismatic shadow of Chairman Mao. We asked the Dalai Lama as to how could he put up with such subjugation. "What choice does a prisoner have?" was his answer.

The Dalai Lama had about half a dozen meetings with Chairman Mao. He found Mao most impressive. The Dalai Lama had felt a magnetic force[3] as he shook hands with him. With such situation he tried to make the best of the circumstances.

On the other hand, the Chinese were just toying with the young Dalai Lama as clearly seen from the narratives of his meetings with Chou En-lai and Chairman Mao. At one point of their meeting in India, with his beguiling charm, knowing full well that the Dalai Lama was exploring the option of not to return to Tibet, Chou En-lai had even said that the reforms in Tibet may even be postponed for 50 years if Tibetans were not ready!

Nevertheless the fact remains that the Dalai Lama did not abrogate the 17-Point Agreement. This has been made out as a strong case for the sovereignty of China over Tibet. His stay in China for about a year and his acceptance of the post of Vice-President of the Steering Committee of the People's Republic of China put a further seal to it. Enforced as this co-existence was, it sure was full of contradictions. We may explain the nature of these contradictions by way of learnt helplessness or Prisoners' Dilemma[4].

A final blow came in the form of Panchsheel. In 1954, when Pandit Nehru visited China, he signed a Treaty that categorically ruled out interference in the internal matters of each other. The Treaty explicitly said that Tibet was a part of China.

To be explicit, stark reality was that from 1950 till his escape, the Dalai Lama was a prisoner in his homeland. Not only his movements were monitored by the Chinese, he had to obtain permission even to move. Whether he himself desired to witness a cultural show or it was being offered to him as a lollypop by his captors, it is absolutely clear that the protocol laid down by the self-appointed masters had to be followed.

General Tan, who was commanding the military base at Lhasa, had invited the Dalai Lama to a theatrical concert. But he laid down conditions for the visit in most unreasonable terms. One of them stipulated that he was to go without his bodyguards. So there was not much enthusiasm on the Tibetan side either. It is, of course, the privilege of the host to decide in the manner in which the guest is to be received. However, dynamics are different when the host and guest relationship is based on hostility. When the host laid down terms that the guest must arrive entirely defenceless, it is enough of a clue that security and defence are surely needed. Friendship is based on trust and mutual goodwill. A relationship of distrust and hostility may still be an on-going relationship; it does not, however, then, subscribe as a friendship but turns into diplomacy. Diplomacy, simply defined, is the art of garnering as much or much more for giving nothing or less. A diplomat is a person who *lies* for the sake of his country is a celebrated pun.

So when the Dalai Lama is required to visit a Chinese military camp, may be to fulfil his own wish to see a cultural show but unarmed and without his customary security, the common man in the streets of Lhasa naturally should have nightmares. And nightmares are scary regardless of the fact whether there was any validity of scary images.

It was this kind of uncertainty and ill-will that saw the eruption of the uprising on 10th March, 1959. The Dalai Lama had procrastinated to go for the show on the excuse of his examinations. Now he had completed his studies. The examination was in the form of dialectics. When enormous suspense hung in the air it is a matter of wonder as to how the dialectics could be carried out about esoteric theories and their relevance in human affairs. It is even more pertinent to wonder how would a New Year celebration and Monlam festival be religiously carried out in such a climate of uncertainty. Does religion provide strength and sustenance at such a moment, or does it only serve as a dope?

But no sooner the examinations were over and the Monlam festival passed, the Chinese pressed for a definite date. The invitation was a command. There was no stalling now.

This made people suspect that this was a covert plan to abduct their leader. Therefore, huge crowds gathered in Lhasa. So violence broke out. The people's collective consciousness was tuned to a single concern about the safety of their God-King. Ngobo started broadcasting messages over microphones from the Chinese camp. He was not accessible to the crowd but they do identify some persons who had been on the Chinese side. One of them was killed. His killing and his dead-body was on display.

Then, Norbulingka, the summer palace of the Dalai Lama, was shelled. To top it up, a message was sent in secrecy saying, "If Your Holiness with a few trusted officers of the bodyguard can stay within the inner wall (of the Norbulingka) hold a position there and inform General Tan exactly which building you will occupy by marking it on the map, they will certainly intend that this building not be damaged." This made the Dalai Lama to conclude that the Chinese intended to destroy the palace and deal with the crowd accordingly. While doing so, his life was seen as endangered, obviously by both the sides. The correspondence that ensued between the two sides is a classic illustration of diplomacy in the circumstances of distrust, despair and distress.

General Tan wrote to the Dalai Lama that since the intrigues and provocations of the reactionaries have caused him very great difficulties, he will do everything possible to rescue him. The Dalai Lama replied, "There is obstruction by people, lamas and laymen who were instigated by a few evil elements and who did not know the facts. This has put me to indescribable shame. I am at a loss as to what to do. .... Reactionary evil elements are carrying out activities endangering me under the pretext of ensuring my safety... unlawful activities of the reactionary clique cause me endless worry and sorrow."

In reply, General Tan was to describe "the traitorous activities of some reactionary elements" and complain that the local government of Tibet was feigning compliance while actually helping them. He also exhorted the Dalai Lama to extricate himself from the dangerous position of being held by the traitors and go over to the Military Area Command for a short stay. The Dalai Lama appeared to be appreciative when he wrote on 16th March that he had addressed a meeting of more than 70 representatives of government officials and asked them to calm down, otherwise his life would be in danger. And this time he signed the letter in his own hand with the informality as, "the Dalai".

There was, thus a façade in order to gain time at any cost. As an experiment in truth how would it stand validation is a matter of conjecture. This was just a survival strategy.

Under the camouflage of these letters whether General Tan was beguiled or deliberately decided not to tighten the noose around the Dalai Lama is difficult to guess. The official Chinese version as told by Chou En-lai[5] is that even after they came to know about his escape, they could have intercepted him. They did not do so on account of a considered judicious decision, not because of their inability. Chou En-lai said that had PLA intercepted him, this would have resulted in the exchange of fire. This could have endangered the Dalai Lama. So far he had acted according to the book. His conduct had not aroused any suspicions according to Chou. In a classic example of perverse arguments he even went to the extent to prove that the Dalai Lama could have escaped from the "evil and misguided elements". Chou also said that they knew about the Dalai Lama's escape and could well have prevented or intercepted him but of their own accord, let him go.

Regardless, this was to turn out as one of the biggest escapes of the Twentieth century. If the Dalai Lama could have stayed in Chinese hands or had he been killed, what would have been history is a fertile ground for fanciful speculation. Such events for sure provide a philosophical backdrop to history.

Enigmas of chance and predestination get sharply focused when one ponders over some of the freak happenings that come to occur which turn out to be the guiding forces of history. Does a single human being have any decisive pre-ordained role so as to shape the future? How does the force of circumstance pick up an individual to be a front rank leader? Philosophizing on such questions, Leo Tolstoy wondered on the role that a single soldier may play to decide the fate of war and peace. To deny any role to an individual's freedom of choice would be a total negation of nature's certain — but difficult to decipher — ways. It would mean that the individual is only a speck of dust or a straw of grass in the wind, floating like jetsam and flotsam amidst the uncertain winds that are equally uncertain in their origin. On the other hand it may not be rationally possible to deductively conclude any particular design deciding the role of any individual in shaping the future. Thus, even when dilemma defies resolution, a rationalist thinker would still extol the virtue of freedom of choice of an individual as a unique attribute of human beings.

At a given moment it appears that history is taking a particular course. But suddenly a freak incident around a single individual takes place in such a way that the course of history changes radically. If there is no philosophical interpretation of such events, there is at least an element of romance and wonder around them. The escape of Princess Anastasia from assassination during the Russian Revolution failed to influence history. Had Mujibur Rehman survived the coup, would Bangladesh be different today is anybody's guess. Yet it is certain that a few of such chances did significantly alter the course of Twentieth century civilization.

Gandhi had a similar escape from a violent mob wanting to lynch him in South Africa. Gandhi's criticism of apartheid had claimed wide publicity before he reached there. He sensed trouble and wanted to disembark from the boat incognito after dark which would ensure his safety. A trusted white friend advised to the contrary. This would be an act of cowardice and show that he was afraid. Why should he attempt his passage stealthily? It was, therefore, decided that he, along with his white friend, will make his way in broad day-light.

As the two of them stepped out of the boat, soon enough Gandhi was recognized by some young people loitering around. They shouted his name and collected a gang. Gandhi was soon to be separated from his friend and cornered where the white youth started boxing him. At this very juncture, the wife of the British Police Commissioner, Mrs. Alexander, happened to pass by. She threw a shield around Gandhi and reprimanded the hooligans.

While they were taken aback, they followed Gandhi to his friend's house. A large crowd gathered, surging on being violent at any moment. Their demand was that Gandhi should be handed over to them. To lynch him to a nearby tree was their aim.

By this time, word had reached Mr. Alexander, the Commissioner of Police. He took the situation in his stride and soon established not only a dialogue but even a rapport with the crowd. Keeping them thus engaged he sent a word to Gandhi with two options: one, to escape in disguise or two, not only to die with his family but risking the life and property of his friend. Gandhi accepted the first one. He was disguised as a white policeman. This involved not only a change of attire but whitewashing his face. Accompanied by a couple of escorts Gandhi made his escape. When the word of his safe transit was passed on to Mr. Alexander he was making the crowd sing songs of how wonderful it would be to lynch Gandhi!

It is interesting to observe Gandhi's own reflections on the diverse stance taken by him in a single day. He reflects, "It is idle to adjudicate upon the right and the wrong of incidents that have already happened. It is useful to understand them and, if possible, to learn a lesson from them for the future. It is difficult to say for certain how a particular man would act in a particular set of circumstances. We can also see that judging a man from his outward act is no more than a doubtful inference, inasmuch as it is not based on sufficient data."[6]

The survival instinct of a politician compels him to change his views like the chameleon who changes its colours. It is commonly interpreted as compromising of principles. But the chameleon changes its colours in accordance to the dictates of Nature. It is an adaptive process. The changing stances of the politician are perhaps adaptive responses to an ever-changing political and social environment. Not only such an adaptation may lead to survival but it probably decides how man may become a Mahatma or a maniac. Justifying his mercurial tendencies, Z.A. Bhutto took recourse to Plato philosophizing that consistency is a virtue of stale minds. While the world is in a state of constant flux and at every moment there is a different dimension; since at least one variable, that is Time, is constantly changing, there are no two absolutely identical situations. A change of attitude, therefore, need not be at variance with what was held as a principle before. Gandhi also seems to be tuned to this philosophical wisdom when he proclaims that it is futile to judge people only by the attitude that they displayed at a particular time regardless of the consideration for the totality of the circumstances. Even after he became "Mahatma", there were several contradictions between his statements at different times. He simply explained that what he said last should be believed.

Historical forces need not be ascribed meaning. There may be no meaning at all and historical forces may be only ghosts in the minds of historians! But it is certain that history devolves around such bifurcation points. The escape of the Dalai Lama was such a point in the history of Tibet.

Before his escape, the Dalai Lama had come to know of the Chinese atrocities and wished that they were not true. They included crucifixion, vivisection, disemboweling and dismemberment. Beheading was common and rows of beheaded skulls were even pictured in newspapers as the fate of those who rebelled. Burning people alive was common. Rebels were tied to the back of powerful horses and the horses were made to gallop till the victim died. In the face of these atrocities, the Dalai Lama had tried in vain for ten long years to buy peace; this not only meant the sacrifice of sovereignty but also of freedom. Now to save his life, he must escape.

So in his own words, "I felt powerless.... The thousands of gilded Buddhas that stood flickering in the gentle light of countless butter lamps were a pointed reminder that we lived in a world of Impermanence and Illusion."

Letters written by the Dalai Lama (Appendix I) were used by the Chinese later on to malign him. At this juncture they did provide a breather of time to think and plan. When the oracle was consulted, he shouted, "Go, go tonight." He even charted the possible route of escape to India before he collapsed out of the trance. The Dalai Lama's own meditative divination provided the same light. He decided to escape into Exile in India.

Before setting out the Dalai Lama went to offer prayers to Mahakala. In his own words, "As I entered the room through its heavy, creaking door, I paused for a moment... a number of monks sat chanting prayers... There was only the glow of dozens of votive butter lamps sat in rows of golden and silver dishes. Numerous frescoes covered the walls. A small offering of tsampa sat on a plate on the altar. A server, his face half in a shadow, was bending over a large urn from which he was ladling out butter for the lamps. No one looked up... One of the monks took up his cymbals whilst another put a horn to his lips and blew a long mournful note. The cymbals clashed together and were held vibrating... I went forward and presented a kata implying not only propitiation but also the intention of return."

The authors see no necessity to seek clarification from the Dalai Lama. An innocent captive surrounded by hostile and violent forces all around has a fundamental unwritten right to secure his survival. A person caught between Scylla and Charybdis has to innovate a way to jump across both. In such a situation, the meaning of the word truth undergoes a semantic transformation. When some facts are camouflaged into projection of different meanings or connotations so as to ensure survival, do they purport to be a lie? A misquoting of fact is a lie, when there is a purposeful motivation to take advantage of the other by hoodwinking. That, of course, is untruth.

However, even if one were to go entirely by the Chinese version, the escape of the Dalai Lama was a tricky and highly dangerous move. Secrecy is not violation of truth. Treading on a truth path is to be vulnerable and vulnerability is directly proportionate to the openness of the dealings. There is no virtue in merely being vulnerable and, in the process be eliminated. As a matter of reflection and counterpoint, one has to look only to the fate of Panchen Lama who stayed behind in China.

If any of such future possibilities were to have a bearing on the actions of the Dalai Lama and his troop which planned his escape, one would be thankful for that diplomatic tact through which precious time was bought. This tact has gifted mankind with the repertoire of half a decade of experiments in truth and non-violence that shall enrich the Twenty-first century civilization. Can we compare the happenings in Palestine, Kuwait, Iran and Iraq with what is happening now in Tibet? And let us compare the response in the form of 9/11 in New York and 7/7 in London to what counter position Tibetans have come to display. This is in spite of their frantic diplomatic efforts at UN being an exercise in vain as we shall see in the next chapter.

REFERENCES

1. The concept of *karmic connection* is deeply rooted in Eastern traditions. Logic and rationality or otherwise, is not to be debated here. Suffice it may to mention that on the basis of Newtonian physics, scientists of the stature of Stephan Hawkins have argued in favour of pre-determinism. Past life and reincarnation have been debated for times immemorial and will remain a matter of faith which modernists might call superstition.
2. Stuart Gelder and Roma Gelder, *The Timely Rain, Travels in New Tibet*, New York, 1964.
3. *Ibid.*, p. 97.
4. Prisoner's Dilemma is a hypothetical situation where a prisoner is faced with a choice between confession and denial with radically different outcomes.
5. Stuart and Roma Gelder, *The Timely Rain, Travels in New Tibet*, New York, 1964.
6. M.K. Gandhi, *Experiments with Truth*, Ahmedabad, 1949.

3
Impotent United Nations

Historical Perspective

Sino-Tibet relations in history; World War, 1944; United Nations Organization is founded, 1946; Tibet ignores the event; India wins freedom, 1947; Peoples Republic of China is established, 1949; Tibet alarmed, initial exercise in diplomacy; China invades Tibet, 1950; Tibet approaches UN, 1950; Evidence of genocide in Tibet, 1957; the Dalai Lama appeals to UN, 1959; Support at UN, 1959-1965; Resolutions by the United Nations, 1959-1965; S. Rimpoche, Kalon Tripa describes further UN efforts as useless, 2005.

The history of Sino-Tibet relations has been of strife and conflict since the times of the 5th Dalai Lama. Though at least once Tibet ruled over China, mostly Tibet has suffered. Uneasy peace was evident in description of their relationship as "the great people of China shall ever be content to live in peace in China and so would the great people of Tibet live in Tibet. In fact, what ever may be the rule in China, Tibet suffered; and so the typical description of the relationship is "whatever may be the colour, white, black or red, cat wants to eat mouse."

Therefore, before we see protracted and desperate diplomatic efforts that were to prove an exercise in futility, let us explore the historical backdrop that brought this about.

Though Tibet had isolated itself, historically Britain and subsequently India and United States have had contacts with it. Tibet leaned heavily on US support not only because of its superpower status but also on account of a relationship that was initiated by the President of United States in 1942. During the Second World War, Roosevelt had personally contacted the Dalai Lama and thanked him for whatever help they received[1, 2]. This was the first diplomatic contact between Tibet and USA. A polite and very cordial letter went on to state:

Washington, July 3rd, 1942

Your Holiness

Two of my fellow country men, Ilia Tolstoy and Brooke Dolan, hope to visit your pontificate and the historic and widely famed city of Lhasa. There are in the United States of America many persons, among them myself, who, long and greatly interested in your land and people, would highly value such an opportunity.

As you know, the people of United States, in association within those of twenty-seven other countries, are now engaged in a war which has been thrust upon the world by nations bent on conquest, who are intent on destroying freedom of thought, of religion, and of action everywhere. We are fighting today in defence of and for preservation of freedom, confident that we shall be victorious because our cause is just, our capacity is adequate, and our determination is unshakable.

I am asking Ilia Tolstoy and Brooke Dolan to convey to you a little gift in token of my friendly sentiment toward you.

With cordial greetings,
Franklin D. Roosevelt

At the time of meeting the Dalai Lama, Tolstoy stated that he was recommending to his government that Tibet be represented at the Peace Conference at the end of war. He also said that US Government had full sympathy for the weak and small countries that wished to retain their independence.

The 13th Dalai Lama died on 17th December, 1933. In a remote village, far away from Lhasa, a child is born on the 6th July, 1935, in Amdo. In 1937, he is considered to be the reincarnated 14th Dalai Lama by thc scarch party according to an elaborate ritual and various signs. The enthronement ceremony takes place on 22nd February, 1940.

Under the tremendous impact of the holocaust of the Second World War, the nations of the world came to an elementary understanding that a way to avoid war has to be found. The flame of idealism was burning bright and a whole new chapter in International Law was written. Fundamental human rights were defined. And as advancement to the charter of League of Nations, the new organization — UN — had power to militarily intervene.

After the death of the 13th Dalai Lama, for seventeen years, Tibet was ruled by two regents — Reting Rimpoche until 1941; and Takra Rimpoche until 1950. This period was characterized by preoccupation with internal political squabbles and intrigues which, to a significant degree, consumed the vitality of the political and monastic elite. There was confrontation between the forces of conservatism and change. The system tried to confront the future without moving out of the past.

One of the fundamental postulates of Tibetan Buddhism is interconnectedness and interdependence. Even Nature is supposed to be a part of one's individual self. Two giant neighbours were undergoing historical mammoth metamorphosis. The Second World War had changed the map of the earth. One simply wonders as to what kind of stupor came upon the Tibetan polity that even in this crucial period, they remained isolated themselves.

The Peoples Republic of China came into being on 1st October, 1949. It was based on two fundamental pillars — nationalism and communism. China had suffered for more than 200 years because of colonial — imperialist design. One of the ideological planks for the communist party was to bring about a United Chinese Nation. Tibet was on the agenda so that it is liberated from its "feudalistic and imperialist hold" and to be reintegrated with the motherland. K.M.Panikkar, the then Foreign Secretary of India, was told by Chou En-lai, "The liberation of Tibet was a sacred duty". Though he promised that the Chinese would secure their ends by negotiations, and not by military actions.

In 1946, when there was a near certainty of India gaining freedom, India had organized a semi-official conference of Asian nations where Tibet was invited. Friction was evident with the Chinese delegation. Nehru had been cautious even then and told the Tibetan delegation not to raise any issues regarding political status[3]. At the conference, in official maps Tibet was shown as separate from China. That was opposed by the Chinese delegation.

However, Tibet did not utilize this opportunity for even a quiet diplomacy. The Dalai Lama told us, that at that time and later, on 15th August, 1947, Tibetan delegates should have met Mahatma Gandhi. He surely would have supported the Tibetan cause. And in his inimical humorous style he says, had they gone and taken the boy Dalai Lama with them, he would have enjoyed a visit to Delhi zoo!

On a similar front, when the United Nations was founded (1946), Tibet almost ignored the event. There was no attempt on Tibet's part to seek admission to the Assembly of Nations. Moreover when India became independent in 1947 Tibetans chose not to attend this major happening.

The Dalai Lama told us that this was a major blunder. Mahatma Gandhi would certainly have persuaded the Indian Government for better and more meaningful relations between the two nations.

When China attacked Eastern Tibet — soon after Mao's historic speech at Tiananmen Square in 1949 — the Dalai Lama was barely 15 years old. In this period of uncertainty the boy Dalai Lama's preparation to rule consisted mainly of the study of religious scriptures. He could not have foreseen what was in store to come. Stuck in the quagmire of political inadequacy and spiritual introversion, Tibet had no experience in diplomacy and there was no way the boy Dalai Lama could have been tutored into diplomatic ways. Cut off from the rest of the world by inaction on their own part, Tibet was aloof, alienated and friendless.

Communist victory in the civil war in China almost set a cat amongst the cage for the Tibetan polity. It was an immediate need that the sovereign status of Tibet be established internationally. So Shakabpa, a clever Tibetan envoy, contrived to travel on a Tibetan passport to US. When they were not accepted at Hong Kong, he fudged the papers to the extent of deceiving the authorities there. In January 1949 he approached Roy Henderson, the American Ambassador and was told that US would strengthen relations between the two countries.

In November 1949, the Tibetan National Assembly, Kashag was reorganized to meet the challenges of the new situation. An important decision was to sanction additional military expenditure. Tibet Foreign Bureau wrote to Ernest Bevin, the Foreign Secretary of Britain, "We would be most grateful if you would please consider extensive aid in the respect of requirement for civil and military purposes." Britain advised through Gould, a British diplomat who wrote to Kashag: "The British Government has lately been rather disturbed by what they call the supine attitude of the Tibetan Government towards China. The outside world would naturally assume that these claims are genuine if they are not refuted by the Tibetan Government. People do not get anything that they want unless they ask for it and ask continuously." So, on 3rd December, 1949, Kashag sought help from Britain for UN membership.

The Tibetans were just waking up to the ways of diplomacy. Their naivety is evident when on 2nd November, 1949, Tibet sent a very naïve letter to Mao tse-Tung demanding an assurance that the Chinese shall not invade Tibet. This was in spite of the advice of Richardson, the British Agent in Lhasa as well as of H. Dayal, the Indian Representative. Both advised caution, which was ignored. Their inexperience is further highlighted by the way they conducted themselves with Nehru.

Tibetan delegations were dispatched to India, Britain, China and Nepal. On 8th September, 1950, Prime Minister Nehru received the delegation for more than two hours[4]. The Tibetans told Nehru they would not go to Peking unless the Chinese guaranteed Tibetan independence in advance. Moreover, they did not trust the Chinese and reiterated their request that India agree to mediate between Tibet and China. Nehru responded bluntly:

'The Government of India will continue the policy of the British period in considering Tibet outwardly a part of China but internally independent. We will request the Chinese not to send their troops into Tibet, but if the Tibetan representatives say that Tibet is completely independent, it will be very difficult to reach an agreement. And as to India acting as a witness to any agreement, that is talk of thirty years ago and is not acceptable in this day and age.'

The Tibetans replied:

'Because Tibet is independent, please do not talk about 'internal autonomy' under China. If Tibet is ruined this will result in great danger for other countries of East Asia and in particular to India. Now India has only about 75 soldiers protecting the trade marts in Tibet, but in future, if India and China share a border in Tibet then you will have to maintain permanently many hundreds of thousands of troops there and this will be great hardship for India. So think not only about the current friendly relations between India and China but think about the long term future.'

Nehru was irritated by this and said sharply to the Tibetans that it was not enough to speak about Tibetan independence: such status had to be proved according to law.

The Tibetans answered: 'In 1914 at the time of Simla convention, Tibet and Britain made a separate treaty which said that Suzerainty of China over Tibet is wiped out and until now we have been acting as an independent country.'

Nehru immediately called the Indian Ministry of Foreign Affairs to ask whether there was such a separate treaty, and then he replied, showing some anger:

'There is no such separate treaty like this and China never accepted the Simla Convention. The Chinese believe that Tibet is a part of China. Tibet thinks that because China did not accept Simla, it is independent but at that time Tibet did not make any clear decisions. That was a mistake. And later when you had the time and the opportunity to do something (about independence) you did nothing and this was a mistake. During this period, China has been very clever and have proclaimed widely in the international community that Tibet is part of China. Now you, the representatives have to be very careful (with what you say and claim) when you begin your talks with the Chinese.'

There was a recent irritation that could have caused Nehru to react so sharply. Tibet did send a congratulatory note on the occasion of Indian Independence. However, they made it clear that they do not accept India as the legitimate successor to British Government. They had raised the issue of the return of areas of Tibetan population that had fallen under the control of British India, viz. NEFA, Sikkim and Darjeeling, Tawang (present Arunachal Pradesh[5]). They wanted them to be returned to Tibet. Such ill-advised claims made by the Tibetan Government ....resulted in the temporary loss of a certain amount of Indian sympathy for Tibet.

The delegation to China almost walked into the jaws of the dragon as we shall see later.

So with the sounds of PLA cadres on their doorstep, the Tibetans started to look for arms and military assistance. This is evident when on 25th February, 1949, a meeting took place between Colonel Srinivasan of India and Depon Kunsangste of Tibet to discuss military assistance. India did commit minimum military hardware and some personnel to train to use them. But it never went beyond that.

On 29th September, 1949, China's National Peoples Congress approved of waging a revolutionary war for the liberation of all territories of China including Formosa...and Tibet. And on 1st October, 1949, Mao proclaimed at Tiananmen Square, "Long live the Chinese Communist Party". Red China was born.

With this backdrop, in November 1949, a Tibetan diplomat met Howard Donavan, a US diplomat at Delhi wherein a request was put that in the event that Mao takes an aggressive attitude and sends his troops inside Tibet ... "the Government of Tibet would earnestly desire to request every possible help from your Government." The response of Roy Henderson, the American Ambassador to India, was affirmative. He had told a Tibeten diplomat that US would like to strengthen relations between the two countries. The US embassy in Delhi advised the State Department that in the event of a communist victory in China, the US should be prepared to treat Tibet as an independent state[6]. The US policy was to cordon off the communist countries with a string of allies and Tibet had a strategic geographical advantage.

In the wake of imminent danger, for the first time, on 3rd December, 1949 the *Kashag* telegraphed the US Secretary of State requesting help for admission to UN General Assembly. When Nehru was consulted on this point by USA, he was categorical to say that it could do more harm than good. It might hasten the communist invasion.

Nehru was a socialist rooted into wild dreams of socialist unity of the whole world. He was a historian. However, he wanted to reshape the history of Asia. He had dreams of 'Hindi-Chini Bhai-Bhai.' In his book, *Discovery of India*, he frankly reveals his disenchantment with this philosophy. And of course he was irreligious. His interest in Buddhism was only to the extent that it was a period of history in ancient India. It was no wonder then that, when the Dalai Lama visited India in 1956 for the 2500th Buddha anniversary celebrations, Nehru was cold to the Dalai Lama's request for asylum. On the contrary he persuaded the Dalai Lama to go back.

At this very opportune time Chou En-lai had also managed to be in New Delhi. He had successfully established a comradeship with Nehru. He managed to get a gist of what was happening between the Dalai Lama and Nehru. This of course would have enormously helped China to understand the mind of the Dalai Lama and the Government of Tibet. Charting out a well disciplined course of action is necessary for success — not only in diplomacy but in all walks of life. Diplomacy further thrives on command and control. This requires 'intelligence' about the adversary. This is exactly what Chou En-lai did when his visit coincided with that of the Dalai Lama. Educated at the Sorbonne University in France, Chou was thoroughly grounded in the wily ways of Western diplomacy. By this visit to India, he displayed a keen sense of viewing his target, its terrain and the time of the day. It was high class diplomacy that even Harvard professors would admire[7]. Subtle elements of diplomacy — ruse, disguise, beguile and surprise — came naturally to him. For instance, at a press conference in India, he addressed a press in Chinese and an interpreter translated into English. There were some informal chats with the media persons following the conference. In the side lines, some of them were making slimy remarks about him in English. Turning his face towards them, he kept talking with the group but abruptly changed to fluent and flawless English, to astonish and silent the other group!

On the other hand, Mao was a rustic and prided in showing himself as such. He had deeply imbibed a strategy for war from a Chinese philosopher, whom he considered his guru[8]. Sun Tzu was a contemporary of Confucius. Sun Tzu has written, "To fight and conquer in all your battles is not supreme excellence, supreme excellence consists in breaking the enemy's resistance without fighting. Know the enemy and yourself, and in a hundred battles, you will suffer no defeat." Taking several cues from Sun zu, Mao had disciplined his soldiers highly: they were not supposed to demand even a cup of tea from civilians of the territory that they had captured. They were to respect local religion, customs and language; as well as ignore all insults and provocations. They were to promise that the only change will be the elimination of heavy taxes.

So, when Mao had reposed his confidence in Chou-En-lai, he must have been sure of Chou's commitment to the aggressive imperialism that characterized this kind of mind set of Chinese throughout the course of history. Chinese historians trace this trait way back to third century B.C. It is the characteristic of China that if a region once acknowledged her nominal suzerainty, even for a short period, she should regard it as a part of her empire for ever and would automatically revive her claim over it even a thousand years after whenever there was a chance of enforcing it[9]. Chou En-lai fully subscribed to this mind-set.

There were other pristine qualities of diplomacy that Chou ably professed. Diplomats are not supposed to have any emotions; in case they happen to have them, they hide till such time that they utilize them in the service of their country. Only emotion that Chou En-lai displayed was charm[10]. He had almost engulfed Nehru as if he was under a hypnotic charm. Another quality was to lie confidently and never feel abashed if found out. Was it not said that a diplomat is one who *lies* abroad for the sake of his country? Of course, Tibetan discovered this soon enough and started to call him Mr. Chew and lie!

The role of Jawaharlal Nehru and his relationships with the Dalai Lama have two faces. As a socialist, from the very beginning of his political career, his sympathies were with China. In 1955 it was considered to be a pinnacle of achievement of Nehru's diplomacy that he signed the Panchsheel Agreement with China. This amounted to a final giving-away of any say in the matter of Tibet-China relationship. But at the same time when the Dalai Lama sought asylum as a refugee in India in 1959 Nehru was to accommodate not only the Dalai Lama but hundred thousand Tibetan refugees. On the other hand, at their first meeting following the escape, of course he fettered and fumed, and hectored the Dalai Lama.

Nehru's reluctance to get involved has to be viewed in a wider perspective. In 1949, independent India was not even a toddler. It was on the brink of a civil war following Partition. Nehru had charted a foreign policy based on non-alignment with either of the power blocs; he was charting a course of alignment with the non-aligned. Despite his vast knowledge of history, he was not sure of the actual status of Tibet; in one press briefing, he has used the word "vague" five times! Westernized that he was, he had to discover even India. While he was a follower of Gandhi, he had nothing to do with Gandhian morality. Even if Nehru was convinced about the moral and legal grounds about Tibet's sovereignty, he was duty bound to look after Indian interests first and last. The avowed principle of diplomacy is to look after the enlightened interest of your own country; morals and ethics are included to the extent that they serve one's own country. The Indian Army, too, was not prepared. It was certain that support for Tibet would have meant a military engagement and definite alignment with USA. It is needless to reflect on the consequences of Indian support for Tibet then. It can only be said that certainly if this had happened, history would have been different.

Added to the above facts in 1950, even China was not a member State of the UN and none of the major powers or neighbouring India was willing to provide any initiative on behalf of Tibet. In 1950, the communications were very poor in Lhasa. So, when on 7th November, 1950 Tibet appealed to the UN, Shakabpa[11] had to cable from Kalimpong. The appeal was most fervently drafted. It said that "There is legal hope that a nation dedicated to peace will be able to resist the brutal effort of men trained to war, we understand that the UN has decided to stop aggression wherever it takes place." The Government of India was vehemently against any discussion at UN. So, the British also toed the same line.

Nehru was persuading the Tibetans for negotiations. On 16th November, 1949 he said at a press conference that "for the last forty years or so certain autonomy of Tibet was recognized by the British government. A vague kind of suzerainty by China was recognized... Things were never clearly defined.... and have remained vague....We deal with Tibet directly but in a vague sense. .... how far it goes one doesn't know."

Nehru used the word 'vague' five times at the press briefing. But the dictates of history were different. Vagueness had worked well for years, but times were changing. With UN becoming an important world body, new rules were framed and old colonial definitions had to be fixed in black and white: whether a state was independent or not. No state could claim to be at the same time under the suzerainty or vassalage of another state and yet to be fully autonomous.

At this time, in December 1949, the Western diplomats in Delhi considered that Mao would not for a considerable time wish to face the difficulty of mounting an expedition into Tibet, where no material advantage was to be derived[12]. So Nehru further said, "India does not feel free to sponsor but Tibet is free to appeal directly. India neither has the resources nor the inclination to send arm assistance to Tibet."

The British were keenly watching the Indian stand. Soon, on November 21, 1949, the British ambassador telegraphed the Home Office, "India had a total hold on Tibetan foreign relations and its stance did not conform to be in the heir of British policy of preserving integrity of Tibet." On November 22, 1949, the US embassy in India wrote to the Secretary of the State expressing concern about Indian tendency to throw up its hand and to say nothing could be done. Acheson, the US Secretary of State, wanted the US ambassador to put pressure on India to realize the dangers of Communist China and unrealism of supine attitude of India.

It appears that Nehru was the sole arbiter of India's stance. Attlee, the then British Prime Minister had personally written to Nehru asking him to define Indian position in December 1949. Sardar Patel suggested to Nehru that he wanted to make useful suggestions in Nehru's reply to a letter from Attlee. Nehru did not comply. Moreover, he ignored the concern that Sardar Patel penned down following a cabinet meeting (Appendix I).

In November 1950, Nehru said "We told Tibetan government that if they choose they could prefer to appeal to UN. We could not however sponsor such an appeal. We might support generally. We cannot go back on an assurance to help; therefore, we may support it generally[13]. I think that in no event should we sponsor Tibet's appeal. I would personally think that it would be good thing if that appeal were not heard in the Security Council or the General Assembly. If it is considered there, there is bound to be a great deal of bitter speaking and accusation, which will worsen the situation as regards Tibet as well as the possibility of widespread war without helping it in the least. It must be remembered that neither the UK nor the USA, nor indeed any other power is particularly interested in Tibet or the future of that country. What they are interested in, is embarrassing China. Our interest on the other hand is Tibet, and if we cannot serve that interest, we fail."

However, on 14th November, 1950, Hector David Castor on behalf of El Salvador, informed the UN Secretary General asking to include the invasion of Tibet to be taken on the agenda. How did a tiny faraway nation got motivated to sponsor the Tibetan cause? It is said that this was at the instance of USA. However, Hector Castor immediately denied.

And soon after, when the Seventeen-Point Agreement was announced, the Tibetan issue lost momentum. US hectored the Dalai Lama very strongly to repudiate the agreement but he vacillated. While US was willing to grant him asylum with at least 100 other Tibetans in his entourage, they were not prepared for a direct overt/covert military involvement as they had done in Korea. Their foremost condition was that India should also comply. This was out of question.

Tibet's fervent appeal to the United Nations was cabled on 11th November, 1950. However, Shakabpa described the relationship as that between a spiritual guide and his lay followers. What would the Western nations understand of this? He also stated that the present invasion is the grossest of the violation of the weak by the strong.[14, 15] Tibetan appeal said that they hoped that the conscience of the world would not allow the disruption of the Tibetan State by methods reminiscent of the jungle[16].

On 13th November, 1950, when Tibet's appeal reached the Secretary General's office at UN, they were totally ignorant about status of Tibet. They considered the letter from Tibetan Government as a communication from a non-governmental organization and thought of putting it into cold storage.

The situation at the UN was typical of the saying: who will bell the cat. However, on 15th November, 1950, El Salvador sponsored the Tibet issue. This is said to be under CIA influence: El Salvador has constantly denied it. The proposed Resolution by El Salvador ran as follows:

1. The general assembly decides to contempt this act of unprovoked aggression against Tibet.
2. To entrust to a committee that will suggest the appropriate measure to the general assembly.
3. The committee to study the appeal made by the government of Tibet and submits a report.

Roy Henderson, the American ambassador wrote to the Secretary of the State that Rao, the Indian Representative to UN, had informed Government of India that no member of the Security Council desired to take initiative regarding Tibet. He suggested that the matter may be broken. However, overwhelming sentiment in the Indian cabinet was, regardless of the effect of India-China relationship, Government of India could not afford to take uninterested position regarding Tibet[17].

In December 1950, Nehru was preoccupied with the obsession of playing a historical role as mediator over the Korean issue. As it took over the United Nations agenda Tibet's appeal failed into obscurity. And, before this came to discussion on 23rd May, 1951, Seventeen-Point Agreement between Tibet and China was signed. World had no idea about its treacherous nature. According to Heinrich Harrer who reported to the US ambassador Henderson, the Tibetans were addressed in harsh and insulting terms, threatened with personal violence, and virtually kept prisoners. They were simply given the choice of signing or accepting responsibility for the immediate and unconditional military advance to Lhasa[18].

Immediately after the announcement of the Agreement on May 26, 1951, Shakabpa met US Counsul Frazer Wilkins in Calcutta (Kolkata now) and ask that the Dalai Lama would want to know:

1. Should Tibet report to the UN?

2. Was the UN still interested in Tibet?
3. What would the US do?
4. Would the US recommend the government of the Ceylon (Sri Lanka now) to give asylum for the Dalai Lama and his followers?
5. Would the US grant the asylum?
6. How would the Dalai Lama be received as a head of the state? Would the US be willing to provide for his expense[19].

As a response, in the middle of 1951, Roy Henderson suggested to the State Department that a secret letter to the Dalai Lama with the following main points may be sent:

1. Communist regime 'determines to obtain complete control over Tibet.
2. Any concession to Peking will serve only to speed up the ceasing of all Tibet.
3. The Dalai Lama should not return to Lhasa nor should send his treasures back to Lhasa.
4. He should leave for some foreign country.
5. His Holiness should send representatives to Ceylon to arrange for the immediate transfer of his treasures to that country. He should seek asylum over there.
6. Failing this United State would offer asylum.
7. He should send a mission to the United State and make a direct appeal to the United Nations.[20]

Within three days of the announcement of the Seventeen-Point Agreement a meeting in secrecy took place between the American Counsul Wilkins and Shakabpa in Calcutta at the instance of the Dalai Lama. The Dalai Lama had asked six specific questions like:

1. Should Tibet report to the UN if current talks were to break, and how should they do it? Was the UN still interested in Tibet and could it be of any help? What would the US do? Would it be willing to grant visa?
2. As Tibet had no official relations with Ceylon, would the US be willing to approach the Government of Ceylon to give asylum for the Dalai Lama and his followers?
3. Would the US be willing to grant asylum to the Dalai Lama and to approximately hundred of his followers? How would he be received? As a head of the State would the US be willing to provide for his expenses?[21]

While the Dalai Lama failed to commit, Taktser Rimpoche had told US Consul in Calcutta that (i) the Dalai Lama did not approve the agreement and (ii) he would soon make a statement disavowing it and other steps[22].

On 11th June, 1951, India indicated if the Dalai Lama decided to leave Tibet, asylum would be granted in India. However, it laid down a stringent condition. It would be a humanitarian gesture and he would not be allowed to engage in any political activities. The US involvement was strongly opposed. The Americans were keenly exhorting the Dalai Lama to take aggressive stance. The British view was that the American suggestions were cynical and dangerous. The result of encouraging the Tibetans to denounce the agreement would be to provide American publicist with some propaganda point but not the Tibetans effectively. It would be a propaganda stunt[23].

Shakabpa informed USA that the Dalai Lama wanted to discuss with the Chinese. Then a secret unsigned, undated letter was delivered to the Dalai Lama on 6th July once again assuring US support in the form of Tibetan self-determination, the Dalai Lama a head of autonomous Tibet and ultimate return to head non-communist state; but India's involvement was vital. Thus the United State offered to help the Dalai Lama to keep the flame of autonomy alive but it hardly materialized.

By August 1951, the Dalai Lama was still waiting for answers from the US. And the pressure from the Chinese was mounting on him to return. He returned to Lhasa from Dromo *via* Yatung. The Dalai Lama left with anti-Indian feelings. At this time there were two possibilities — if the US help would have materialized he was to go to India immediately but if it were not to be, then he should return to Lhasa. The Dalai Lama withheld the public repudiation of the agreement in the hope of renegotiating a more favourable treaty later on.

The Tibetan initiative by El Salvador faded away into the catalogue of diplomacy in vain. A month later, Chinese troops marched into Lhasa soon followed by the occupation of all the major cities of Tibet.

On 1st October, 1951 Mao congratulated Deng Lieu when they came to Beijing to celebrate the first anniversary of the communist republic complementing them that the liberation had been unexpectedly smooth and without a problem.[24]

A lot of water flowed down the Brahmaputra after this. The Dalai Lama went to China with the hope that the Seventeen-Point Agreement will be so implemented that Tibet will have full autonomy. He came to India once again, in the hope that he will be granted asylum there. How Chou foiled this has been seen earlier (*vide supra*).

Apart from genocide in other places, at the time on 10th March, 1959 uprising in Lhasa alone, at least 90,000 Tibetans were killed. US expressed profound sympathy with the people of Tibet in face of the barbaric intervention of the Chinese imperialists to deprive a proud and brave people of their cherished religion and political autonomy and to pervert their institutions to the communist ends.[25]

The Dalai Lama abrogated the Seventeen-Point Agreement after escaping to India in 1959. He was now determined to appeal to UN. US support was assured. However, Nehru was reluctant, probably based on his own experience about Kashmir. The Dalai Lama was surprisingly pleased when Nehru told him that though the measure is not going to be fruitful, the Dalai Lama may appeal. India is a free country.

The Dalai Lama, on 4th September, 1959, at the Indian Council on World Affairs publicly pointed out that India's position on the legality of the McMohan line depended upon its recognition of Tibet as a State capable of entering into international agreements. He said that "if Tibet did not enjoy international status at the time of the conclusion of the Simla Convention, it had no authority to enter into such an agreement. Therefore, if you deny sovereign status to Tibet, you deny the validity of the McMahon Line." In regard to suzerainty, the Dalai Lama pointed out that "suzerainty does not imply loss of international personality". And, on 9th September, 1959, he appealed to the United Nations.

In 1956, Hungary was overrun by the Soviet Union. Hungary was a UN member and the matter was discussed at UN; though to no avail. Yugoslavia was the only Communist country to support Tibet; the Western Bloc called it another Hungary. In the meanwhile, on 25th July, 1959, the report of International Commission of Jurists was published.[26]

The report on Tibet's appeal to the UN was prepared by Indian international lawyer, Purshottam Trikamdas. It examined the issues of China's obligation to abide by its own system of national and regional autonomy to allow freedom of religious belief and protection of religious institutions, to permit free trade and to respect the property of the Tibetan people. The report examined the issues of violations of human rights and the question of genocide, based upon the 1948 Genocide Convention. On the question of Tibet's legal status, the Commission came to the conclusion that Tibet was an independent country and the report reached the tentative conclusion that "the events in Tibet constitute *prima facie* threat to and a breach of the fundamental legal principles, which the International Commission of Jurists stands for and endeavours to promote and protect. From the present report their emerges also, it is submitted, a *prima facie* case of the worst type of imperialism and colonialism, coming precisely from the very people who claim to fight against it.[27]

The US advised the Dalai Lama to highlight the Chinese communist perfidy and brutality. To achieve maximum world impact, Tibet should focus on outrages and the atrocities committed against Tibetan people and the denial of human rights.[28]

The Dalai Lama wrote to the British for support. On 18th September, 1959, the British, French and the US diplomats met. Gyalo Dhundup and Shakabpa lobbied in Britain. On 28th September, 1959, Tibet's question was proposed to the UN by Ireland and Malaysia.

The USSR and Romania opposed it. New Zealand and El Salvador strongly supported. Krishna Menon argued on behalf of India and said that no purpose will be served by discussion. It said nobody is going to send an army to Tibet to fight China. It apprehended reactions on the Chinese government which are more likely to be adverse to Tibet and the Tibetan people.

Moving the resolution, the Irish representative stated that, "We repudiate the contention advanced by the Soviet representative that, as the people of Tibet have not always since the beginning of time been able to resist being treated as subjects by a stronger power, the case of Tibet is dead, never to be revived. Indeed to admit that contention would be to destroy the basis upon which most of our member nations have established the right to live in freedom and to govern themselves in accordance with the wishes of their own peoples."[29]

Malaysia pointed out that the small states were dependent upon the United Nations for support against large states and, therefore, they should support the principles of United Nations intervention on behalf of the rights of the small nation such as Tibet, "Since once the barrier of world public opinion, freely expressed in this Assembly, is down, it will only make future violations much easier".[30]

This advice might have been taken by Nepal, but Nepal submitted an opinion that avoided any challenge to China's status or its actions in Tibet, echoing the Chinese propaganda, "If one speaks of human rights and their suppression in Tibet, we should first try to find out what human rights the Tibetan people have enjoyed through the centuries and which of these human rights have been denied to the people of Tibet today. Even Tibet has to be viewed in the context of the new, changing, revolutionary Asia." Nepal voted against the inclusion of the Tibet's issue.[31]

The Chinese Nationalist Formosa insisted that Tibet was a part of China but voted in favour of Tibet in the General Assembly. New Zealand said that it would be an abdication of the responsibility to decline to take action.

The position of Malaysia was dictated by the Communist revolt in Malaysia itself. There were ethnic clashes between Malaysians and Chinese. The Chinese population in Malaysia in 1959 was 37 per cent. Their sympathies were with PRC.

The Irish motivation was genuine sympathy: "Those who also have struggled here in the cause of any oppressed people or victimized minority should think very carefully before they decide to ignore the call of the Tibetan people. By ignoring that call they would be weakening the very source to which they look for redress and weakening also the moral force of their own appeals. The question of Tibet is a test case, a challenge to this Assembly. If, despite the charter, a powerful country may force its will, with impunity and without protest, upon a distinctive people one-hundredth part of its size, by what principle would it be denied the right to impose its will by force upon a nation one-tenth or one-half of its size."[32]

Primarily emphasizing the human rights issue but also mentioning the autonomy and freedom of Tibet, first ever UN resolution on Tibet was passed by the General Assembly on 21st October, 1959. It was a moral victory.

Around this time, Chiang Kai Shek declared that as soon as the puppet communist regime on the Mainland is overthrown, the people of Tibet will be free to express their desire and the government will assist them to realize their aspirations in accordance with the principles of self-determination.

In diplomatic matters sometimes trivialities do matter. This is humorously illustrated by the following. In 1960 the Dalai Lama sent New Year's greetings card to the British Prime Minister and the Foreign Secretary, causing a great deal of confusion and debate in the Foreign Office. The FO instructed the High Commissioner in Delhi to inform the Dalai Lama of the receipt of the cards. The High Commissioner, ever mindful of diplomacy, wrote back to the FO saying that he could not reply to the Dalai Lama's card because it would be seen as establishing formal contact with the Tibetan government in Exile. He advised that the Prime Minister's office and the FO should send a direct reply by ordinary mail. The FO, mindful of its position, immediately objected to the suggestion, claiming that since the offices of the Prime Minster and FO were higher than the High Commissioner in Delhi, a direct letter would mean that they had given higher recognition.

Following this, in February 1960, Christian Hector, an American diplomat wrote to the Dalai Lama "As you know, while it has been the historical position of the US to consider Tibet as an autonomous country under the suzerainty of China, the American people have also traditionally stood for the principle of self-determination. It is the belief of the United States Government that this principle should apply to the people of Tibet and that they should have the determining voice in their own political destiny."

On 8th August, 1960, the Second Report of International Commission of Jurists was published. So, on 29th September, 1960, the Dalai Lama wrote to UN for assisting restoration of Tibetan independence as well as in holding human rights abuses.

By an overwhelming majority, the vote in UN was carried that the Tibet issue may be taken up for discussion at the General Assembly. Ireland moved the resolution and once again argued most fervently as a line of argument that all of us who have lived under foreign rule have rejected in relation to ourselves, a line of argument that would have kept half the nations in this assembly in servitude for ever and prevented the world from ever discussing our condition. Looking around this assembly, and looking at my own delegation, I think how many benches would be empty here in this hall if it had always been agreed that when a small nation or a small people fell into the grip of a major power, no one could ever raise their case here; that once they were a subject nation, they must always remain a subject nation. Tibet has fallen into the hands of Chinese People's Republic for the last few years, for thousands of years, or for a couple of thousands of years. At any rate, it was as free and as fully in control of its own affairs as any nation in this assembly, and a thousand times more free to look after their own affairs than many of the nations here.[33]

John Kennedy came to power in 1961. And India was then on collision course with China over the border issue. This seemed to augur well for Tibet.

Continuing the debate in the General Assembly, on 26th September, 1961, Malaysia and Thailand argued that the issue of Tibet on the ground that it is alleged that is a dead issue, should not be discussed.... We see no logic in this...the outrage still continues.

The word to include the item for discussion was passed with 48 in favour and 14 in opposition. So the issue was discussed again on 19th December, 1961 in the General Assembly. The American delegates said that the United States government does not accept the contention that once a people are held in bondage in the communist colonialist empire they lose all further rights to self-determination and the violence of the Chinese communists attacks on the principle of self-determination for the Tibetan people reveals their guilty knowledge that the communist system would be repudiated in Tibet if the Tibetan people has a free choice of their destiny on these two charter principles, human rights and self-determination.[34]

The Communist Bloc argued that this was a Cold War issue. Even the tiny state of Albania was vehement in protesting against "intolerable interference by the UN in the internal affairs of People's Republic of China". China was comfortable in not being a member of UN.

The debate was on expected lines and acrimonious. However, the United Nations General Assembly passed the resolution on 20th December, 1961 by 48 in favour and 14 against (Appendix II). Once again the moral issues were highlighted. The principle of self-determination was mentioned.

China paid no heed to the resolutions. Instead, the torture of the Tibetans got so extreme that in 1962, the Panchen Lama, who had remained in Tibet presented Chou En-lai with a detailed report that came to be known as 70,000 Character Petition. This was so highly critical that Panchen Lama was subjected to "struggle sessions" and was detained for 14 years under virtual house arrest. In December 1964, the Panchen Lama released a further report on continued violations of human rights in Tibet[35]. The Dalai Lama had still some faith left in UN; there was nothing else he can do. He once again appealed to UN. It was an exercise that was a virtual repetition of the previous resolutions. Philippines was a fresh addition this time who argued that "Chinese communist plan to destroy the distinctive character of the Tibetan nation is nearing completion". India came out more openly in favour of Tibetan autonomy. The Indian delegate, Zakaria, even tried to explain the Indian stand during previous debates.[36]

A resolution was once again passed by the UN General Assembly by majority on 18th December, 1965 on similar lines to the previous ones. And it remains on the UN records without any follow up action. That is the power and potency of United Nations! Recently, in 2005, Samdong Rimpoche was asked: Why should Tibet once again not move the UN? His reply was that the UN is an agency that has no potency to implement its own resolutions. They have said what is right and what is wrong. What is the meaning now to ask them to say it again?

In retrospect, was Nehru right in asking the Dalai Lama not to take recourse to UN? Yes, he was right that nobody is going to send an army to Tibet. But, not only Tibet's efforts at UN added a chapter in the history, it also put on record that at this stage of human civilization, might is right and internationally, even rule of jungle can prevail. It is seen to recur: history repeats itself. Idealism, morals, human rights, international law, and, lastly, conscience, all remain empty words in the play of aggressive political forces. What happens is finally the art of the possible. That is what diplomacy is all about and that is the game Tibetans seem to be engaged in at present.

REFERENCES

1. Melvyn C. Goldstein, *A History of Modern Tibet, 1913-1951; The Demise of the Lamaist State*. Berkeley, 1989, p. 402
2. U.S. Foreign Relations, China 1942, 103.91802/687 *Letter from President Roosevelt to Dalai Lama*, dated 3 July, 1942.
3. According to at least one source, the Tibetan Delegation did meet Mahatma Gandhi and asked his advice about how to advance the case of Tibet's sovereignty. Mahatma is said to have assured them that the maps at the conference show Tibet as an independent nation. This shall be the proof. However the maps were withdrawn.
4. Zhwa sgab pa (Shakabpa) Dbang phyug bde Iban. (History of Tibet), pp. 417-18, 1976. Quoted by Melvyn C. Goldstein, *A History of Modern Tibet, 1913-1951; The Demise of the Lamaist State*, Berkeley, 1989.
5. Mullik, B.N. *My Years with Nehru: the Chinese Betrayal*, Bombay, 1971, p. 54.
6. Foreign Relations of United States, Telegram 893.00 Tibet 11-2249, November 22, 1949.
7. Gene, Sharp, *The Dynamics of Non-violent Action*, New York, 2000, p. XIX
8. Clubb, O.E. *Twentieth Century China*, New York, 1978.
9. Majumdar, R.C., *Fate of Tibet*, New Delhi, 1999, p. 261.
10. Nehru was the older of the two and posed himself as the elder statesman. Given to megalomaniac dreams, at the first Afro-Asian Conference on Non-Alignment, Nehru took the prerogative to introduce Chou En-lai to various statesmen like President Nasser and President Tito. Chou fumed internally. However, he swallowed his pride and reserved his spite till 1962 when he taught Nehru and India a lesson without ever telling Nehru what statesmanship is.
11. Shakabpa was not well versed in English. The appeal was in elegant English. It is said that it was drafted by one Mr. S. Sinha, an Indian diplomat at Lhasa. Tsering Shakya, Tibet and League of Nations, *Tibetan Journal*, X 13(1985), pp. 48-56.
12. Kalzang Diki Bhutia, *Tibet Issue at the UN: A Case Study in Informal Diplomacy (1950 - 1965)*, Jawaharlal Nehru University, New Delhi, 2000.
13. SWJN, Cable from Nehru to Rao, Indian representative to UN, Services 11, Vol. 15(2), p. 347.
14. Bureau of His Holiness the Dalai Lama — *Tibet in the United Nations, 1950-1961*, UN document no. A/1559.
15. The Dalai Lama, *My Land and My People*, London, 1962, pp. 228-232.
16. *Ibid.*, p. 228.
17. Kalzang Diki Bhutia, *Tibet issue at the UN*, New Delhi, 2000 p. 146.
18. *Foreign Relations of United States*, Volume VII, Part II,1951, pp. 1689-91 and Henderson to the Secretary of the State, 11 June 1951, pp. 1707-1708.
20. *Foreign Relations of the United State*, Vol. VII, Part 1(1951), pp. 1612-13.
21. *Foreign Relations of United States*, Volume VII, Part II, 1951, pp. 168-91.
22. *Ibid.*, 793B006/1651m telegram BI, 541, dated 26 June, 1951.
23. British Foreign Office document 371/92997.
24. W.D. Shakabpa, *Tibet: A Political History*, New Haven, 1967, p. 301.
25. Kashag, *Contemporary Archives*, XI, p. 16802.

26. Chanakya Sen, *Tibet Disappears*, New Delhi, 1960, p. 412.
27. International Commission of Jurists, *Question of Tibet and Rule of Law*, Vol. IV, 1959.
28. Warner W. Smith, *Tibetan Nation: A History of Tibetan Nationality and Sino-Tibetan Relations*, New Delhi,1961.
29. General Assembly Fourteenth Session, 20th October, 1959, UN DOC. A/4237, in Tibet in the United Nation, Bureau of His Holiness, New Delhi, pp. 96,100,101.
30. *Ibid.*, p. 93.
31. *Ibid.*, p. 103.
32. Tibet in United Nations 1950-61, UN Doc., p. 834.
33. Tibet in United Nations 1950-61, p. 251.
34. Tibet in United Nations 1950-61, pp. 269-78.
35. International Commission of Jurists, 21, 1964, p. 42.
36. Mehrotra, L.L. *India's Tibet Policy: An Appraisal and Options*, New Delhi, 1997, p. 41.

4
A Rebellion Crushed: A Tragic Experiment with Non-Violence

The pragmatic view of any conflict resolution would be to use whatever means that result in maximum advantage with minimum efforts. The deployment of the means is decided by the art of the possible. This perspective is value neutral. No particular inherent virtue is ascribed: what results in the greatest good of the greatest number of people is good.

Buddhism takes the same kind of view. Though non-violence is a fundamental tenet, it does not totally rule out the use of violence. If violent methods were employed so that lot more violence can be prevented, it is a just tool. In one of the *Jatak Katha,* Buddha is a sailor on a boat. The captain of the ship is planning to kill all five hundred occupants of the boat in order to capture a treasure that the ship is carrying. The sailor Buddha comes to know of the captain's plan and kills the captain. A minimum violence has succeeded to save so many.

The Dalai Lama has focused on non-violence, that has won him the Nobel Prize. However, when a violent option was exercised by the tribesmen of the provinces of Kham and Amdo, refined dialectics were beyond their comprehension. Historically, Tibetans have been a martial race. Given the rough terrain and harsh weather of Himalayas, they are built sturdily and can withstand extremes of the situations easily. And this is certainly the case with the tribesmen from Amdo and Kham. They had little understanding of the politics, diplomacy and Buddhist discourse. They only understood conflict and injustice. A terrible wrong has been done to their land, their people and their lama. The only recourse was to revenge in blood. If they did not know sophisticated warfare, they knew guerrilla tactics well. If and when this gets compounded with refinements from a sophisticated agency like CIA, the least they can do was to inflict terrible harm on the enemy. Their story reveals the little known fact that Tibet had an option to violent struggle. The story is as full of valour and romance as that of *Azad Hind Fauz,* the National Revolutionary Army led by Netaji Subhas Chandra Bose. They run parallel to the end. On the other hand, the beginning has much in common with the Mukti Bahini of Bangladesh. The latter succeeded because of the support from India while the rebellion failed in Tibet because of lack of support from the neighbour!

The first confrontation occurred towards the end of 1954. The Chinese were pushing with reforms which the peasants in Kham thought to be interference and imposition. The Tibetans saw the reforms as a subversion of their value system. The reforms meant that all that was precious in their world view would be destroyed.

It was a tradition that every Khampa carried a weapon and some had access to guns too. When the Chinese insisted on surrendering of the weapons, a revolt broke out that was ultimately to catapult into a national rebellion. Though this was comparable to the 1857 uprising in India, it did not have organization or leadership. However, there was support from Chiang Kai-Shek of American weapons that were air dropped.

Chinese took the extreme step of bombing a monastery which had 3000 monks and many rebels.[1] Other monasteries also feared the same fate. And armed resistance from such other loci in both the provinces of Kham and Amdo brought about a situation that at one time they were totally without governance from Chinese.

We may recall that even under Chinese occupation before March 10, 1959, there was some sort of a Tibetan army. Most of the cadres of the army sought refuge in what was called North Eastern Frontier area of India after the escape of the Dalai Lama. And some of the cadres continued to function as guerillas within Tibet. At this time, the Dalai Lama's elder brother, Gyalo Thondup was in Darjeeling and now he planned a closer involvement with the CIA. What was previously a limited support now culminated into a planned roadmap to a possible insurgency leading to independence of Tibet. This was amply supported by the aristocratic community settled in Kalimpong. This provided a base to liaison with the CIA as well as the Kuomintang.

Two of the Dalai Lama's brothers, Gyalo Thondup and Thubten Norbu, had established links with CIA. And Gyalo Thondup took the leadership of the rebels. An elaborate plan was charted so that a select few would be trained in guerilla warfare by the CIA in USA. About 500 men were selected — based on their martial nature, physical stature and ancestry, i.e. either tribal chieftains or their progeny. The men represented at least one district in Tibet's provinces. And after the training in the American bases, they were air-dropped within Tibet's border. There they were to organize the National Volunteer Defence Army.

The National Volunteer Defence Army was composed of young Tibetan youths in the refugee camps, people working at the road building sites that was to link Tibet with main land China. But the bulk came from the defiant militant tribes from Amdo and Kham. Initially there were no modern weapons and they carried only large knives and outdated rifles. They had no military training. But now there was a realistic possibility of large scale CIA support. The Tibetan youths in the refugee camps were dreaming to do some kind of magic sacrifice so that there can be a free Tibet. To push a tank through the columns of Chinese soldiers was one of the dreams towards attainment of their goal. They believed that people who have stayed behind and still aiming to dislodge the Chinese were the best and, only the soft found an easy way into India.

Around this time there was a popular protest sung as a chorus in the streets of Lhasa:

> We would rather have the Dalai Lama than Mao tse-Tung
> We would rather have the Kashag than the Uyon Lhen Khang (PCART)
> We would rather have Buddhism than Communism
> We would rather have Ten sung Mag mi than the PLA
> We would rather use our own wooden bowls than Chinese mugs.

The hope got strengthened following the defeat of India at Chinese hands in 1962. Initially India was reticent to support. The Tibetans in India were refugees and they were obliged to the Government of India so as not to cause them inconvenience. The scenario became totally different after 1962.

A full scale rebel uprising thus came about and it was named *four-rivers-six-ranges.* This came to be known as National Volunteer Defence Army (NVDA). The Tibetan nationalist rebels had modern weaponry now supplied to them along with radio operators and secret coding method. Their weaponry included MI rifles, mortars and silencers. They also learnt parachuting, rock-climbing, and river-crossing. And, of course, the refined arts of espionage were also taught to them. Finally, they were to be ready to rise up in revolt at the shortest signal so that all such units functioning in tandem can bring about upheaval. The individual cadet had only a limited knowledge of the operation. Only the select few leaders and the CIA had the full knowledge of all the rebel bases that spanned entire Tibet.

Gyalo Thondup's diplomacy with USA had worked well. During 1957 to 1962, Tibetans would be picked from the refugee camps and smuggled out of India to what was then East Pakistan (now Bangladesh). One has to remember that these were the days of Hindi-Chini Bhai-Bhai policy and the Indian border security would have a hostile watch on the Tibetans.

The story of the assaults by the guerillas is the story of brave people who took their lives in the palm of their hand and looked face to face in the eyes of death. The Dalai Lama narrates a small story of the valiant guerillas[2]: "The old lama who had recently escaped from Tibet in 1970s tells as to how he had observed an encounter from his hermitage, high up in the mountains in the remote part of Amdo. A small posse of six horsemen had attacked a PLA encampment several hundreds strong just near the bend of a river. The result was chaos. The Chinese panicked and started shooting wildly in all directions killing large number of their own troops. Meanwhile, the horsemen, having escaped across the river, turned back, and approached from a different direction, attacked again from the flank before disappearing into hills. I was moved to hear of such bravery."

Gyalo Thondup was convinced that only the US will help then and, the only way to deal with Chinese was the hard way[3]. (Pala, who was the personal secretary to the Dalai Lama in 50s and arranged all the audiences then, meticulously saw that no rebel leader can approach him; when did the Dalai Lama come to know is difficult to guess). As the leader of NVDA, he established a vast espionage network throughout Tibet in late 60s and early 70s. This made their operation very fruitful. (It was through this route that it was known about the Chinese shifting of the main nuclear base to Tibet). The fighting in both the provinces of Kham and Amdo got intense and numerous freedom-fighters with their numbers running into tens of thousand had joined hands in guerilla warfare. They would procure arms not only from the Chinese after ambushing them but also by raiding the Tibetan government ammunition store-houses.

On October 20, 1962 China invaded India. After slapping a humiliating defeat, they retreated on November 21. Thereafter, India with CIA collaboration established a special frontier force. It was no longer necessary now for CIA and Khampa operations to be carried out *via* East Pakistan and the NVDA could function from New Delhi itself. Once a week a joint meeting of the officers of CIA, Research & Analytical Wing and NVDA will be held. The data operated through radio signals, it was analyzed and the strategy planned. And it was thought that the area of Mustang bordering Nepal and China was the best location for the operation. Mustang had a height of 15,000 ft where there was a plateau; the situation of this strategic height was similar to the advantage that the Pakistani army enjoyed during Kargil war. There was only a single valley through which any approach could pass from Mustang to North in China and to South at Kathmandu. Moreover Mustang was close to the only road connecting Lhasa to Ladakh. A General named Baba Yeshi was the commander. He had his headquarters at Mustang.

The period between 1962 India-China war and 1971 was indeed critical time for military hope for Tibet. During this time if India would have thought of relinquishing its honour that was lost in 1962, Tibet may have reason to revolt as CIA was still backing them. However, for India it turned out to be a critical period of transition. In 1964 Nehru died a broken man. This was followed in 1965 by a war with Pakistan. While negotiating peace, India had to give away military gains on a platter because of Soviet intervention. And this took the toll in life of Lal Bahadur Shastri. Indira Gandhi's ascent to power was not unchallenged. Morarji Desai was a strong contender to the prime-ministership in 1965: once again he challenged Indira Gandhi in 1969 and the Congress party had a vertical split. With this sort of political situation, India was not in a position to dabble into matters of wider and long-ranging interests.

In July 1971 Henry Kissinger took a secret flight to Peking[4]. USA had recognized the importance of trade and commerce with the largest populous nation in the world. China and Russia axis had already split. Richard Nixon changed the foreign policy of the Cold War. Instead of a barricade around the communist countries, now there was a shift — to go behind the barricade. While this would facilitate trade and commerce, the mixing up of the economies was thought to be a better way to break communism now. And China was willing to raise the "bamboo curtain". Henry Kissinger's mission to Peking brought about a US-Chinese rapprochement. The CIA, therefore, cut off its support to Tibetan guerillas.

For guerillas, territory is most important in their strategy. Towards that they were utilizing their bases in Nepal. Nepal was frightened by what happened between China and India in 1960s. If China was to deal with Nepal in the manner that it did with India, Nepal would be in a position similar to Poland *versus* Germany in Second World War. Nepal could be run over by PLA in a couple of days! So far, it was clinging to India for support. But in 1970s it got big-brotherly attitudes from New Delhi and decided to balance its relationship with China. For more than 12 years Nepal had allowed the guerillas to function from Mustang. Now they decided to expel them.

But the worst of all, there were internal differences in National Volunteer Defence Army. Gyalo Thondup, who was *de facto* the Commander-in-Chief of NVDA, decided to remove the Commandant General Baba Yeshi and replaced him with General Gyatso Wangdu, who was trained in United States by CIA. The Government at Dharmashala tried to pacify Baba Yeshi and appointed him as Chief of Security to the Dalai Lama. Yeshi was not reconciled. Basically he was made to be a guerilla warrior. But now his war efforts took a U-turn. He organized a guerilla group of his own and started attacking the rival group led by Wangdu.

China was getting worried about the operations of guerillas from Mustang. Mao tse-Tung himself told the King of Nepal to stop the operation of Khampas or face the worst consequences.[5] So Nepal made a determined effort to quell the rebel activity. Now the fate of the resistance was sealed as it was torn between internecine fights, pursuit by the Nepalese army and depletion of CIA support. It finally culminated in the surrender of Baba Yeshi to the Nepalese Government. Baba Yeshi was a broken man, dishonoured by his own men and a failure in the service of his nation. With tears rolling down his cheeks he surrendered himself to Nepal and bartered for asylum. In return, he gave full account of activity of National Volunteer Defence Army to Nepal.

Even today, with 50 years history behind them, the Tibetan communities in India do identify themselves along the original lines as to what province they belong to. Baba Yeshi belonged to Kham. There was also a split in the refugee settlement along the provincial origin. Refugees from these provinces sympathized with Baba Yeshi and perceived it to be a conspiracy within the Central Tibetan Government at Dharmashala. This went to the extent that some of the refugees stopped their one-rupee-a-month contribution to Dharmashala.

Nepal tried to barter with General Wangdu too. They offered a rehabilitation package. The Khampas refused. By chance there was the arrest of NVDA's officer Lhamo Tsering by Nepal. He was held as a hostage. However, even this bait did not result in surrender of Khampas. Seeing the impossibility of any breakthrough and an obvious impasse between Nepal and Khampas, the Dalai Lama decided to intervene. He saw no hope of their survival unless they surrender.

There was no possibility of a war between China and India nor was there a possibility of war between China and the then Soviet Union. There was no uprising in the Chinese mainland either. And the guerillas were trapped between the devil and the deep sea — between China and Nepal. The Dalai Lama thought it worthwhile to seek peace thorough utilization of non-violence, since Nepal had offered not only amnesty but rehabilitation. The immediate loyalty of the militia was to the chief of the tribe but the Dalai Lama's voice was the final command.

The Dalai Lama sent his emissary, Takla to Kathmandu. Takla was asked to go along with Lhamo Tsering, the arrested rebel leader, to contact the guerilla base. From there on Takla went alone and addressed the assembled Khampa chieftains. Takla said that the life of Lhamo Tsering was at stake and he can be saved only if the guerillas were to surrender. It is said that the guerillas had a good laugh at this. They retorted that now that they knew where their comrade in arm was held, they would raid the post and free him that very night.

Noticing their stubborn resolve, Takla then played tape-recorded message of the Dalai Lama. And the tragic consequence started to unfold. This caused anguish, confusion and muddle headedness. Panchen, one of the heads, was the first to speak. He said that they have carried on guerilla warfare on scant support for over two decades against the powerful Chinese. If they never thought of surrendering to the powerful Chinese, where was the question of giving up against paltry Nepal? For a Khampa, his weapon is a part of his own self. Giving up a weapon is like giving up a part of one's body. On the other hand, he cannot think of disobeying the Dalai Lama's orders.

There were two options open now, either to push inside Tibet and fight till death or to obey the Dalai Lama's appeal. Wangdu and other senior officers decided to go along with the second option.

This was followed by a tragedy to be followed by another tragedy and yet another. Rather than submitting to a shameful surrender, Panchen took his life by cutting his throat. He was followed by some other leaders. Once the Khampas laid down their weapons Nepal broke its promise. Instead of amnesty and rehabilitation, the guerillas were apprehended and put into jail.

Wangdu had yet not surrendered and, with the remaining guerillas, he made a desperate bid to cross over to India. He was pursued by Baba Yeshi's men, now in the service of Nepalese army. Before Wangdu could cross over to India, he was caught in a pincer attack between the Nepalese troops and Baba Yeshi's faction. Except for a very few that could cross over to India, Wangdu along with his troops was massacred. And the irony of the entire tragic incident was that Bába Yeshi flew from Kathmandu by a helicopter to identify Wangdu's body!

Lhamo Tsering and other Khampa leaders who had surrendered according to the Dalai Lama's appeal languished in Nepalese jail for 7 years. This was indeed a tragic end to the valiant guerillas warfare and more tragic was the outcome of an appeal by the Dalai Lama in the service of non-violent means.

The silver lining to the fighting spirit of the Tibetans is the Special Frontier Force. The force was created during the Indo-China war of 1962. While at its inception it was thought to be the future army of Free Tibet, it was one of the plans that in the event of war with China, the Special Frontier Force would try to seize Tibet. Such a role was denied by destiny to the Special Frontier Force. But they had a different reward coming their way during 1971 Bangladesh war. This time they turned into a vanguard for the Indian army in the form of the Mukti Bahini and were instrumental in winning independence for Bangladesh.

Now the Special Frontier Force has been renamed the Establishment 22. Their rolc was well publicized following Bangladesh war. However, there was nothing known about the women cadres. An expedition to Mount Everest was dispatched on March 18th, 2005. It is known that two of the ten participants were Tibetan women. Dechen Lhamo and Pema Choedon are paratroopers belonging to the Special Frontier Force. They are skilled in guerilla type mountain warfare and martial art. Dechen Lhamo was raised in Nepalese hills while Pema was brought up in a Tibetan refugee camp at Behrampur, Orissa. Special Frontier Force has contributed indirectly too. Lobsang Yeshi, the son of a SFF soldier is now the International Vice-President of Tibetan Youth Congress (TYC) and carries the flag of Rangzen.

Let us juxtapose Tibetan situation to India. The score of the militancy on the Indian side of freedom struggle is not so tragic and futile. During the Second World War Subhas Chandra Bose, broke away from the Gandhian path of non-violent agitation and took the support from Japan. He even contacted Hitler on the basis that an enemy of the enemy is the best friend. Hitler is said to have guaranteed full support to Subhas Chandra Bose. However, Mahatma Gandhi declined this route and argued that Nazis would be worse masters. When Japanese marched into the then Burma, Azad Hind Fauz joined them in armed action. In the minds of Indian youth of that time, Subhas Chandra Bose was an idol and earned the epithet, Netaji. Netaji died in an air-crash. Following the conclusion of the Second World War, cadres of Azad Hind Fauz were captured by the British troops. A trial was conducted in New Delhi at Red Fort. But all of them were acquitted. It is said that insurgency by Netaji had made British realize that India may also rise in another War of Independence like 1857.

Though for a brief period, during the emergency years of 1975 to 1977, George Fernandes along with the journalists Vikram Rao, Kirit Bhatt and other socialist comrades created an underground group with the aim of destabilizing the autocratic Indira Gandhi government. They aimed at blasting vital installations or bridges. They procured dynamite from the quarries nearby Baroda. The plot leaked out and about 11 of them were jailed with the charges of treason that attracted a life-sentence or hanging. Following the victory of the Janata Party and the victory in election of

George Fernandes (while he was in jail) – all the Vadodara Dynamite Case prisoners were granted free release. All of them came out as heroes and George Fernandes was made a central minister.

There are other smaller instances that cannot be compared to insurgency but are in marked contrast with what happened to Tibetan militants.

In early 1970s Jaiprakash Narayan had declared retirement from politics and has given away himself to Bhoodan Movement of Vinoba Bhave. This movement was entirely on Gandhian lines. Vinoba had thought that a non-violent transformation of class struggle can be brought. This was through a mass movement called *bhoodan.* People holding large chunks of land should give them voluntarily to the landless. He had toured the entire countryside with this mission. Just after this period, Jaiprakash's attention was drawn to the dacoits of Chambal valley in Madhya Pradesh. The people who had suffered atrocities from upper class society took to revenge and the ravines of the Chambal river provided them with impenetrable hideouts. The police were ineffective against them.

Jaiprakash Narayan single-handedly took up the challenge of reforming them. He succeeded and most of the dacoits surrendered even without any barter of amnesty. An interesting personal reminiscence may be narrated here. One day in the early morning we were surprised to see our friend Dr. Damodar Nene accompanied by a tall hefty man of about 6 ft 4 inches strolled into our house. When we showed surprise at the unknown towering figure, he just gave a hearty laugh and with a sprite touched the top of the doorway with one of his feet! He was a reformed leader of the Chambal dacoits! The story speaks of the real charisma of non-violent Jaiprakash Narayan. Unarmed and unaided he had established contacts with the dacoits, forayed into their hideouts without any security and talked to them. He had tended to their hurt feelings, and rather than living like hunted dogs, persuaded them to join the civil life as independent Indian citizens. Of course, they had a record of loot, burglary and murder. Jaiprakash could persuade them to surrender to the law and be ready to be prosecuted.

When they did so to the utter relief of the Madhya Pradesh government, there was a show of proceeding according to the law. However, the towering influence of Jaiprakash Narayan at that time taken together with that of Dada Dharmadhikari, who had voluntarily relinquished the Chief Ministership of Madhya Pradesh and remained in the Sarvodaya movement, had its say. All the dacoits were rehabilitated to live a free life as ordinary citizens.

There was another instance of banditry in the Chambal valley in late 1990s. Phoolan Devi branded as bandit-queen had suffered grave atrocities and became a dreadful dacoit. She attained international notorious fame because of her dreadful past and awesome image as a bandit. After she gave herself to the process of law, she won parliamentary election and sat in the parliament as its member.

Compared to all these, the valour, courage and dedication of the Tibetan guerillas have so far gone waste, and even met with a tragic end. One may as well wonder, if resorted to giving up arms in the service for non-violent means by the Dalai Lama was to result in suicides because of the lost pride, or long languish in the jails, why not to die in the service of the motherland fighting against the enemy? This is the question that only freedom fighters like Bhagat Singh and Sukhdev can answer.

This leads us to philosophical reflection on ends and means. For Mahatma Gandhi use of non-violence as a tool towards righteous ends turned out to be a mammoth experiment and it ended in such a surprise that the British Empire yielded to a frail man. That was indeed the survival of the weakest. For Jaiprakash, it was a small but beautiful experiment and that too succeeded when he put his life at stake. Such experiments provided software systems for the evolution in conflict resolution. Noble spirits like Martin Luther King and Leh Valecha were inspired and used the tool successfully.

A question is being frequently asked: What if Hitler was ruling India? What could non-violent Jews do against him? Gandhi succeeded because of refined sense of justice of the Labour Party as well as the commitment of Roosevelt and Americans to the ideals of freedom and liberty. The world has seen the worst holocaust in the history of mankind in the form of Second World War and its recent memory gave a transient message: "Never Again". Non-violent struggle has worked for Indian independence. However, has even a single year elapsed after the foundation of UN when the war is not being waged somewhere in the world?

Man by nature is aggressive and violence has yielded desired results to him when might was on his side. Take the case of China. As of now, they have got away with murder – genocide. Tibet hoped that the conscience of the world nations would be aroused by their suffering. Most nations, including US — the champion of freedom, liberty and justice — know that what was done in Tibet, is as per the rule of jungle; they would rather do business with China than worry about the historical atrocities or the fate of Tibetan civilization. China will hold 2008 Olympics merrily!

The resolution of the paradox is provided by Mahatma Gandhi. For him, there is no alternative to non-violence; that is the only tool, regardless of results. Rooted in his bearings that thrive on the teachings of *Bhagwat Gita*, means were the ends[6] for him. When the whole of mankind will come to believe and behave according to this logic, then Brahmaputra will truly be said to have changed its course. On the other hand, a few decades, though appear to be a long time for individuals, may be just a breathing time for historical forces. Can anyone tell with certainty that the fight for a Free Tibet is finished? Could we have foreseen what happened in Soviet Russia? It required philosophical foresight of a visionary Rohit Mehta[7] to forecast in 1935 that the Soviet Union cannot survive. With due humility, we clearly perceive that Tibetan Spirit cannot be dominated for ever; it is bound to assert again and again.

REFERENCES

1. Tsering Shakya, *The Dragon in the Land of Snows*, London, 1999, pp. 141-184.
2. The Dalai Lama, *Freedom in Exile*, London, 1990, p. 139.
3. Subsequently when his stand softened, China called him a friend and he did shuttle between Beijing and Dharmashala to liaison.
4. Henry Kissinger, *The White House Years*, New York, 1980.
5. John Avedon, *In Exile From The Land of Snows*, New York, 1984, p. 126.
6. Aldous Huxley, *The End and Means*, New York, 1950.
7. Rohit Mehta, *Theosophical Socialism*, Adyar, Madras, 1935.

5
Tibetan Youth Congress — Torchbearers of Rangzen

Historical Perspective

Valiant Tibetan youths organized themselves as a political and cultural body and founded Tibetan Youth Congress (TYC) on 7th October, 1970; Tenzing Geyche was the founding president who later served as the personal secretary to the Dalai Lama; patronized initially by the Dalai Lama; constitutionally independent of the Government in Exile; planned to demonstrate before Chinese Embassy in 1977; Met Jaiprakash Narayan; Gateway to Janta Government; Confrontation with Kashag; Leaders absorbed into Central Tibetan Administration; differences with the Dalai Lama; Five-Point Peace Plan and Strasbourg Proposals framed in 1987 that accept Tibetan autonomy against independence; Confrontation with official policy; TYC does not rule out violence; Does not subscribe to Strasbourg Proposals; Does not follow middle way approach, 2005; Committed to Rangzen (independence).

Patronage from Government in Exile withdrawn completely following the referendum in 2008; The official policy is to be an Autonomous Tibetan Region within Chinese Republic; Contradictions continue; Elected Kalon Tripa, Lobsang Sangay was once upon a time TYC President.

While most of the young refugees found their sustenance from road building sites across India, a few fortunate ones got the means to study and went to colleges. Some refugee families belonged to the aristocratic class. Even before the escape of the Dalai Lama in Exile, their children were studying in Kalimpong and other Indian cities. They had seen the working of the political system and parties in India. With their modern education and inspiration from the freedom movement in India, they thought of organizing a platform of their own and Tibetan Youth Congress was founded in October 1970 with the following objectives:

1. To dedicate oneself to the task of serving one's country and people under the guidance of His Holiness the Dalai Lama, the Spiritual and Temporal Ruler of Tibet.
2. To promote and protect national unity and integrity by giving up all distinctions based on religion, regionalism or status. It advocates independence from China of Tibet, including the three provinces of U-Tsang, Do-toe, and Do-med.
3. To work for the preservation and promotion of religion and Tibet's unique culture and traditions.
4. To struggle for the total independence of Tibet even at the cost of one's life.

In 2005, there were more than 1,30,000 Tibetans surviving in India in 30 refugee camps. Tibetan youngsters study in about 100 Tibetan schools. More than 400 monasteries and cultural centres have been built in India. There is even a contingent of about 5,000 Tibetan soldiers serving in the Indian army, manning the Siachen Glacier frontiers. Their military service may not allow them to join political organizations, but almost all the Tibetan youths from the community are members of TYC.

When TYC was founded, Tibet was almost forgotten world over. Tenzin Geyche Tethong, once upon a time Personal Secretary to the Dalai Lama was the founding president. Other founders, viz. Lodi G. Gyari, Sonam Topgyal and Tenzin N. Tethong have subsequently held important positions with Government in Exile. The Dalai Lama delivered the inaugural address. True to his democratic style, he had no objections when the Congress drafted a constitution that made TYC an independent movement of Tibetan youth. This was a democratic bifurcation point from Tibetan Central Administration. Henceforth, they shall have no control over everything Tibetan, be it in India or elsewhere in the world. Little would have the Dalai Lama known then that the baby is going to outgrow its parents as well as benefactors when it really comes of the age. Let us see how.

The Tibetan youths have seen the functioning of the youth wings of various political parties in India. They have known that this is a pathway to the building of future leadership. Buddhist as they are, they liked the dialectics, and, democracy also thrives on the dialectical discourses. The organization gave the youths a platform to not only question the happenings of the past but also to raise their doubts about the government in Exile. Thus since its inception, the Tibetan Youth Congress while owning its allegiance to the Dalai Lama, is in a state of creative tension with the Tibetan government and even with the Dalai Lama himself.

Tibetan Youth Congress (TYC) came to limelight with a spectacular success in 1977 when they secretly planned to demonstrate in front of the Chinese Embassy in New Delhi. The news leaked out and there was only a limited fight with the police outside the embassy. The police did not allow the majority of the Tibetans to leave the refugee camp. Even this limited scuffle got media attention and the word spread around. It charged up thousands of refugees in and around New Delhi. They spontaneously had a large demonstration and precipitated indefinite hunger strike. Their immediate demand was to implement all the resolutions that were passed by the United Nations (See Appendix II).

During those few days in March 1977, the limelight that the Tibetan movement gathered was unprecedented. And, this was concurrent with a major event at the national level. This was a crucial watershed election time when Indira Gandhi was voted out of power. And here was a chance opportunity for Tibet since many of leaders that were to form the new government were those who had championed Tibet's cause loudly inside and outside the parliament. Jaiprakash Narayan though ailing was the king-maker in the emerging political scenario. He along with his socialist friends had almost adopted the young Dalai Lama in 1959. The Dalai Lama's faith in the Gandhian socialist/spiritual JP, as he came to be called, was such that the Dalai Lama handed over whatever funds that he had mustered while escaping from Tibet to JP. A Trust with JP as the president was formed. (No wonder that with idealist JP, with hardly any expertise at managing the money, it soon disappeared).

Tempa Tsering[1], Jamyang Norbu and Lodi Gyari[2], along with a few others, ventured to meet JP. Nobody would have thought that they had any chance. They implored the secretary with the password — Tibetan refugees. The gates immediately were wide open. They briefed JP. He was highly supportive and, even promised the TYC leaders that he would secure the backing from Morarji Desai, the Prime Minister designate. The newly elected leaders support reconciled the Tibetans. They called off the fast and one of the senior most leaders, Acharya Kripalani offered orange juice to seven Tibetans who were fasting unto death. When open support to Tibetans was on display, many politicians went to them and pleaded their backing; maybe to be on the right side of the tide.

While Tibetan Youth Congress leaders were jubilant with their breakthrough and subsequent patronage by many politicians of Janata Party who were to be in the subsequent Government, Kashag and the government in Exile were not only not so enamoured of their eccentric unauthorized initiative but were annoyed with them. The Kashag response was a rude shock to TYC activists.

It is not difficult to understand the Kashag's reaction. They charged the TYC leaders with recklessness and unthoughtful actions so as to endanger the refugee settlement. This brought out a confrontation between the TYC and Kashag. The chaos continued for quite some days when the Tibetan Youth Congress heckled the ministers and elected deputies. The diffusion of the confrontation was also in an incomprehensive manner. The top founding members of the TYC resigned from its central committee. Strangely enough some youth leaders were in high government positions. And the list of those who made to the top posts is impressive. Sonam Topgyal has been the prime minister. We have seen about Tenzing Tethong. Lodi Gyari is the envoy at Unites States. And, the list is long.

Was the confrontation because the youth leaders had stolen limelight? Did they really harm the Tibetan cause by their preemptive actions? Whom did they actually embarrass? The answers to these questions are difficult to gauge but the very incident is an illustrious example of freedom of democratic action. The subsequent restitution of the youth leaders to the high government offices also sent a clear message that it is the ebullient invigorated and effervescent youth that is the real salt of any nation. It is through their steam that the political actions will get propelled. Of course, tears will be shed and the hearts broken in the confrontation between the old guard and vanguard.

The confrontation has been focalized since the Dalai Lama announced Five-Point Peace Plan in 1987 at Capitol Hill and further elaborated them as Strasbourg Proposals at Strasbourg, France on June 16, 1988. This hit worse than a bombshell to many Tibetans, particularly the youth. They were flabbergasted. Though the older generation was dumb folded, the youths were angry and they spoke from their mouthpieces: Tibetan Review and Rangzen. Speaking on behalf of most Tibetan youths, Phuntsog Wangyal was to argue meticulously under the title Giving- up the Struggle[3]. He said:

> "It would be no exaggeration to say that there is not a single one who does not yearn for Tibet's independence.... The only question is that some see the issue of independence as realistic, and others as unrealistic. It is a myth to claim that gaining independence is a more difficult task now than it has ever been during the past three decades."

He equated the belief in ultimate goal of independence to their belief in Buddha. "In fact, independence is perhaps small as an aim compared to enlightenment, and may definitely be more realistic from an individual point of view than the attainment of Buddhahood in ones lifetime." Regarding its effects on the morale of all, but especially upon that of activists, he observed:

> "This would be a crushing blow. So many Tibetans have fought all their lives for this one issue, and now, overnight, find that they have to change, and for no good reason. How would they feel, I wonder, those who laid down their lives in the name of Tibet's freedom — the more than one million who perished since China occupied Tibet, those who died in October 1987 and March 1988, or those who are still being arrested, imprisoned and tortured — if they heard that independence was no longer held to be realistic, and that Tibet was destined to remain for ever a part of China? Was the whole of their sacrifice just a waste?"

Along with the large Tibetan community in Switzerland, the Tibetan Youth Congress and Tibetan Youth Association (the largest independent Tibetan political organizations in India and Europe) made very strong protests against this statement, in the presence of the Dalai Lama in Switzerland. They declared emphatically that they would maintain their belief in independence and would fight to the end to attain it.

TYC apprehended that the statement released at Strasbourg seemed to be a direct product of non-Tibetan views, and of those opinions prevailing over Tibetan views. It was thought so because the Dalai Lama was engaged in hectic diplomacy with the West during this time. And he had suggested the name of a European lawyer, Michael van Walt van Prag, as one of the negotiators with China following Strasbourg Proposals. Of course, China protested vehemently about his inclusion and, this time rightly so. TYC argues that nobody except the Tibetans has a right to speak on behalf of Tibet. That Michael may have exercised considerable amount of legal acumen and knowledge about international law in influencing the Dalai Lama, says the TYC leaders, and is evident from his book, *The Status of Tibet*. TYC thinks the book is pro-Chinese. Without naming him, the article further said:

> "Yet the issue at stake here is Tibet and the future of the Tibetan people. Therefore, the Tibetans' feelings and their determination must surely be the primary consideration behind any move the Tibetans take. If the Tibetan people have neither the will to fight nor the hope to believe in their cause, no amount of Western support or pressure can conjure up a positive result for Tibet.... So it seems

> that this proposal was influenced less by Tibetan views and more by the advice of foreigners[4]. It was rather telling that, at the time of issue, the statement was available in English and French, and a few days later in German, but not in Tibetan. Subject to a number of last minute changes, it was formulated and written in a bland and sophisticated prose, which ordinary people will find impenetrable, and therefore, only a rich source of confusion[5]."

TYC viewed the shifting stance not only to the desperation felt by the Tibetans in power to return to the motherland but also to the foreign hands. They argued that while Tibetans are busy in diplomacy, when they seek support internationally they do so on the camouflage of moral grounds. The monolith of China has also at its commands powerful diplomacy that binds interests of trade and business. TYC believed that the same foreign powers which are apparently helping the Tibetans could also be pressurizing the Dalai Lama to wrap up a deal.

This was evident by the diplomacy and counter diplomacy of several eminent statesmen. Edward Heath, the former British Prime Minister following a sponsored visit by the Beijing as well as Jimmy Carter, the former American President, are said to have, according to TYC made heavy-handed attempts to make the Dalai Lama compromise[6]. Even Lord Ennals who had checked the international legal conference on the status of Tibet and has been one of the prominent nominators for the Nobel Prize, is quoted as saying to the Chinese, "to show imagination in the administration of their oldest territory"[7]. This is in spite of the fact that Ennals in his report, "Tibet in China" has categorically said that the most outspoken calls for the independence came from within Tibet.

TYC has total distrust of China. They are just not enamoured by any of the agreements, treaties, or declarations that the Chinese government may make. They are themselves aware about the fate of the 17-Point Agreement and believe that the Sino-British agreement before the handover of Hong Kong will meet the same fate. The Chinese had promised democratization to Hong Kong before hand over by the British. Then they said it will be in 2007. Now they are saying 2012! Most people in Hong Kong believe that they have been sold out. If they were to be given an option of British citizenship, the herds of Chinese from Hong Kong would have flocked to UK.

It was a fact that the Tibetan people were not consulted, and that, even when they were, it was within such a short period that they did not have time to consider the subject in any depth. It was argued that such a vital shift demanded a referendum[8]. It called out for more time for reflection and discussion in order to arrive at a greater consensus. This time was not given.

The bitterness was amply conveyed when he further wrote: "It will, for a start, undermine the will to fight for independence. At, the best of times this is a very difficult and frustrating occupation, and in Tibet it is very risky. It is not something that Tibetans need to do to make their lives more comfortable."

Various factors have historically worked as causes of divisiveness in Tibetan society, the most significant being regionalism and sectarianism. Yet the question on which Tibetans have been 100 per cent united all along is that of independence. Now there were factions who held that the Dalai Lama is the protector and knows best what course to follow. TYC surely and certainly disagreed when it came to independence. This has divided Tibetan polity. This is just what the Chinese have been waiting for.

It is quite evident that the effect of this statement on the Tibetans was miscalculated. The Dalai Lama has always said that the ultimate goal was the happiness of the Tibetan people, and the Chinese could now say, that the Dalai Lama also believed that it was they who would make the Tibetans happy. It looks as though the Tibetans have given up.

Therefore, in many ways this statement represented a great diplomatic achievement for the Chinese and the biggest setback for the Tibetans.

Probably the most compelling motivation for the Dalai Lama has been his dedication to finding an answer to the Tibetan question during his lifetime. This may have led him to go too far. This has happened in case of Indian leaders just prior to 1947. Aged as they were, they got too anxious to win independence while they were at the helm and India was partitioned.

It was said that there was a compulsion to act fast so that population transfer may stop. But the Chinese have not committed at all about stopping it. In that case, why should Tibetans abandon their claim to independence? When decisions are in the hands of the Chinese, whatever freedom the Chinese hand out today can be withdrawn tomorrow.

The Chinese did say that there was nothing new in the proposals. They have never accepted Tibetan independence anyway, so what have the Tibetans given up?

The proposals were issued at Strasbourg. No country ever makes important announcements from foreign regions, unless they are joint statements. Some say it was a tactical move. The Western countries have been the main corridor for Tibet. But why did they forgot that one of the main reasons the UN filed the appeal of Tibet, cabled by Shakabpa in 1950 was that it was sent from (Kalimpong) a foreign land? Western sympathizers having special interest in Tibet were also perplexed about what Tibetans are standing for.

In conclusion, Phuntsog Wangyal said, "One hundred years from now, history will judge us in a harsh way. One does not want to be a part of the group of people who left Tibet, led a comfortable life in the world outside, and gave up the future of their country. Who would want to be part of such a history?"

After the Strasbourg Proposals, the important questions were: How would the Tibetans remain confident and assert that the Tibetan people do want independence? How will they remain united to fight for it?

These questions have been answered by time itself. Now in 2006, TYC asserts that because of its democratic set-up and freedom to choose, no individual or group, however large or small, amongst the Tibetans in Exile has the right to decide the future of Tibet. And the Dalai Lama subscribes to this view, since innumerable times he has said that "the Tibetan people themselves must be the ultimate deciding authority". Therefore, Tibet's future must be decided by the Tibetan people as a majority, and until that majority can fully exercise their will, no such decision can be taken. TYC was unanimous that it should be reversed or abandoned at once.

Tashi Tobgye Jamyangling, another TYC activist, voiced the same views but in much harsher tones. The Tibetans are soft spoken up to a fault. And the revered Dalai Lama is never spoken of in derogatory language. Jamyangling must not only be very angry but partly out of senses when he referred to this act as "A Political Menopause."[9] He said:

> "What most Tibetans would care to know is that the statement was made by the Dalai Lama. If so, then it is the last word. And that shall remain national character till the Dalai Lama exists. He dared to ask further "How on earth are we ever going to decide our political and social destinies after His Holiness is no more? The Tibetan struggle must go on without His Holiness the Dalai Lama, and that the Strasbourg statement must be viewed as a statement meant for public debate and determination, and not as commandments that require every believer to live and die for."

Ironically, as a TYC functionary, Tashi was one of the members of the first official fact finding delegation sent by the Dalai Lama in 1979 to China. The delegation covered some 15,000 kilometres by road across Tibet. He wrote, "I saw thousands of blistered Tibetan hands, and I listened to hundreds and hundreds of people who suffered so very much under the Chinese. This experience changed my entire life! For the first time in my life 1 realized that China has not won and that Tibet was stronger than it had ever been for over a century."

He was critical of the Dalai Lama explaining co-existence with China on the basis of interdependence, "What we must also understand and accept is the fact that this sense of interdependence comes not, in almost all cases, from love for mankind or Bodhichitta, but rather, it surfaces from the very depth of man's survival instinct....Modern politics is a selfish science which leaves very little or no room for lasting comradeship and fidelity. The point is that where there is gain, there is no shame.

Exhorting his countrymen that freedom shall not be available on a platter but only through "the will to fight, let there be fire in our eyes, and let the very depths of Tibetan emotion be stirred....rise against our common enemy. Let us not pretend to love our enemy, because we don't. Let us not pretend that the Buddha's Dharma and Marxism have anything important in common, because they don't."[10] This is the most severe criticism of the Dalai Lama that we have yet come across from a Tibetan.

Before the Tiananmen Square massacre, there was some hope since Deng was pursuing moderate policies. In August 1989, Jamyang Norbu wrote in *Tibetan Review*, "In Deng's grave new world, an illusion dies."[11] For about a decade Deng's policies were towards moderation. This liberalization culminated into the demonstration by the Chinese students at the Tiananmen Square. The subsequent demolition of the demonstration by the brutal use of force is one of the most ugly and grotesque chapter in Chinese Communist history. Tanks were rolled over the squatting students and regime took pride in releasing coloured photographs of student's heads flattened by the tanks.

However, a good thing happened. The Chinese themselves did not respond favourably. And after waiting for a long time, the Dalai Lama and Kashag withdrew the proposals.

Now the Tibetan Youths once again realized that the communist system has only one aim: that is to strengthen communist dictatorship. All totalitarian systems so planned their organizations that the totalitarian might alone survive. If they seen to be giving any kind of message that the people — the sub-systems within the system — have any role to play in reforming or transforming the system it is just a façade. The illusion is allowed so long as it serves the strengthening of the fascist trends. TYC gave up all the hopes of any moderation from the Chinese and affirmed their commitment to independence. Now they do not want to forget for ever that China has the dubious distinction to have recorded the largest massacre in the history of mankind (sixty million were killed between 1949-1970, according to the *Guinness Book of World Records*). No matter if Hu Yao-Bang has apologized.

It does not matter to them when he attributes such acts to the Gang of Four that has been ousted. They will never trust the Chinese.

This has given a signal to the Indian Government. Even though the Dalai Lama has constantly appealed to them that they should not indulge in any unlawful or violent activities, it is now clear that the youths may not listen to all that the Dalai Lama may say. Delhi police was wary of the ebullient temperament of the Tibetan Youth and sensed that they may create trouble during the visit of the Chinese Premiere, Li Peng in 1990. Most of them were rounded up and put into a temporary custody.

The Indian Government went a step ahead in asking the Dalai Lama to move out of New Delhi. Apart from the insult to the Dalai Lama, (against which we protested through the columns of *The Times of India*), it revealed an important fact about the Indian stance. We have seen earlier that in Nehru's times, when the Dalai Lama was in New Delhi, Chou En-lai had managed to be there. That time Nehru had utilized his presence for some sort of a negotiated settlement. Now the Indian leadership was clear that they have no role to play between the Dalai Lama and the Chinese.

The fiery youths of yore have matured into pragmatic past middle age group by now. But the train is ever moving and the newer entrants are no less firebrands. The membership now is 30,000. Let us have a look at them.

Soon after the 10th March, 2005 watershed-event (see Chapter 14), when we met some of the executive members of TYC they appeared like any other Tibetan youth. Within minutes, we could see the fire within them. When asked why were they not seen at the function, they said they had taken a remote seat as per their position. Why there was no Rangzen? And, why there were no leaflets? Simply because, they were not wanting to embarrass the Central Tibetan Administration. They knew what was about to come. But for them nothing has changed including their wish not to displease the Dalai Lama to the extent they can. The Dalai Lama may tread on whatever course he thinks appropriate to the present times. Tibet is a nation first. The Dalai Lamas came later to protect the nation. TYC will fight for the independence unto the last. They are non-violent today but they have not totally forsaken violence as a tool.

And we were in for a surprise soon after our return from Dharmashala. We had met this frail maverick of an activist, Tenzin Tsundue, in late 2004 at a symposium organized by the Tibetan Youth Congress at Baroda. He was bubbling with unease. Though he is born in India and could have obtained an Indian citizenship, Tibetan blood is flowing hot in his veins. So he carries a refugee status. After finishing his studies at Loyola College, Chennai, the call of the motherland was so powerful that he crossed over to Tibet from Ladakh. He fell in Chinese hands and after three months in prison they found him hot enough to throw back to India. As a writer and a poet, he reflects the yearning of a child who is tired of waiting for the mother.

Tsundue is a model of the new generation Tibetan youth. He respects the Dalai Lama as a son who would respect his grandfather. In the matter of future of Tibet, he is absolutely clear that only Tibetans have a right to decide about the future course and not even the Dalai Lama can write off Tibetan independence.

In April 2005, when there was an abrupt silence in his response to our correspondence, we were wondering what has happened to him. On March 10th he had opted to be in Mumbai to organize a function in support of Tibetan Independence. This had to be called off since the supporters said that when the Dalai Lama has backed up there is no point. Tsundue, however, must be preparing to make history of some sort.

Tsundue gave some clues as to what he was up to when he wrote in *Tehelka*, on 9th April, 2005: "I can never think of being party to the corrupt Communist China. I studied the *Bhagavad Gita*; my *karma yoga* is to fight for an independent, free, liberated, Tibet, while my *guru* His Holiness the Dalai Lama preaches a compromise with China.

"I am excited that in few days China's Prime Minister is to visit India with a huge business team. For me he is the head of Communist China, which invaded my country and continues to rule it with tyranny. Why do more than 3,000 Tibetans escape to India every year, running from Chinese persecution? Now is the time to protest China's occupation of Tibet directly to Wen Jiabao. Lathi-charges, jail, long drawn-out court cases, I am ready to face everything, but I will not keep silent". And he showed it by his action.

On Sunday, 11th April, 2005, when the Chinese Premier, Wen Jiabao visited the Indian Institute of Science at Bangalore, Tsundue was there to welcome him from the second floor balcony with a Tibetan flag, a banner with large display, "Free Tibet", shower of pamphlets and anti Chinese slogans. The display was dramatic. He could disrupt the official welcome for about 15 minutes when he was whisked away by the security. The message was two-fold — India is a democratic country and in spite of security, people do get away with shouting slogans for freedom. For the Chinese Premier it was a reminder that however smooth may appear the dialogue with India, till the issue of Tibet is not resolved, the Tibetan youth will not yield.

Since their presence is world-wide, they grab at whatever opportunity occurs anywhere. For instance, they had organized hunger strike at the UN. And when the Chinese were trying to market Buddhism in the form of Buddha's statues in New York, Lhadun Tethong, Canadian born daughter of former foreign minister of Tibet, along with numerous activists mobbed the exhibition with placards that the exhibition was of looted articles! The exhibition had to be winded up. However, independence is not won by such protests, that at least the Chinese know far too well.

Non-violent though it is, Buddhism does permit a selective violence in the service of greater good. We have already mentioned the story in *Jatak Katha* about Buddha. Christianity prescribes the offering of the other cheek. The Dalai Lama too, has offered the other cheek. The Tibetans have no third cheek but the youths have two powerful hands. The BBC news described the Congress as "radical but influential". The Chinese state Xinhua News Agency was of the view shared by several Chinese Tibetologists that the group was a *terrorist organization*. The TYC has denied Chinese accusations that it would resort to *suicide bombing* to achieve *independence.*[12]

How powerful the young Tibetan hands can be against the militant power? Their answer is as powerful as "that were of Veer Savarkar and Bhagat Singh". We were happy to note their knowledge of Indian history but were surprised when TYC members argued that the Hindu God Krishna also had to resort to violence when all other options were exhausted.

The Dalai Lama asks them that if they were to turn to militancy, where are they going to get the arms. One angry young Tibetan told us, he may not know the answer, but the Chinese should know. They may as well put the question to Bin Laden. If there is a will there is a way. So far they have not turned to violent militancy, mainly because of the Dalai Lama's pacifying grace. And in their fire-splitting writings and thoughts, thus far there is no saber-rattling, it is just rhetoric. Unless they perform, by whatever way, they will be judged by history not by the speeches they make but by the action and the result they deliver.

It is said that youth is usually brash and seldom wise. However, it was Mahatma Gandhi who said that the youth is the very salt of the nation. We believe after meeting these self-sacrificing faultless youths (no smoking, no alcohol, living away from family or long bachelorhood, yes, and some starvation) that they have the potential to provide a viable alternative to the moderate policies of the Dalai Lama. It is for them to prove, as yet.

Just when this chapter was being edited, we were visited by two TYC members. One of them, Penpa Tsering, called himself a former political prisoner of China. We renamed him a freedom fighter. At the age of 17, he participated in a demonstration against Chinese and was sentenced for four years in the worst of jails. He endured all kinds of tortures including ruthless thrashing to get information of accomplices, standing on the ice for days and touching live electric wire. He escaped to India during the fifth year of his sentence when he was on parole. Out of thirteen young men who climbed through the Himalayas, eight died of starvation. They went hungry for days and at times boiled their boots and belts as food.

After his refuge in India, Penpa Tsering joined an organization — The Gu Chu Sum Movement of Tibet. It is said to be a welfare organization. But the name translates as 27 (September), 1 (October) and 7 (March) Movement. It is named after three biggest uprisings in Tibet. Would Penpa Tsering be content to look after the welfare only?

Penpa Tsering had come with Lobsang Yeshi, International Vice-President of TYC. He wanted to know the opinion of the local youths about the middle way policy of the Dalai Lama. All seventy participants at the meeting were unanimous that there is no middle way; there is only one way and that is Rangzen.

Lobsang Yeshi proved this by appropriate action within two days. On 6th December, 2005, when the Dalai Lama was to address the Indian Parliament[13], protesting against killings of three monks in November in Tibet, TYC members surrounded the Chinese Embassy in New Delhi and some entered it by jumping over the walls[14]. Thirty-eight youths were apprehended by Delhi police. The news were on most of the channels of national TV.

The stay of Tibetan young guests acquainted our grandchildren with the freedom fight. They were so excited. So when Tibetan youths were marching in silent protest on 10th December, 2005, the Human Rights Day, they joined the march and proudly held the Tibetan flag high!

The protest in Delhi had even far reaching response. On 11th December, 2005, BBC covered human rights situation all over the world. Tibet was covered for ample time to emphasize that a mere protest attracts a jail detention for three years in Tibet. So does carrying a portrait of the Dalai Lama. The story was covered by three correspondents who had personal exposure to Tibet situation. While they narrated their story, BBC utilized the latest clips obtained from New Delhi. We were proud of our recent guests!

We had seen a Tibetan flag in Dharmashala office of these youths. Under the word Rangzen, there were numerous signatures in blood. Since then we believe that TYC members are capable of highest sacrifice. Let December 6th, 2005 event be a harbinger of such deeds. The Goddess of Revolution is only expiated by the blood of youth and that is the standard prescription of revolution.

In the final analysis, where there is patience, and will to succeed, perseverance will pay regardless of the costs.

Baroda TYC Protesters on Human Rights Day, December 10th, 2011

REFERENCES

1. Tempa Tsering manned the Delhi Bureau of Tibet when we last met him in 2006.
2. Lodi Gyari is the Head of the delegations (five till 2006) sent by the Dalai Lama to Peking for negotiations.
3. Phuntsog Wangyal, "Giving-up the Struggle", *Tibetan Review*, September 1988, p. 9.
4. This is an indirect reference to Michael van Walt van Prag, a lawyer and a trusted friend of Tibet, whom the Dalai Lama had mentioned as one of the negotiator.
5. *Ibid.*
6. This is only partly true. Following their on-the-spot visit to China, these statesmen had written to the Dalai Lama. They did not agree to some of his views. But there was no question of heavy-handedness (See Chapter 7).
7. *The Independent*, 11th April 1988.
8. As long as the Dalai Lama was the temporal head (2011), the sole responsibility rested upon him when he acts without a referendum. Now a referendum is held and, he has relinquished his sovereign status.

   Such a referendum was planned in 1995-96. There were four points to it. All the Tibetans were to vote on one of the course of future actions, viz. (1) middle way, (2) self-determination, (3) independence, and (4) satyagraha based on Gandhi's model. A year of preparation was decided. The Tibetan Youth Congress members undertook upon themselves, along with peoples deputies and other NGOs in informing the masses about the options. After a year of education and canvassing it was decided that more time was needed still and it was defered till August 1997. By that time Tibetan Youth Congress itself had hardened its stand. For them there was no option to total independence. They, therefore, campaigned for the withdrawal of the referendum. The government in Exile conducted an opinion poll. Over 66 per cent of the population said no to the referendum and the parliament in Exile had no option but to withdraw the referendum at that time.

9. Tashi Tobgye Jamyangling, "The Tibetan Challenge, The Political Menopause?" *Tibetan Review*, 1989, p. 2.
10. This is a direct confrontation to what the Dalai Lama has been saying.
11. Jamyang Norbu, "In Deng's Grave New World: An Illusion Dies", *Tibetan Review*, August 1989, p. 8.
12. Wong, Edward (22 November, 2008). "At Exile meeting, Tibetans Debate Independence". *The New York Times*, 23 April, 2009; Wax, Emily (23 November, 2008). "Exiled Tibetans weigh freedom struggle". *Washington Post*. Retrieved 23 April, 2009. Mishra, Pankaj (December 18, 2005). "The restless children of the Dalai Lama", *New York Times*, 23 April, 2009; " "Tibetan Youth Congress" is pure terrorist organization", 10 April 2008; "Tibetan Protester dead", *BBC News*, April 29, 1998, 23 April, 2009; Lakshmi, Rama (16 April, 2008). "Tibetans in India Facing Tight Security for Torch", *Washington Post*, 23 April, 2009; Tim Luard (25 April, 2006), "Fathoming Tibet's political future", *BBC News*, 23 April, 2009; "Tibetologists consider "Tibetan Youth Congress" a terrorist pro-independence spearhead", *Xinhua*, 4 May, 2008; "Tibetan exile group in India denies Chinese accusations", *USA Today*, 24 April, 2008.
13. This was for the first time that the Dalai Lama was invited to address the Indian Parliament. It did not materialize since there were no proceedings because of ruckus over corruption in high places.
14. History repeats itself. Just as it had happened in 1977, the TYC president Kalsung ran into rough waters following this incident and resigned.

6
Nobel Peace Prize — Open Sesame!

After the passing of the third UN General Assembly resolution in 1965, there was no real change, internally as well as diplomatically. It appeared that the issue of Tibet is lost for ever. When China started emerging as a colossal world-market, most Western countries also got wary of the Dalai Lama. Head of no major power was willing to see him. However, the Dalai Lama never lost hope and never gave up. He continued to tour round the globe. If diplomacy was difficult to execute, there was a lot of teaching to do in the service of the suffering humanity.

A real breakthrough came in 1987. The Nobel Peace Prize was announced. At the time of announcement, the Dalai Lama was in United States engaged in a scientific workshop at the Mind-Life symposium (Chapter 11). While the participants at the workshop were jubilant to receive the news through a phone call, the Dalai Lama, true to Buddhist temperament, took the news with equanimity. The Dalai Lama's response was that the real winners of the prize were the people of Tibet. They have steadfastly pursued a peaceful path of struggle and suffering. At that moment, there were violent upheavals in several countries and a notion was gaining ground that peaceful change was not possible. The idea of non-violent revolution was receding as too idealistic. For the Dalai Lama, the prize was an overwhelming proof to the contrary."[1]

Generally a prize is supposed to decorate the recipient. Nobel Prize for Peace has gone either to statesmen who have brokered peace or the activists who contributed on a global scale. The Dalai Lama falls in both the categories. However, the stature of the Dalai Lama and the length of his efforts are unsurpassed by any.

The Prize is awarded by the Nobel Committee on the recommendation of eminent people who have excelled in specified fields. A look at the list of people (Appendix III) who sponsored the Dalai Lama's nomination and their citations are truly illuminating. They were from all the continents.

They were statesmen, government functionaries, authors and creative people from a wide spectrum. Everyone had a novel look at the personage of Dalai Lama. All these facets assembled together made a composite whole of several aspects of the personality that the name of Dalai Lama symbolizes as a jewel. The world woke up and the cause of Tibet was written all across the globe in the minds and hearts of people who cared.

The idea to nominate the Dalai Lama first took shape in the summer of 1985. A medical doctor Arthur Crum, regardless of his unawareness of protocol, was the first onc to send a letter to the Secretary for the Nobel Prize Foundation. He wrote:

"Since my letter to you of May 3, 1985, I have not received Post Office notification of delivery. I feel so strongly about the Dalai Lama's candidacy and his worthiness for nomination for the Nobel Peace Prize that I am taking the liberty of sending another copy to the Committee.

It is unequivocally and strongly felt that the Dalai Lama's receiving the Nobel Peace Prize would do so much to further World Peace and would be illustrious to the Nobel Committee. Since his 25-year Exile, he has quietly and persistently advocated peace in every way possible and recognition on the scope symbolized by the Nobel Peace Prize would do so much to further the cause you both represent."

The closing date for the nominations, February 1 of each year, had long expired. Undeterred, he sent the nomination. He was encouraged by the response that the Secretary decided to keep the letter on the file.

When the nominations were compiled in 1986 there was a consorted worldwide effort by numerous statesmen, intellectuals, activists and religious leaders (Appendix III). The protocol for nomination includes several categories of people who may nominate citing the reasons.

Dr. Arthur Crum took up the matter further with the office of Tibet. On August 2nd, 1985, he wrote to Mr. Tinley Nyandak at New York, with hints at dinner diplomacy:

"I understand that one of the most effective ways to accomplish placing a name in nomination is Item (g), that is, to be nominated by a former Nobel Prize Winner. I have indirect access to Bishop Tutu, Winner of the 1984 Nobel Peace Prize. This could develop into one of the most significant means of putting His Holiness' name into nomination. I am in the process of arranging to have Bishop Tutu dine with me the next time he visits the United States. I feel I could better present the case of the Dalai Lama's nomination in person rather than by correspondence. Also, someone from your office made the important point that knowing someone in the Norwegian Parliament would have great importance, which comes under item (b).

In addition, I have already put in motion, at a private dinner meeting with Dr. Robert Polk, on Monday, July 29, my strong recommendation of the Dalai Lama for the clergyman of the Year for the Society of the Family of Man Award. Remember, this is the route Bishop Tutu took before gaining the Nobel Peace Prize. Dr. Polk told me to put my recommendation in writing to him. I am presently composing this letter which I will send to him on Monday and a copy to you. He further suggested that to give added weight for the Dalai Lama's selection from the Board Members, I should also write to Jay Hershinson, Vice Chancellor for Public Affairs, University of New York. Dr. Polk feels Jay would recommend. You will be getting follow-up correspondence on all these matters next week. Kindly inform Chuki Wangdu about this activity with Mr. Hershinson, as I understand she conducts her department work under him at the Chancellor's office."

An MP of the Green Party was at the Kalachakra initiation at Bodh Gaya. He got the information and wanted the members of the Green Party to be associated. They were late when they contacted Nobel Office. But the nomination was already on, so they argued that they would like their names associated with the nominators.

As the word spread, the wife of the 1968 Peace Prize winner, Rene Cassin, was also keen to support the nomination. Buddhism considers the environment as much a part of self as the inner mind. It has to be conserved and protected the same way. This has a great appeal to the Green Group in France as well as Europe. Together with Rene Cassin, there were a number of French personages who met the Dalai Lama during his visit to France that year and joined the sponsors.

Great care was exercised that no Tibetan organization, as such, has nominated or campaigned for the Dalai Lama.

The nominations can turn into a hagiographical anthology. The most powerful advocacy was from Robert Thurman, Prof. of Religion, Amherst College, Massachusetts:

"It is my honour and delights to place in nomination for the Nobel Peace Prize the name of His Holiness Tenzin Gyatso, the Buddhist Monk and the Fourteenth Dalai Lama of Tibet. I understand from Mr. Frederick Hyde-Chambers of England that there are quite a few nominators for His Holiness this year, but that each of us is to submit a nomination individually.

His Holiness has served the Tibetan people as their spiritual and temporal leader since he was installed in 1951 at the age of sixteen (five years earlier than usual due to the calamitous nature of that time). For thirty-five years he has embodied the highest ideals of peace and compassion in his person, steadily deepening and strengthening his own understanding and action (I can personally testify to his own efforts and growth, as I have known him personally now for twenty-one years). He has represented them in his teachings and writings, enabling tens, perhaps hundreds of thousands of people to understand their own problems with anger and violence and to make progress towards developing a happier attitude and more peaceful behaviour. And he has upheld "non-violence" unceasingly in his political role as the sole leader acknowledged by the Tibetan people, either in Exile or under the Chinese occupation. During a terrible time of violent persecution, Exile, and dislocation of all Tibetans, he has succeeded, in restraining the inevitable impulses in his people to terrorism, violence, or self-destructive despair. He has kept up their hope, led them in building new communities to preserve the best of their traditional culture, and never gives up in patient negotiations with various Chinese regimes to restore the happiness of his main population in Tibet.

This is how he manifestly embodies peace to all who meet him, and these are the accomplishments for which I sincerely consider His Holiness an eminently worthy, insightful choice for the honour of the Nobel Peace Prize.

Although I do not know anything about the formal policies of your Committee, it is clear that the conferral of this great honour plays a significant role in some cases in actually influencing an ongoing course of events by assisting an outstanding representative of peace to conduct his or her work in a wider sphere, touching and benefiting a larger circle of people. I have in a number of academic papers on past and present Dalai Lamas analyzed the ways in which His Holiness serves various constituencies today and might serve more widely in the future, as I believe he inevitably will. I will summarize that analysis for you here, so you can better judge the great impact on world peace this nomination proposes. I will be brief but thorough, for it seems to me, important that His Holiness' unique situation must be carefully elucidated in order to present the argument supporting his nomination.

Firstly, His Holiness now most closely serves the Tibetan people, both those refugees in Exile who keep the culture alive and those still in Tibet who suffer under a fundamentally unrelenting, genocidal occupation. He is a saving parent to them, helping them keep their lives together after devastating losses. He has been an enormous practical help to them, a protector, spokesman, and a provider. He has been an indispensable spiritual beacon for them, a teacher and an example. Those still in Tibet look to him with greater devotion than ever, his personal upholding of their plight to a world preoccupied with matters supposedly larger than individuals or tiny nations, their only hope.

Secondly, other Buddhists under Communism or in Exile from it are served and deeply moved by His Holiness, as a wellspring of hope. His visit to Outer Mongolia in 1979 was an occasion of tremendous outpouring of faith and joy on the part of a people under anti-Buddhist ideology for almost, fifty years. When refugee communities of Vietnamese, Chinese, or Cambodian Buddhists invite His Holiness to their gatherings, national differences are soon forgotten and universal Buddhist familiarity is affirmed. In the democratic Asian nations there are still free Buddhist populations in the area from Japan and South Korea, Indonesia to Sri Lanka and India. His Holiness has been invited to most of these countries and is received with great respect by the authorities and heartfelt fervour by the faithful. In Europe and America, His Holiness is revered by several hundreds of thousands of Western Buddhists, irrespective of the type of Buddhism they espouse. Historically, Buddhist institutions avoided structure centralization, so they have nothing organized as a "Universal Church". Yet His Holiness emerges in modern times as one of a very few Buddhist leaders with global visibility with whom all Buddhists can identify.

Thirdly, His Holiness is recognized by all the important leaders of other world religions as one of the truly accomplished religious practitioners, philosophers, and institutional leaders of any religious tradition. Speaking for Buddhism, especially the Messianic Buddhism of the Mahayana, his message always rises above specific dogmas and ideologies to go to the heart of religion, the benefit and salvation of humans and other living beings — love, compassion, tolerance, wisdom, humility. He is thus a major force in keeping religion itself alive in a secular age, and serves all religious people everywhere. He is very well respected in Hindu/Muslim/Sikh India, the country that has so generously sheltered his people, often called upon to mediate in inter-religious assemblies. And he is admired as a spiritual, mystical, and saintly celebrity by the general public in all the Western countries, though sensitivity for the political concerns on the part of host governments has kept him relatively muted in speaking out in his social role as representative of a people. Former Senator Paul Tsongas once remarked to me, emerging from an audience, that His Holiness seemed to him to be "one of the last world spiritual leaders whose image and mystique remains intact and untarnished, a great potential force for good."

Fourthly, His Holiness is outstanding among religious leaders for his attitudes and actions concerning non-religious or even anti-religious people. He refused the offer of outside aid to fight the Chinese invasion in 1950, during the time of the opening of the Korean War and a general Western movement to "contain" Mao's progress. Instead he went to Peking, met all the major leaders, studied their ideas, and strove for eight years to cooperate with them in reforming aspects of Tibetan society. In 1959, realizing that "reform" meant complete abolition of Tibet's religious culture, he fled with many followers, fearing what might happen to his people if anything happened to him and seeing Exile as the only means to preserve some seeds for the future. But still he never condemned the basic good intentions of the Chinese Communists. He found compassion in their ideals, while crying out against violence and cruelty in their practice. He still does not condemn China, still insists there can be and will be a time of good relations after the atrocities have ceased and the errors have been rectified. He still offers a helping hand of Buddhist insight into the processes of selfishness and their transmutation into selflessness to those he refers to as "sincere communists," that is those whose primary concern is for the welfare of the community. And while he admires the free West and its religious liberties and industrial progress, he never tires of urging that "money is to benefit human life — human life is not for money," and that they should make more effort to get along with their ideological rivals. (I will never forget the conservative William Buckley's initial exasperation and eventual amazement with His Holiness when he interviewed him at length on "Firing Line," when His Holiness could not be pushed into a blanket condemnation of "Red China," "communism," "atheism", and so on. When instead, the meaning of "free world" was examined as per the actions of the West, it became clear that this was a man whose religious commitment to peace and moderation was not a matter of dogmas, institutions, or general ideologies, but was a matter of a compassionate heart attuned to the immediate human reality.)

This brings us to how His Holiness will serve the world even more effectively in the future, as people world-wide begin to realize the many levels of mediation, his spiritual presence, intelligence, and warm heart, can effect. If we analyze the main threats to our planet today, we can conveniently isolate at least four main axes of conflict: (1) between capitalist and communist industrial peoples, so-called "First" and "Second" worlds (presently responsible for the prospect of nuclear holocaust); (2) between these two as a group and the "Third World" peoples (North and South, rich and poor, often combined with various racial polarities); (3) between modern mass states and traditional small nations; and (4) between scientific and religious worldviews (and in this same vein, between different religious worldviews). His Holiness the Dalai Lama is in a natural position to help mediate all these conflicting polarities. In fact he does so everyday in his writings and discourses.

Firstly, in regard to communism and capitalism, he has solid ground in Buddhist ethics to agree with the ideal of economic justice of the former as well as with that of social and political liberty of the latter. Most importantly, he persuasively argues that neither system can work well without a special educational stress on unselfishness and compassion, the cement needed to hold any society together. Without selflessness and compassion, capitalism becomes savagery, and communism becomes systematic oppression of the individual. Both systems need to avoid fanaticism and develop tolerance of each other, remembering their own ideals and first principles. In historical record, the Buddhist doctrines and institutions have the greatest proven experience in educating peoples in selflessness, compassion, and tolerance. Though not every unholy war was avoided, Buddhism lacks the concept of a "holy war".

Secondly, he joins leaders of other faiths in trying to awaken the consciences and also consciousnesses of the rich nations, to share their wealth, because it is right and meritorious, and also because it is in their own long-term self-interest to do so. His Holiness also has a natural potential to inspire the poor nations to control their hatred and resentment of the rich, showing the example of Tibet as a land of simplicity and frugality by choice, holding up the Buddhist principles of non-violence and tolerance. This level of rich/poor conflict is not such a priority today as the poor nations have not yet gotten nuclear teeth. But all too soon this particular mediation will be more and more crucial.

Thirdly, the modernity/traditionality conflict results in various kinds of ecological disaster, as well as in the destruction of all "non-governmental" peoples, such as the Native Americans, and tribals planet-wide. Here the contribution of Tibetan culture is important, as it is a traditional culture in some respects that yet has the sophisticated, classical, Buddhist "Inner Science" perspective that allows it to adopt certain beneficial aspects of modernity without destroying its ecological or cultural base. Tibet created a unique educational system for developing an "inner modernity," during the very centuries since the Renaissance in which the West developed the "outer modernity" that gives us now our civilization, and the power to obliterate ourselves. His Holiness is very eloquent on the complementarities between the "Inner" and "Outer" Sciences, and is uniquely qualified to reconcile the best in the modern and the traditional. The complex and skilful way he represents his tiny people and their world religion, to keep them from being crushed under the clumsy giant of modernizing China, without surrender and without violence, contains many lessons for both moderns and traditionals.

Fourthly, the religion-science dichotomy interconnects very deeply with all of the previous conflicts, and His Holiness is a leader among leaders in re-articulating spiritual values and visions in ways acceptable and even compelling to "secularized" scientific-minded people. As an infini-theistic tradition (neither theistic nor atheistic), Buddhism does not propose any reason-faith dichotomy, and has millennia of experience in mediating between various theisms and atheisms, as it has encountered them in many different cultures and eras. His Holiness is a product of a rigorous intellectual training in logic, epistemology, and metaphysics, and has been an avid student of Western "outer" sciences since his youth. And so he can marshal powerful philosophical resources to support a spiritual perspective, on scientific as well as religious grounds. At the same time, he is self-critical of the archaic elements of his own and others' religious worldviews and so scientific people tend to find his perspective balanced and constructive.

This Christmas in Bodh Gaya, India, I heard His Holiness lecture two hundred thousand Tibetans, approximately one quarter from Tibet itself, the others from the Himalayan countries and India, about love and compassion. He was elucidating the "Tolerance" Chapter of Shantideva's *Guide to the Bodhisattva Life* (8th century India), a long and intricate section on how to develop real compassion for one's enemy. Many of the Tibetans had lost loved ones, liberty, land, health, and many of their life's opportunities. They were mostly simple people, and he spoke to them straight from the heart yet with a compelling intelligence. I thought of Mahatma Gandhi as His Holiness explained how the real fight was against the inner enemy of their own intolerance and anger, how proud he was of them for their enduring with patience in the main, how they must keep clear that evils committed against them were the fault of the enemy's confusions, greed, and anger, and not the fault of the enemy himself, who himself was the first victim of these negative passions. He truly reached those people. They returned to Tibet resolved to endure and prevail. And I thought of Martin Luther King as His Holiness powerfully reminded those in Exile of their responsibility to use their freedom to develop their insight and character for the time of re-building that must come. It is remarkable that there is a man like this alive today, still putting his life and heart into the non-violent yet indefatigable resolution of life and death conflict, trusting the ancient truth that only love ends hate, only compassion stops violence, relying on the supremacy of the moral force of truth.

For these reasons, I think this nomination is vital, timely, and creative, as well as wholly worthy. Such a major figure who puts his life on that line should be recognized, encouraged, and honoured as much as possible. And so I close my nomination of His Holiness the Dalai Lama for the Nobel Peace Prize. Please be assured that I stand ready to serve the Committee in its information-gathering process, should that be required."

As expected, China protested. It vehemently opposed the King of Norway meeting the Dalai Lama and threatened that, if he were to do so, bilateral relations may suffer. Norway explained that Nobel Prize is awarded by Nobel Committee; it is a non-political matter. But once the prize is announced, it is customary for the King to receive Nobel Laureates and they see no reason to make an exception. On the occasion of the award of the Prize, the Dalai Lama acknowledged as:

"I believe my selection reaffirms the universal values of non-violence, peace and understanding between all members of our great human family. We all desire a happier, more humane and harmonious world, and I have always felt that the practice of love and compassion, tolerance and respect for others is the most effective manner in which to bring this about.

I hope this *prize* will provide courage to the six million people of Tibet. For some forty years now Tibetans have been undergoing the most painful period in our long history. During this time, over a million of our people perished and more than six thousand monasteries — the seat of our peaceful culture — were destroyed. There is not a single family, either in Tibet or among the refugees abroad, which has gone unscathed. Yet, our people's determination and commitment to spiritual values and the practice of non-violence remain unshaken. This prize is a profound recognition of their faith and perseverance.

The demonstrations which have rocked Tibet for the past two years continue to be non-violent despite brutal suppression. Since the imposition of martial law in Lhasa last March, Tibet has been sealed off, and while global attention has focused on the tragic events in China, a systematic effort to crush the spirit and national identity of the Tibetan people is being pursued by the Government of the People's Republic.

Tibetans today are facing the real possibility of elimination as a people and a nation. The Government of the People's Republic of China is practicing a form of genocide by relocating millions of Chinese settlers into Tibet. I ask that this massive population transfer be stopped. Unless the cruel and inhuman treatment of my people is brought to an end, and until they are given their due right to self-determination, there will always be obstacles in finding a solution to the Tibetan issue.

I accept the Nobel Peace Prize in a spirit of optimism despite the many grave problems which humanity faces today. We all know the immensity of the challenges facing our generation; the problem of our population, the threat to our environment and the dangers of military confrontation. As this dramatic century draws to a close, it is clear that the renewed yearning for freedom and democracy sweeping the globe provides an unprecedented opportunity for building a better world. Freedom is the real source of human happiness and creativity. Only when it is allowed to flourish can a genuinely stable international climate exist.

The suppression of the rights and freedoms of any people by totalitarian governments is against human nature and the recent movements for democracy in various parts of the world are a clear indication of this.

The Chinese students have given me great hope for the future of China and Tibet. I feel that their movement follows the tradition of Mahatma Gandhi's *ahimsa or* non-violence which has deeply inspired me ever since I was a small boy. The eventual success of all people seeking a more tolerant atmosphere must derive from a commitment to counter hatred and violence with patience. We must seek change through dialogue and trust. It is my heartfelt prayer that "Tibet's plight may be resolved in such a manner and that once again my country, the Roof of the World, may serve as a sanctuary of peace and a resource of spiritual inspiration at the heart of Asia."

The Kashag celebrated the 15th Anniversary of the Conferment of the Nobel Peace Prize to the Dalai Lama, when Buddha was quoted as:

And when individual rights are violated, we all know that if one is not able to protect it by relying on the forces of inner strength, morality and non-violence, no amount of wailing before any country, nationality or famed organizations can restore or safeguard the human rights. As Lord Buddha said:

> "One is the protector of one's own self,
> Who else can be one's protector?"

Kashag issued a similar statement on 10th December, 2009, the twentieth anniversary of the conferment of the Nobel Peace Prize, as:

His Holiness the Dalai Lama has been making tireless efforts to realise the cause of the Tibetan people in general, and in particular to preserve and promote the unique language, culture and religion of Tibet, as well as to promote world peace, inter-religious harmony, basic human values, environmental promotion and universal responsibility throughout the world. So great and unimaginable is his contribution in these fields that he has been granted over 100 awards and certificates of merits by the countries and organisations/institutions across the globe. This year alone, he has received many awards and honorary certificates, viz. Honorary Citizenship of Warsaw City, Poland; Honorary Doctorate from the University of Marburg, Germany; International Freedom Award from the National Civil Rights Museum in Memphis, USA; Prize for Love and Forgiveness from the Fetzer's Institute, Vancouver, Canada; Honorary Doctorate from the University of Calgary, Canada; Tom Lantos Human Rights Prize, USA.

Today marks the 61st year since the Universal Declaration of Human Rights was announced there is not only is there no protection of the basic human rights in the world, but also like a big insect eating a smaller insect.

On 1 October this year, China celebrated 60th anniversary of the founding of the People's Republic of China. During the celebration an awe-inspiring and large-scale parade of military hardware was carried out. It was a warning about the brutal suppression that can result by the Chinese Government. It was aimed particularly to the protesters in East Turkistan, (Chin: Xinjiang) and whole of Tibet.

From March 2008 until today, 228 Tibetans have died under the crackdown, out of which we have names and other personal details of 118; 371 Tibetans were given jail sentences; 4657 Tibetans were either arrested or detained; 990 Tibetans have disappeared and 1294 were injured during the peaceful protests. Who knows how many other Tibetans were killed; jailed or are being tortured?

We are especially concerned about the young Panchen Lama, Gendun Choekyi Nyima, who was forcefully arrested by the Chinese Government since as a child, thus disregarding UN Convention on the Rights of the Child. Though twenty years old now, he is denied of the basic rights and to date his whereabouts remains unknown. We urge that all the innocent political prisoners, including Gendun Choekyi Nyima, be released immediately.

According to reliable information in various global media, two Tibetans, namely Lobsang Gyaltsen and Loyak who were associated with the peaceful protests in Lhasa last year were executed. Three other Tibetans, namely Kangtsuk, Tenzin Phuntsok and Penkyi (female), who were given death sentence with two-year reprieve, were also executed.

Looking from another side, since the large-scale peaceful protests in Tibet last years, many Chinese lawyers, intellectuals and general public who were not fooled by Beijing's propaganda, have come out with open reports. In spite of Chinese Government's severe blockage of news media, the number of articles written in the internet in support of Tibetan issue is increasing.

From 6 to 8 August this year, International Sino-Tibetan Conference was held in Geneva, Switzerland, and in the final document 'Finding a Common Ground', it states "the root cause of the Tibetan issue is not a conflict between the Chinese people and the Tibetan people, but rather the autocratic rule of the People's Republic of China in Tibet and its cultural genocide in Tibet. The Beijing government's claim that 'Tibet has always been a part of China' is factually incorrect; and everyone present at the conference highly respects the Dalai Lama's Middle Way Approach."

On 18th and 19th of November this year, the fifth World Parliamentarians' Convention on Tibet was held in Rome, Italy, and according to its Rome Declaration: "International pressure must be applied in order to start a meaningful dialogue between the representatives of the Dalai Lama and the Chinese Government; [and] express support for the substantive negotiations between the Chinese Government and the representatives of the Dalai Lama towards a meaningful resolution of the Tibet issue, with the Memorandum on Genuine Autonomy as the realistic and constructive basis for negotiations."

This year again, eight Nobel laureates made a statement in support of His Holiness the Dalai Lama and the Tibetan people, which mentions: "We urge the Chinese government to take immediate and constructive steps to resolve the status of Tibet and an end to the oppressive policies that continue to marginalize the impoverished Tibetan in their own land. By implementing law that are enshrined in the Chinese constitution for a legitimate and meaningful autonomy for all Tibetans, the Chinese government will make great strides in securing peace and unity in their land."

The United States government announced an appointment of Mrs. Maria Otero as a Special Coordinator for Tibet issues on 1st October, 2009. On 17th November, 2009, Mr. Barrack Obama, the President of United States, at a press conference with Chinese President Hu Jintao at the Great Hall of People in Beijing has urged Chinese government to start a dialogue with the envoy of His Holiness the Dalai Lama.

Unity of nationalities is the very basis of a nation's stability whereas the stability of China is the basis of World Peace. The importance of this fact cannot be denied by any. The Central Tibetan Administration headed by His Holiness the Dalai Lama is a free spokesperson of the 6 million Tibetans. Because of that, the concerned members of the People's Republic of China were repeatedly explained that to resolve Tibetan issues, we will hold on to Middle Way Approach seeking solution to the Tibet issues within the present Constitution of the People's Republic of China.

Moreover, to make Twenty-first century a century of cooperation and dialogue, nations and peoples should co-exist harmoniously with each other. Where there is conflict between nations and peoples, they should not stand against each other; rather they should have wisdom to resolve their differences through a peaceful means. A peaceful method is not only in accordance with the need of the time but it also goes well with the desire of the people for universal values such as equality, freedom, democracy and human rights. It is clear that the present Chinese leaderships have to respect the call from the international community in the long-term interest of the Tibetan and the Chinese people and, to secure stability for China.

Speaking on Indian foreign policy, the Prime Minister Dr. Manmohan Singh has said, "I think the respect for fundamental human rights, the respect for the rule of law, respect for multi-cultural, multi-ethnic, multi-religious rights, I think those have values. So, even the Indian perforce with regard to the GDP might not be as good as the Chinese, certainly I would not like to choose the Chinese path'."

There were some murmurs that Nobel Peace Prize was an effort at secret diplomacy to malign China through the back door. But democracy thrives on freedom of speech and action. Somebody may invent a theory as to how the idea was planted in the mind of Dr. Arthur Crum. Freedom, liberty and justice survive only in democracy where it is concurrently known that nobody can fool anybody for all the time. If there were intense efforts by those who wanted to serve the cause of Tibet, they did so within the parameters laid down by the Nobel Committee. And to suggest that Nobel Committee can be manipulated, is hard to pass on. The Nobel Committee works in the service of the ideals that are laid down by them and they found no better person than the Dalai Lama (though there were numerous nominations that year), so the Prize was awarded to him.

The leaders of Western Europe, UK and the President of USA have, till the Nobel award, been reluctant to talk to the Dalai Lama. What the Chinese called as wealthy and influential friends of the Dalai Lama have, thereafter very strong arguments to impress upon and persuade their leaders not only for the sake of, truth, culture, civilization, religion and spirituality, but also in terms of accepted Western norms of equality, fraternity, freedom, democratic rights and international law.

The Nobel Prize was another important milestone for Tibet. Now the Prize was a valid passport to the corridors of most nations. Open Sesame! And wide they were the doors open now! They had the stamp of the values that democratic nations cherished.

REFERENCE

1. The Dalai Lama, *Freedom in Exile*, the Autobiography of the Dalai Lama of Tibet. London, 1990, p. 290.

7
Resurrection of the Phoenix

Historical Perspective

The negotiations with China in 1970s yield no results; China sticks to its Five-Point Proposal; The Dalai Lama persists with his religious activities in USA; acquires many friends who turn to collaborators; United States Congress invites him to address, 1987; The Dalai Lama makes Five-Point Proposals at the Congress address with main emphasis on non-violence; proposes that Tibet be a zone of Ahimsa; Formulation of Strasbourg Proposals, 1988; the Dalai Lama launches a major diplomatic initiative, writing to the statesmen world over and, is a continuous process now: Marshal Law in Lhasa, 1988, tepid response from Chinese; Kashag and the Dalai Lama withdraw Strasbourg proposal; Nobel Peace Prize, 1989; Bill Clinton elected as US President, 1992; Strong support to Tibet; Several Congressmen and Senators veer around Tibet; Conference of International Lawyers on Tibet establishes Tibet's status as an invaded and occupied nation; The London Report, 1993; Conditioning of MFN status with human rights by Clinton Administration, 1993; European Union sends a delegation to China to verify human rights situation; Resolutions by US Congress, German Parliament, 1996, European Parliament, 1997 and others; the Dalai Lama writes to Jiang Zemin, President, PRC,1998, he is not seeking independence; Jiang Zemin visits US, declares his willingness to negotiate with Tibetans, 1998; Appointment of Tibet diplomat by US; Jimmy Carter suggests a compromise formula, 1999, following a non-official visit by a delegation from Jimmy Carter Center to China in 1998; Britain, France, Human Rights Commission of UN concerned about the boy, Gedhun Choekyi Nyima. Panchen Lama, 1999; Several parliaments and European Union pass more resolutions; calls for voting against China's bid for 2004 Olympics, asks for withdrawal of World Bank loan offer; conditions that EU may recognize the government in Exile, 2000; US suggests negotiations, 2001; Wen Jiabao in Washington, 2003; Dick Cheney in Beijing, very strong public statement ever made, 2004; Resumption of negotiations with China, no concrete results, 2004-2011.

Diplomacy consists of choosing the most appropriate of several options. It requires the intellectual ability to generate many options. After the options are laid out there is a projection into the future, where the enlightened interests are utilized as the sole instrument for choice. A statesman has a sagacity to be able to browse on the dialectical, discursive dialogue, both with his advisers as well as within himself. The sagacity and the wisdom of a statesman reflect in his ability to choose an action that should be appropriate with the present and future interests of his people and State. History does not judge a statesman by the virtues and merits of his opinions. Moral and ethical code has been written down since ages and, for the Dalai Lama it is compacted in the form of Buddha's teachings. His statesmanship would then reflect as to how he applies the Buddhist philosophical postulates in the service of his people and the State.

Apart from the intellectual process, any choice is influenced further by the personality and character of the statesman in question. It is influenced also by what is the nature of the objective at a particular time and place. All of these, viz. charisma of the persona as well as the nobility of the cause, contributed as to how friends were found and people got influenced in the service of Tibet.

The love for truth and compassion for the oppressed had found several protagonists for Tibet. This was particularly so after the International Commission of Jurists confirmed genocide[1] in Tibet four times. And, other judicial commissions had also endorsed the findings. The openness, frankness and clarity, and not the least, the sense of humour of the Dalai Lama had won him numerous friends internationally.

An intangible development came to the rescue. By this time, the West had developed great appreciation of Tibetan culture and religion. For the agnostic West, Buddhism had tremendous fascination since it insisted on dialectical rationalism. The refined interpretation of the mind was a new psychology for healing of the West that suffered from Freudian interpretation of self; seeking meaning only in the service of self-gratification and ego. Buddhist doctrine preached an alternative in the form of caring and compassion; sharing and giving. If this was not *nirvana* it was freedom from the shackles of ego and healing of the mind. There were several Buddhist centres, many of them manned with Tibetan lamas in Europe, USA and Canada. They are flocked not only by the disturbed agitated youth, but also by the powerful and perturbed people. This has generated a large popular support in the form of awareness about the Tibetan struggle and their just cause.[2]

The Chinese position in 2006 is that atrocities have been a matter of anachronistic history. The mistakes were committed and have been apologized for. And during the Cultural Revolution, not only Tibet, but entire China had suffered. As regards the fundamental human rights, the concept is only suited to the developed Western nations; a developing society cannot afford to have such luxury.[3]

And the Chinese argue to their nationalities: given the liberty, right to dissent and freedom, look, what has happened to Russia that was once a superpower! The Politbureau and the Party knows what is best for China. The fundamental human rights and such concepts are really meant to subvert and break China. And these restrictions are not applied discriminately in Tibet only. They apply to the entire country. And this has given you progress. This is distorted logic and violates the axiomatic principles of justice.[4] In a just society, each person should have an equal right to the most extensive total system of basic liberties. This has to be compatible with a similar system of liberty for all. But it makes no sense to say that Hans Chinese would also be punished for carrying a photograph of the Dalai Lama. Further, social and economic inequalities may exist in most societies but they have to be so rearranged that they are the greatest benefit of the least advantaged. How many Tibetans are governing the Tibet Autonomous Region?

The Marxist philosophy that liberty has to be restricted in the service of the State till such time that the State will wither away is fundamentally incorrect. Freedom and liberty are the principal appetites of soul. And the State shall never wither away; power corrupts and absolute power corrupts absolutely. Liberty can be restricted only for the sake of liberty. A less extensive liberty must strengthen the total system of liberty shared by all. Above all, less than equal liberty must be acceptable to those with the lesser liberty. Will Tibetans — or for that matter any nationality — ever accept to be second class citizens?

The booming economy is being showcased not only to the West, but to the Tibetans too. Five Star hotels, race courses and shopping malls are there because of Marxist economy. If the Party crumbles and democracy was to be implemented, all these will disappear. But who is rich in Tibet now? What are the advantages to the ordinary Tibetans? The bulk of the riches are with Hans Chinese migrants.

Equality is prior to the principle of efficiency and maximizing the advantages; and fair opportunity is prior to everything else in the operations of economy. Even a temporary inequality for the lesser privileged Tibetans can only be accepted if it were to eventually enhance their opportunities. After all, the suffering can it be ever imagined that a Tibetan will become the Head of the Chinese State? Even after full assimilation, Tibet will always be in the position of erstwhile like East Pakistan. Mujibur Rehman, even after winning elections, could not head the State and it had to crumble.

For any country to be cohesively united, all social primary needs — liberty and opportunity, income and wealth, and the bases of self-respect-have to be distributed equally. There is no injustice in the greater benefits earned by a few provided that the situation of the persons not so fortunate is thereby improved.[5] A society is rightly ordered and, therefore, just, when its major institutions are so arranged as to achieve the greatest net balance of satisfaction summed over all the individuals belonging to it. Only that situation is best which procures the greatest happiness for the great numbers, and that is worst which in like manner occasions misery. While the Dalai Lama is in the pursuit of the greatest good of the largest number of Tibetans, does anybody need any further proofs of the misery of the Tibetans? This is elementary and has appealed to all sensible people so now, friends of Tibet are spread all over the globe. This has resurrected the phoenix.

With this preamble, let us now see as to how this happened. The principles are well spelled out and most nations incorporate them in their constitutions. That Tibet is an independent nation and deserves identical consideration with any other was soon forgotten after the UN General Assembly passed the last resolution in 1965. While so many nations had shed tears at the sufferings, nobody moved a little finger. Tibet was thought to be a lost case. A civilization was wounded and crushed; it was only the ashes that remained of a nation. The Dalai Lama was left in the lurch, doing welfare activities for the refugees and giving religious teachings.

The tradition to go to East in search of meaning is well established. In not so affluent times as of now, groups collectively contributed money and sent their emissaries to explore mysticism, for instance Paul Brunton, author of 'A Search into Secret India', came to India. In similar vein, Robert Thurman came to Dharmashala in seventies to study Mahayana Buddhism. Later, he was to be a professor at Amherst. Subtle and intangible happenings may indeed be the forces of history when, in 1979, the Dalai Lama found first hiatus to the hearts of Western audiences through this route. He visited USA on in September 1979 ostensibly on an invitation to explore Tibetan Buddhism before a university audience. Little may he have realized that this would lead to a recurring event that culminated in his meeting, Al Gore[6], Bill Clinton, George Bush Sr. as well as the present incumbent, George Bush Jr. and many statesmen in Europe. His public talks brought him close to many eminent politicians and influential people. He seemed to be a master craftsman in the art of how to win friends and influence people. The issues of fundamental human rights, environment and self-determination were emerging as fashionable currencies in the USA and the West. The Tibet issue rested basically on these values. Popular appeal cascaded into tremendous support from various Congressmen that culminated into a major event.

The cultural diplomacy was making now a foray within the US Congress. The unique nature of governance in the United States made it possible that the State Department of the Government of United States was not involved in the Tibetan issue. Personal contacts and advocacy with nearly a hundred members of Congress brought new development. In 1985, these Congressmen sent a letter to the Chinese President asking to hold direct talks with the Dalai Lama. This catapulted into passing of a Bill by the Congress on 18th June, 1987. The Bill declared that Tibet is an occupied country and endorsed the stand of the Exile government. The passing of such a Bill was possible through a consorted cooperation between the avowed anti-communist Congressmen like Senator Jesse Helms and liberal Senators who were primarily concerned with moral and ethical issues like Senator Claiborne Pell.

On 21st September, 1987 the Dalai Lama addressed the human rights caucus at US Congress. There he enunciated five points by which the Tibet issue can be resolved:

1. The transformation of the whole of Tibet into a zone of peace;
2. Abandonment of Chinese population transfer policy which threatens the very existence of the Tibetans as a people;
3. Respect for the Tibetan people's fundamental human rights and democratic freedoms;
4. Restoration and protection of Tibet's natural environment and abandonment of use of Tibet for the production of nuclear weapons and dumping of nuclear waste; and
5. Commencement of earnest negotiations on the future status of Tibet and of relations between the Tibetan and Chinese people.

The Dalai Lama noticed that within the audience there appeared to be a number of people who seemed to be Chinese. He was quick to spot them and pointedly asked them as to who they were. They were from Xinhua, the official Chinese News Agency. Beijing was keenly taking notes of the Dalai Lama's peace offensive now.

It is for the first time that he labelled the entire Tibet as a zone of *Ahimsa* and, the zone of *Ahimsa* meant that –

1. The entire Tibet – Greater Tibet – would be demilitarized;
2. There will be no manufacturing, testing and stock piling of nuclear and other armaments;
3. The Greater Tibet would be transformed into a natural park or biosphere protecting wild-life and plant-life, preservation of eco-system with a policy of sustainable development;
4. Any technology that were to produce hazardous waste should be prohibited; and
5. There will be promotion of such arms that were dedicated to peace and to the protection of all forms of life.

This kind of pragmatic Buddhism was assured to find favour with the Western sensibilities of the time. It had great strategic advantage incorporated for India too. India with its traditional hostility towards Pakistan is ill-affording to maintain military balance on two fronts. The huge Indo-Tibetan border in the North with its susceptibility into border skirmishes is costing India dearly. Given the demilitarization of Tibet, India's gain will be huge in terms of actual savings on the military build-up along the border as well as the intangible gains of peace.[7]

Only if the Chinese were willing to give up their grip on Tibet would they see justice in the Dalai Lama's proposal. As expected, the Chinese had already protested before the beginning of the visit and asked USA, "to take measures to prevent the Dalai Lama from engaging in any political activities in the United States against the interests of China." United States rebutted such a charge on the ground that the Dalai Lama was free to visit United States in his private capacity and there was no official US involvement.

On 22nd September, only a day after the Dalai Lama's address, 8 Senators wrote jointly to the new Chinese Communist Party Secretary, Zhao Ziyang asking him to accept the Dalai Lama's proposal and begin negotiations on that line. Thus, Tibet had come to acquire strong support within the influential political circle. The phoenix had come to life and it had now to find wings to fly.

It is interesting to notice how the American diplomacy is woven around double talks. A year before in October 1986, the US Congress had revised the US Export Import Bank Act. This could have hardly been a matter of international diplomatic interest. But Beijing was quick to note that in the list of the countries that come under the compass of the Act, Tibet was listed as a separate country. Only when Beijing formerly protested that the State Deputy said it was a technical lapse. In the same vein, while the Congressmen and the Senators were staunchly backing the Dalai Lama, the State Deputy, on 14th October, 1987, said that the Dalai Lama has conducted activities not consistent with his status as a respected religious leader. The State Deputy publicly disowned any official support for the Dalai Lama's 5-Point Peace Programme.

On 20th September, a day before the speech at Congress, there was a pro-independence demonstration in Lhasa by 21 monks from Drepung monastery. They carried the Tibetan National Flag and shouted slogans demanding Tibetan independence. Within 4 days, on 1st October there was a second demonstration by a group of monks from Sera monastery. This time they were also joined by some lay people. That makes the whole exercise a diplomatic effort in tandem.

At this juncture, China was promoting a policy of "Open Tibet". That had increased the Western tourist members visiting Lhasa. Tourists had grown into thousands. Potala Palace is a site for tourist attraction. The Chinese had viewed tourism as a means of earning a fast buck and they were probably imperceptive of the impact that the tourists can carry about a lost *Shangri-La.*

This was evident when we came to view a video cassette secretly taped by an American journalist and a medical doctor disguising themselves as ordinary tourists with only cursory interests of sight-seeing. They extensively filmed their interviews with several ordinary Tibetan people. This they passed on to the ABC Television which scheduled its telecast at prime time.

And this was done in a very dramatic manner. The channel invited the Chinese Ambassador to America to brief its audience about the developmental programmes in Tibet. The telecast began with the Chinese ambassador showing video clips in grandiose style about the Western style of living in Lhasa including the horse races. He showed new housing and factories. And he concluded by saying that this was the development. The ABC correspondent then took over with sarcastically polite remarks of showing some alternative models of development. Clip after clip showed various scenes of atrocities, enforced sterilization, tales of sufferings of the common Tibetans. After each view of the clip, the commentator would repeat the question, "and is this also what you call as development?" The Chinese Ambassador was aghast at the scoop and then left speechless. There was visible fading of the colour on his face as he just gathered enough composure to say, "This sure is a mistake somewhere .... This is an aberration" etc.

Coming back to the demonstrations by the monks in 1987 at Lhasa, this too was witnessed and photographed by the Western tourists. As the demonstrators were detained in a police station, several hundreds Tibetans gathered outside to demand their release. The situation almost turned into a prototype of *Chauri-Chora* of Gandhian era. The demonstrators burnt the doors of the police station and in the process at least one Tibetan was badly burnt. He was carried as a martyr by the demonstrators. This was witnessed by hundreds of onlookers. In the police firing by the Chinese into the crowd 8 to 10 people were killed. The tourists even photographed the scene that showed the police aiming at the demonstrators from the rooftops.

Congregation of the events of September and October 1987 was seen by the Chinese as a meticulously concerted attempt "to split the motherland".

After the incidents of October 1987 recurrent demonstration took place in Lhasa and elsewhere. The Chinese thought to counter this by taking a hard line against the Dalai Lama. Once again they made the mistake of showing clips of video film of Dalai Lama's address to the US Congressmen so as to prove him a "*splittist*". The clips showed the warm regard the Congressmen showed towards him. While the Chinese thought that they were giving concrete evidence of splittist activity of the Dalai Lama, the clippings carried a different message. The people interpreted them as a clear evidence of the support of the US Government. Moreover, the enthusiastic welcome and the attention showered on him by the Congressmen who were seen to be surrounding him further strengthened the Tibetans devotion to him.

Again, when the Dalai Lama was invited to address the European Parliament in the following year in 1988, there was vehement protest by the Chinese government coupled with threat and retaliation by cancelling the invitation to the European Council President to visit China. This also backfired on the Chinese since it generated a lot of news leading to greater public awareness. The European Parliament withdrew the official invitation but true to the Western liberal tradition, every member of the European Parliament was within his right to invite the Dalai Lama and hold a private meeting at the European Parliament. Thus the Chinese protest did the work of propaganda for the visit. The Dalai Lama visited the European Parliament on June 16, 1988 and made a statement that came to be known as Strasbourg Proposal. He now elaborated on the 5-Point Peace Proposal that he had first made at the Capitol Hill. For the first time the Dalai Lama agreed to give up the demand for the total independence of Tibet.

Thus, in 1988, the Dalai Lama addressed the European Parliament and announced the Strasbourg Proposals. The charismatic maverick, Petra Kelly had taken the issue in Germany fervently so that German Bundestag also passed a resolution favouring Tibet. The European Parliament followed with identical support (Appendix IV).

It is elementary that after the Dalai Lama, dropped the demand for independence, China had no hurry now to negotiate. How could the Dalai Lama be so naïve? The proposals were idealistic and noble, but without any return and totally contrary to what Tibetans would perceive as their self-interest.

While the Proposal appealed to the Western sensibilities, it was in the natural style of the Chinese to raise objections and issues of trivial nature and to stall the negotiations altogether. They objected to a lawyer of a foreign nationality to be a part of the negotiating team. They also objected to the venue as Geneva and demanded that it should be Beijing. And, finally, they wanted to negotiate directly with the Dalai Lama and none else.

The Chinese objections on the surface appear to be reasonable. When we delivered some lectures on Tibet issue in England in 2001, many members asked us as to what is wrong about the Chinese objections. They pointed out that, in the negotiations with the British, Mahatma Gandhi was willing to walk more than the half way. Did he not go all the way to England in the times when transport was to be by sea, to attend the Round-Table-Conferences? Did he ever shy away from directly representing Indian National Congress to empower him? The Dalai Lama, even though he has given over the powers of governance to the *Kashag,* is a sovereign in a position not enjoyed by other sovereigns. Is it not that for Tibetans his word would be the last word?

We explained to our British friends the dissimilarities between the two situations. Though the British Government was imperialist, they were guided by certain norms of legality and decency. When there was a massacre at Jalianwala Bagh, they had appointed a judicial inquiry where even an Indian judge was appointed. When this judicial commission gave a report against General Dyer he was called back. Apart from this there were several instances of gentlemanliness and decency exercised by the British to other leaders. There is an instance that one evening when Maulana Abul Kalam Azad was playing tennis in the jail, the jailor came over and stood at a discreet distance till the game was finished. He then approached the Maulana and informed him that his wife had died and the Government had issued orders for his immediate release on parole. Of course, the Maulana refused the parole. There is another instance when a youth had fired at a Governor in Pune at point-blank-range and yet could not be convicted for want of evidence. And the Governor, on the release of the young man from jail, had congratulated him for his bravery.

Let us revert to the Sino-Tibet dialogue. To imply strongly that the Tibetans mean official bilateral talks, "a deputy minister of the Tibetan government," Ala Jigme Lhundup, delivered, on 25 October, 1988, the Tibetan reply to the Chinese message of 23 September. The "Tibetan government-in-Exile" suggested that they were willing to hold the first round of talks with the Chinese government on the future status of Tibet in Geneva in January 1989. "Deputy Minister" Ala could not meet the Chinese Ambassador in New Delhi and so delivered the message to Councillor Zhao Xingsung. Zhao asked Ala whether the Dalai Lama would participate in the talks, to which Ala replied negatively. However, the "Tibetan government had earlier announced the formation of a six-member negotiating team" of which Ala is one of the members. The Chinese councillor also enquired if a Dutch international lawyer was a member of the team. The Tibetan minister replied that he was "one of the three aides assisting the team and not one of the negotiators."

The Chinese Vice Minister of State Nationalities Affairs Commission, Chen Xin stated in November 1988: "the Dalai Lama was "insincere" towards the proposed talks in Geneva because the Lama was not going to attend the talks personally. We have never recognized the government in Exile headed by the Dalai Lama. That is why we will only hold talks with the Dalai Lama himself and will not hold talks with a so-called 'government' delegation sent by the Dalai Lama." Chen also pointed out the inclusion of a foreigner in the Tibetan delegation "contravenes the principle adhered to by the Central People's Government." The objections raised by China were: (1) independence cannot be the basis for negotiations; (2) the negotiating team must represent His Holiness the Dalai Lama; and (3) there should be no foreign participation in the negotiation.

Four months later, at the Second Session of the Seventh National People's Congress, Ngapo Ngawang Jigme, a former leading aristocrat and official and now Vice-Chairman of the National People's Congress Standing Committee, repeated Chen Xin's statement. After raising three objections, Ngapo said, "We welcome the Dalai Lama to return to China so long as he renounces advocating the independence of Tibet and contributes to the unity of the nation and the country and to the building of the motherland and new Tibet." This stand, he concluded, "had been repeated time and again by Deng Xiaoping and the central government, and it remains unchanged today."[8]

On 12 April, 1989, the Bureau of His Holiness the Dalai Lama issued clarifications: "We have conveyed to the Chinese government that (1) the framework for negotiations proposed by His Holiness the Dalai Lama refers specifically to the positive notion of association with the People's Republic of China; (2) the Tibetan negotiating team has been appointed by His Holiness the Dalai Lama; (3) There is no foreign participation in the negotiating team. There are both Tibetan and non-Tibetan advisers to the team. It is quite natural for the team to seek advice from qualified persons regardless of their nationalities."

Before the dialogue can go further, martial law in Lhasa was imposed on 7 March, 1989 and all contacts with China were cut off. However, just around pro-democracy demonstration, Beijing sent a message to the Dalai Lama. The message said although the Chinese government disagreed with the Dalai Lama's Strasbourg Proposal as the basis for negotiation "at the same time they still insist they want dialogue."

This obviously was a carrot; concerned about the protest catapulting into Lhasa. The Dalai Lama preferred to join the global wave of condemnation rather than profit from the opportunity offered by Peking. In May 1990 a Chinese government official stated, "The Central Government has upheld an open attitude towards the talks with the Dalai Lama and we have never changed our eagerness to hold negotiations." He blamed the Tibetan leader who "has closed the door on negotiations himself by cutting all these healthy contacts".

So from 1987 till 1989, there were sporadic but repeated anti-Chinese demonstrations. (They continue till today: most tragic being self-immolations – 13 so far.) This culminated on 5th of March, 1989 into largest anti-Chinese agitation since 1959. There were riots for three days and the police fought street battles with Tibetans. During three days between 75 to 750 Tibetans were killed. If these were allowed to go up to March 10, Tibetan National Uprising Day, the consequences could have been dire. The Chinese, therefore, imposed martial law throughout Tibet on March 8.

There was, thus, a temporary break in the negotiations. The gist of the Strasbourg Proposal was that the Dalai Lama gave up the demand for independent Tibet. He had then veered to the genuine autonomy without any prospect of getting it. This bewildered several Tibetans and the reaction to the proposal was of anguish and dismay. However, the Chinese response was nil. And the Dalai Lama as well as *Kashag* declared the proposals void after waiting for about a year.

On the other hand, the route of direct negotiations through Gyalo Dhondup had also floundered. The fact finding delegations revealed disturbing situation and a tremendous devotion to the Dalai Lama.

The West had woken up to the Tibetan cause. Not only Chinese atrocities were projected on the television channels worldover, benevolent, compassionate and charismatic figure of the Dalai Lama was blooming in the media. He came to meet numerous statesmen and corresponded with them.

How this diplomacy contributed to the Tibetan cause is evident from the dialogue and correspondence that the Dalai Lama had with various statesmen.

From Edward Heath, MBE, MP, House of Commons,
UK to the Dalai Lama

25th May, 1985

I have now returned from a twelve-day visit to China which I indicated to you on 5 February, 1985. I had the opportunity of discussing Your Holiness' position with the Chinese leaders and they confirmed to me that the situation remains exactly as they described it to you in Five Points Plan discussed with your delegation in Peking. Perhaps I may give you my personal impressions.

The Chinese leaders appeared to me to be perfectly neutral in their attitude to this question. They do not wish to do anything to persuade you to return to China, nor do they wish to deter you from returning. It is a question, the answer to which they leave entirely to Your Holiness. When in your Statement of 16 December, 1984 you said, "The very fact that the Chinese are insistent that I return and stay in Peking clearly indicates that there are still problems inside Tibet, I must comment that I do not find the Chinese leaders "insistent". Indeed they have no way of insisting that Your Holiness should return to China. Further, I must add that I received no impression that the Chinese leadership is worried about problems inside Tibet."

The situation inside the Peoples Republic of China is changing very rapidly. Development is proceeding speedily. The public relations with the outside world are being greatly widened. In these circumstances they can afford to maintain their present attitude indefinitely.

Encouraged by the response to Strasbourg Proposals, the Dalai Lama launched a major diplomatic initiative that is a continuous process now. The Dalai Lama wrote to the President George Bush Sr. in September 1987:

Dear Mr. President,

Unfortunately, the situation inside Tibet remains volatile. It will be engendered by 43 years of Chinese occupation continues to escalate in the hearts of the Tibetan people. Despite the failure of the Chinese government to respond positively to any of our past initiatives, I am continuing my efforts to open a channel of communication with them.

Very recently, the Chinese government contacted my brother, Gyalo Thondup, and asked that he goes to Beijing to "explore possibilities." While I cannot be certain that anything concrete will emerge from the meeting, in the hope of advancing the interest of the Tibetan people in even a small way, I have authorized him to make the trip. He is in China at the moment. I will inform you of the results of his efforts whatever the outcome.

I would like to thank you for signing into law last year's Congressional resolution acknowledging Tibet's status as an occupied country. Your actions can significantly bolster the morale of Tibetans everywhere. At the same time, Mr. President, the Tibetan people, particularly those inside Tibet, were deeply hurt by the United States' failure to support the Tibetan resolution at the February meeting of the U.N. Human Rights Commission in Geneva.

Jimmy Carter, the President of United States replied to the Dalai Lama on 9 October, 1987:

Your visit to my home was a pleasure and very helpful to me in understanding from your perspective recent history and current circumstances in Tibet.

Since then, I have received your letter of 28 September, enclosing your congressional statement and requesting that I assist in the initiation of exploratory talks between your representatives and officials of the Chinese government.

As I informed you, the position of the Chinese is that this is an internal matter which does not involve foreign nation or even "foreign individuals who are their friends." In spite of this, I have found them to be quite interested in your private views as relayed to us after your visit to Plains.

I would be glad to meet with Dr. Van Walt and so that he might answer a few of my questions which explain to me in more detail what degree of autonomy you consider to be necessary for you to return to people in Tibet. If there seems to be some promise of accommodation, I might then consult with the Chinese in an unofficial pre-mediation phase to determine if further specific talks would be possible and advisable.

I look forward to hearing from your representatives. Best wishes in your search for peace and service for those whom you represent.

The Dalai Lama further wrote to Jimmy Carter on September 9, 1991:

President Carter,

Thank you very much for your letter of August 28, 1991. It is very kind of you to receive my representatives. I am grateful and encouraged by your great interest in and growing concern for the Tibetan issue.

We have made great effort during the past eleven years or so to find an understanding with the Chinese authorities. And, as you know, even after over three years since I presented my Strasbourg Proposal in 1988, the Chinese have failed to respond concretely and officially. In fact, over five months ago, on March 10 this year, in my annual address to commemorate the Tibetan National Uprising, I said that unless the Chinese came forth with some concrete response within the near future I would be compelled to consider my last proposal ineffectual. An official statement to this effect has also been issued by the Kashag, the Tibetan Cabinet in exile.

At this point I do not have any definite plans to present to the Chinese. With the Strasbourg proposal invalid, I have left the table clear for alternative suggestions. (You are aware; many Tibetans have been deeply disappointed with my last proposal.) I am at present in the process of collecting ideas from amongst the Tibetans as well as from our Western friends. Moreover, under the new Charter recently adopted by the expanded people's deputies which is a kind of a mini constitution, fully democratic and which is to govern our administration while in exile, I need to consult and discuss these important matters with the people's deputies. Nevertheless, the gross violations of human rights inside Tibet, the massive transfer of Chinese population into Tibet, and the destruction of the Tibetan environment are extremely urgent and grave.

Jimmy Carter replied:

Please let me know when and if you feel that I can be of help either to consult with your representatives, to participate in drafting a tentative agenda for peace talks, or a substantive message to Beijing.

You have my continuing respect, admiration and best wishes.

This was further buttressed by many senators writing a joint letter to the President. USA Senators (24) to the President on November 1, 1991 as:

Dear Mr. President,

On October 9, 1991, at Yale University, His Holiness the Dalai Lama delivered an important address in which he spoke about a visit to Tibet. The Chinese government has in recent years invited the Dalai Lama to return for a short visit.

We believe the Dalai Lama's approach to resolving the question of Tibet through dialogue, understanding, and a steadfast insistence on non-violence deserves the support of all world leaders. We commend you for your meeting with the Dalai Lama this spring, and believe that the meeting can begin a new and principled policy towards Tibet. We call upon you to support the Dalai Lama's proposal to visit Tibet and to directly raise this issue with the Chinese leaders on the earliest possible occasion.

Sincerely,

Daniel Patrick Moynihan, Claiborne Pell, Paul Simon, Jesse Helms, Alfoose M. D'Amato, Christopher J. Dodd, Edward M. Kennedy, Harris Wofford, Pete V. Domenici, Dennis DeConcini, George J. Mitchell, John F. Kerry, Richard G. Lugar, Alan Cranston, Bill Bradley, Paul David Wellstone, Joseph R. Biden, Jr., Charles S. Robb, John D. Rockefeller, James M. Jeffords, Larry E. Craig, Paul S. Sarbanes, Dave Durenbefger, Herb Kohl.

Taking the matter further, George Bush Senior to the Dalai Lama on November 3, 1991 as:

Thank you for your recent letter reporting on your trip through Mongolia and the Baltic nations. I share your joy at the developments leading to greater freedom and democracy in the countries you visited. Their new-found liberty is an accomplishment that stands as a banner of faith and a signal of hope to people throughout world.

It was an honour and a pleasure to discuss these basic human values with you during our meeting in April. I have followed your most recent visit to the United States with interest. Your tireless commitment to the welfare of the Tibetan people and to the principle of non-violence has earned not only my great respect, but also the deep appreciation of the American people.

I believe that dialogue with China is important..We are engaged for the long-term with China for the sake of protecting American interests, for the sake of democracy and freedom, and for the sake of all the people in China.

USA Senator Jesse Helms, taking the matter further in the same vain, to the Dalai Lama:

November 5, 1991

"I shall always continue to support your efforts to lift the dark blanket of oppression from the Tibetan people.

With great admiration and affection."

The concern for Tibet by the Clinton Administration came only weeks after the Dalai Lama met President Clinton and Vice President Gore as well as many Members of the House and Senate. The Congress, in 1991 declared Tibet to be an occupied country. Now the senators also began to support Tibet. So, there was bipartisan support for the Tibetan people's non-violent struggle for human rights and self-determination.

Then the concern for the oppressed Tibetans did find several protagonists globally. Numerous international Tibet support groups came into existence[9]. Several eminent persons though not in any official position came to sympathize the cause. Some of them we shall see later (Chapter 9). Here just one classic illustration about the functioning of the democratic system is narrated. In 1992, an influential American lady, Elsie Walker, wrote to the Dalai Lama that several congressmen, senators and public figures have concerted their efforts to put pressure upon the US administration and the government. It appears that Elsie Walker had considerable influence with George Bush. When she wrote to him, he appreciated her analysis on June 15, 1992, as "profoundly in depth and thoughtful". He also kept an open mind to meet the Tibetans that year. George Bush Sr. went to the extent of canvassing support. He wrote to Elsie Walker Kilborne, a cousin:

June 15, 1992
Dear Elsie,

Thank you for sharing with me your profoundly sad and thoughtful analysis of the situation in India and China concerning the conditions of Tibetans in those countries. I appreciate hearing from you and value your assessment of the likely direction of the dialogue between the Chinese and the Tibetan people.

Meanwhile, I will keep an open mind about the meeting with the Tibetans towards the end of the summer.

Bill Clinton regretted to the Dalai Lama in 1992:

Although we have not come as far as I would have hoped, I believe that progress has been made with the Chinese in the area of human rights. It is my wish that this progress continues in a constructive fashion. Your role in this progress will not be forgotten.

With this backdrop, the Dalai Lama took a major initiative to write to Deng Xiaoping, to dare to trust, in 1992:

"For meaningful negotiations to take place it is essential to have mutual trust. Therefore, in order to create trust, it is important for the leaders and people of China to know of the endeavours I have made so far. My three representatives carry with them a letter from me, accompanied by a detailed note of my views and my efforts through the years to promote negotiations in the best interests of the Tibetan and Chinese people.

On my part, I have put forward many ideas to solve our problem. Now it is time for the Chinese government to make a genuinely meaningful proposal if you wish to see Tibet and China live together in peace."

Since China was unyielding to various overtures, the position in the eyes of international law has to be clearly and finally established. It has remained "vague" since Nehruvian times. So, several legal groups congregated to hold an International Jurist Conference in 1993 on Tibet. Their agenda envisaged reference to history, distinction of Tibetans as people by themselves, the right of self-determination, and human rights. These were to be examined with reference to international law. Lord Ennals, who was one of the sponsors for the Dalai Lama for Nobel Prize was the chairperson of the conference. The happenings, then and thereafter, on the international arena appear to be so co-coordinated as if history had orchestrated them in advance!

The conference not only discussed the jurisprudence, but went into the details of evidence as regards to:

1. Self-determination of the Tibetan people;
2. Key to Tibet-China historical events;
3. Tibetans as a distinct people;
4. Is Tibet part of China?;
5. Relevant territory of Tibet, population transfer;
6. Impact of population transfer;
7. Political self-determination;
8. Economic and environmental self-determination;
9. Social and cultural self-determination; and
10. Denials of human rights to Tibetans.

Their conclusions were in absolute favour of Tibet. Titled as the London Statement on Tibet[10], they arrived at the following:

They followed strictly standard legal and judicial procedures. So they invited the Chinese to present their point of view. The Chinese retorted through their ambassador in London, Ma Yuizhen, that this was interference in the affairs of "big family of the Chinese nation"[11]. He said that the theme violates the respect for the sovereignty and territorial integrity. He wanted the conference to be cancelled. Justice Michael Kirby replied that the organizing committee decided to confer regardless of the Chinese position and have carefully gone through the entire material supplied by them by the Chinese Ambassador (15 documents). A report, now known widely as London report was published following a conference of international lawyers on issues relating to self-determination and independence for Tibet, at London[12] on 6-10 January, 1993, as:

1. That there can be no serious dispute that Tibetan civilization has long and distinct history and is in danger of disappearing;
2. Tibet was before 1949-1950 an independent state for the purposes of international law;
3. Since the military action of 1949-1950, Tibet has been under the alien occupation and domination of the PRC and has been administered with the characteristics of an oppressive colonial administration. There is alien rule by China that is not distinguishable from colonial occupation;
4. The invitation to join the Republic was an acknowledgement by the Republic of China that Tibet was not, as such, a part of the Republic and would need an act of self-determination to join it. No such act of self-determination has ever occurred. China has imposed its rule upon Tibet; and
5. The evidence demonstrates that there is a consistent serious violation of universally recognized human rights in Tibet.

In their recommendations there was a major clause to commence genuine negotiation to facilitate the exercise of the Tibetan people's right to self-determination and a clarion call to all the governments of the world to take up the question of Tibet with regard to the Tibetan people's right to self-determination. They proposed a further gesture at reconciliation. They suggested a meeting in Beijing with professional lawyers and jurists from China to consider "these matters in an atmosphere of friendship and good faith". This was not answered by the Chinese side. Though nothing concrete in terms of proposed bilateral meeting emerged, this conference provided a tremendous buttress to the Dalai Lama to vindicate his position. He can now talk to the Europeans on the platform of jurisprudence and international law too.

The Dalai Lama was now received by almost all the leaders of the free world. By 1995, there were several Tibet-friendship groups in Europe and elsewhere. They were spread out in Belgium, Czech Republic, Canada, Denmark, Finland, France, Germany, Hungary, Lithuania, New Zealand, Norway and Sweden. They worked out a concerted plan of influencing the parliamentarians in their countries so that they may sponsor legislations in support of Tibet. They also organized inter-parliamentary debates. This way the objective of keeping the issue of Tibet alive was more than achieved.

Though these statesmen were weary to displease and confront China, they could at least impress the Chinese to talk to the Dalai Lama. The Chinese had shut the doors for negotiations after the Tiananmen Square happenings. Therefore, there was a flurry of activities on the Western Front. Several parliaments in addition to the European Parliament passed resolutions in support of Tibet and called upon China to open up negotiations.

The decision to include a separate condition on Tibet in the Executive Order for Most Favoured Nation (MFN) in trade relations to China, and its wording, were hotly debated within the US Administration. Outside factors which played a role were large-scale demonstrations in Lhasa (1988-89) and subsequent statements by the Dalai Lama persistently renouncing violence and public support that was generated thereby. Beijing made some gestures, such as token release of Tibetan prisoners, in an attempt to avoid a strong condition on Tibet. The final condition — that China must make significant progress in protecting Tibet's distinctive religious and cultural heritage — is largely in keeping with the emphasis of the Dalai Lama. Only a few weeks ago (1993), while in Washington, the Dalai Lama stressed to US policy makers that his foremost goal was the survival of the Tibetan people and Tibetan culture and the greatest threat was the Chinese population influx.

Meanwhile, Rajiv Gandhi, the then Indian Prime Minister, visited Beijing. Both the governments were keen to avoid another war. Rajiv Gandhi's visit assured China that Indian stand on Tibet issue remained unchanged and China and India moved closer in terms of resolving the long standing border issue. It also raised a moot question silently: how long a refugee will be able to remain in the guest country[13]? Chinese had not moved at all from their earlier stand. Almost in desperation, the Dalai Lama wrote a long letter to Deng clarifying that he is not for independence. There was no answer. An alternate strategy had to be evolved. It generated through numerous friends.

The award of the Nobel Prize, persistence of the Dalai Lama on non-violence and, reports of International Commission of Jurists brought Tibet into frontline focus worldwide. Earlier, the Dalai Lama was respected as a spiritual and religious leader but was a political pariah. No leader in the position of power of any country would want to meet him. The King of Norway was the first one to receive the Dalai Lama, in spite of the Chinese protest, as it was customary for Nobel Laureates. Thereafter, a dialogue developed with many important world leaders and all the US presidents from Jimmy Carter to George Bush, Jr. And now, he has met Barak Obama several times.

There were no more cobwebs or confusion about Tibet now. The world had come to acknowledge that Tibet is on the verge of being wiped out as a nation. Even Russian President Putin included a Buddhist diplomat in his delegation on his visit to China and the Dalai Lama warmly commended him. And now there was no unanswered question as to who will bell the cat. US has emerged a singular superpower. And it spoke once again with same clarity as did President Roosevelt to Winston Churchill. If imperialism was out of date in 1947, it is much more so now in the Twenty-first century. Fundamental human rights came to include the right to self-determination. US President George Bush was almost like a Tibetan spokesman. Senator Feinstein had said something similar. And Collin Powell made some plain talk.

Jimmy Carter had set the ball rolling for a compromise formula. After the visit of a delegation from the Carter Center to Tibet in November 1998, he wrote to the Dalai Lama on February 16, 1999, as:

"As you know, a delegation from The Carter Center visited Tibet last November. We might enhance understanding of Chinese government policies towards the Tibetan-inhabited regions and of the attitudes that have been expressed by you.

You will note that their viewpoint is different from many Tibetan views and, at the same time, it does not agree with some Chinese assessments about the situations there. Ambassador Harry Barnes plans to be meeting with you. He will share them with you then:

(a) Would an unequivocal statement by you that Taiwan is part of China be helpful to your purposes? (You may recall that I did that when I established diplomatic relations with China in 1979.)
(b) Does your expansive territorial definition of Tibet make the attainment of other objectives more difficult?
(c) Would an emphasis on attaining religious goals in Tibet be more productive than the preset focus on political issues?

(d) Do you think it would be helpful for you to call on international development agencies and interested nations to help accelerate development of vocational schools, public health, and environmental programmes in the Tibetan Autonomous Regions?

I am also sharing some of the points raised in this letter with President Jiang Zemin."

US Congressmen Tom Lantos, John Edward Porter, Gephardt, Newt Gingrich, Charlie Rose and Ben Giiman also wrote to the Dalai Lama on February 23, 1993 as:

"As leaders of the Congressional Human Rights Caucus, we invite you. We can think of no clearer example than the one set by the Tibetan Government-in-exile where the leaders of a nation have made the respect of fundamental human rights and the value of peaceful negotiation the central focus of their policies.

This year also marks the fifth anniversary of your first visit to the U.S. Congress when you presented your Five-Point Peace Plan to members of the Human Rights Caucus.

Over the years, the Congressional Human Rights Caucus has grown to become one of the largest bipartisan organizations in Congress with over 220 Congressmen and Congresswomen – a majority of the House Representatives – participating in Caucus authorities."

Warren Christopher, a member of Human Rights Caucus wrote to the Dalai Lama on April 27, 1993 as:

"As you know from previous visits to our country, Americans have long had a special interest in Tibet's culture and its people. Your dedication to non-violence and to whom you are spiritual leader have justly earned your world-wide recognition."

The diplomatic initiative was pursued worldwide. The Dalai Lama wrote to Douglas Hurd, M.P. on May 25, 1993, as:

"I have said many times in the past, whether intentionally or unintentionally, displacement of Tibetans is taking place in Tibet as a result of the massive influx of Chinese mainly in the bigger towns of Tibet. Moreover, the recent arbitrary arrests of several Tibetans in conjunction with the EC Ambassadors' delegation to Tibet highlight the gravity of the human rights situation in Tibet."

Thereafter, Clinton conditioned MFN to China on Preservation of Tibetan Culture in a press note on 28th May, 1993, as:

"Washington, DC — Today President Clinton announced that among the conditions placed on the future renewal of China's Most Favoured

Nation trading status is significant progress in protecting liberty, distinctive religious and cultural heritage.

The President's report accompanying the Order, which will be released soon is said to discuss the influx of Chinese into Tibet as a threat to Tibet's heritage."

In a very strong statement issued this morning by Senator Patrick Moynihan, the Finance Committee Chairman said, "Today President Clinton has made history. He has told Congress that the movement of Chinese to Tibet threatens Tibet's unique identity and culture.... He has told China that significant progress must be made in protecting Tibet's unique identity or he will effectively severe trade with China."

Bill Clinton to Charlie Rose, canvassing support for Tibet, as:

June 5, 1993
Dear Mr. Chairman, House of Representatives, Charlie Rose

Thank you for your letter regarding your concern for the Tibetan people and the subject of conditioning China's Most Favoured Nation (MFN) trading status on human rights improvement.

The treatment of Tibet and its people is of deep concern to me and is an issue of high priority in our relations with China. The charges that the Chinese Government is implementing a policy to support the immigration of Han Chinese to Tibet are especially troubling. I strongly believe that the Chinese Government should respect the economic, social and cultural rights of the Tibetan people and have pressed the Chinese Government to begin a dialogue with the Dalai Lama.

As you know, last week I announced conditions on renewal of MFN status for China, including that China must take measures to protect Tibet's distinctive religious and cultural heritage. I believe that by speaking with one voice, the Administration and Congress sent a strong message to China that it will be held accountable for its human rights record.

This was directly acknowledged by the Dalai Lama writing to Bill Clinton on June 8, 1993:

I would like to congratulate you on your recent announcement conditioning future renewal of Most-Favoured-Nation trading status to China on human rights improvements in China and Tibet.

The entire world looks to your great nation to lead the struggle for universal human rights. Your Executive Order sends a strong message to the Chinese government that, the United States Administration and

Congress care deeply about the welfare of the Chinese and Tibetan people that together you will hold China accountable for its repressive acts in China and Tibet.

I strongly believe that the broad condition in your Executive Order relating to the protection of Tibet's religious and cultural heritage will in the long-term bring about the desired results to improve conditions inside Tibet. I am very pleased that the issue of population transfer was raised accompanying Report.

Furthermore, I am greatly encouraged by the priority your Administration has placed on the resumption of the dialogue between the Tibetans and Chinese in your report.

Correspondence was multilateral as seen by Jimmy Carter writing to the Dalai Lama on August 4, 1993, as:

"President Clinton and I were touched by our meeting with you in April, and the important issues you raised were factored into. The language on human rights in the Executive Order and the accompanying report to Congress reflects our deep concern for the welfare of the Tibetan people.

As you know, I feel strongly that the Chinese Government should respect Tibet's distinctive religious and ethnic heritage."

Once again. Multilaterally, Bill Clinton to the Dalai Lama on November 23, 1993, as:

"Thank you for joining us for our 10th Anniversary Celebration of the Caucus. Your commitment to the cause of human rights is an inspiration to us all, and your presence was a great honour."

The Dalai Lama replied to Bill Clinton on December 2, 1993, as:

"I would like to offer my congratulations to you and your Administration in illustrating such global leadership on trade, proliferation and human rights at the Seattle summit.

I deeply appreciate your personal call for negotiations on the issue of Tibet during your meeting with Chinese President Jiang Zemin in Seattle. Even though it was publicly reported that President Jiang did not immediately respond positively to your call for negotiations, the fact that you personally brought up the matter sent a very powerful message to the Chinese leadership."

Once again. Multilaterally, Congress of United States to the Dalai Lama wrote on February 22, 1994, as:

President Clinton called upon President Jiang to respond by beginning substantive negotiations with you or your representatives.

You confirm our understanding that you or your representatives are ready to meet with senior Chinese leaders for substantive negotiations at anytime and without preconditions.

(Senators) George J. Mitchell, Thomas S. Foley, Robert Dole, Richard A. Gephardt, Robert H. Michel, Daniel P. Moynihan, Charlie Rose, Claiborne Pell, Benjamin A. Gilman and Jesse Helms.

In reply, the Dalai Lama to the Speaker Foley on March 4, 1994:

Dear Speaker Foley,

I am writing in response to the letter of February 22, 1994 from you, Senators Mitchell, Dole, Moynihan, Pell, Helms, and Representatives Gephardt, Michel, Rose and Gilman.

While it is the overwhelming desire of the Tibetan people to regain their independence, over the past fourteen years I have repeatedly and publicly stated that I am willing to enter into negotiations and to work from an agenda that does not include independence, in response to Deng Xiaoping's statement in 1979 that "except for the independence of Tibet, all other questions can be negotiated." I remain committed to this stand. As I have stated in my Five-Point Peace Plan and subsequent proposals, negotiations should address all issues which threaten the distinct religious, cultural and national identity of the six million Tibetan people has consistently attempted to confuse my position.

I am grateful for the tremendous support that the issue of Tibet has consistently received from the U.S. Congress and the new dynamic engagement by the Administration on the issue of negotiations.

The Dalai Lama to Bill Clinton:

December 1, 1994

Since June we have learned of a tightening of security and crackdown on monks, nuns and suspected independence or human rights activists. This repression has now been extended to include even those Tibetans who are engaged in establishing private funded schools and teaching the Tibetan language. Furthermore, series of new measures have been introduced to increase political control of the monasteries and other religious activities.

Of special concern to me is the decree compelling Tibetan Communist Party members and cadres to bring their children back from India, where they are studying in schools run by our Exile Administration. Failure to comply with this decree would result in expulsion from the Party or denial of salary raises and other penalties. Hundreds of thousands of Chinese students are allowed to study abroad — a large number of them being the children of cadres and leading members of the Chinese Communist Party. In the face of this general practice the measures adopted in Tibet constitute a blatant discrimination against Tibetans.

I have attempted to appeal to President Jiang Zemin to reconsider this measure on humanitarian grounds. Unfortunately, the Chinese Embassy in New Delhi has returned my letter objecting to the letter-head used. Nevertheless, in the past they had not objected to the letters I had written to their leaders on the same letter-head. There is definitely a hardening of Chinese policies with regard to Tibet.

Some of my friends contend that this hardening of Chinese policies is a consequence of the decision to delink trade and human rights. In Tibet the Chinese authorities have seized the opportunity to launch an extensive campaign to portray this as a decisive Chinese victory over the US-Administration in order to dishearten and demoralize the Tibetans.

The Dalai Lama browsed the proposed Tibet Act, 2001 before the Congress as:

Dear Congressman Lantos,

I am writing to express my deep appreciation to you, once again, this time for your leadership efforts concerning what I understand to be an important legislation on Tibet. My Special Envoy, Lodi Gyari, has shared with me a draft copy of the Tibetan Relations Act of 2001, as well as details of your most recent conversation.

While it is my customary practice not to comment on legislation before Congress or other parliamentary bodies, I believe that this effort not only will provide renewed hope to my people but also will certainly convey the message to the Chinese leadership that the United States support for Tibet is serious and determined to bring about a negotiated solution.

As Lodi Gyari has conveyed to you, I believe that it is vital to my own efforts in dealing with the Chinese government that the international community, especially through governmental expressions, recognize and respect Tibet's separate and distinct identity, as you have done in this bill. This message in no way contradicts my commitment to finding a negotiated settlement. It is, after all, China that is intent to eradicate Tibet's national, cultural and religious identity, and my Middle Path approach that would safeguard it and yet accommodate China's sovereign interest. You have only acknowledged historical fact, which cannot be changed and no one should be permitted to distort.

I understand that you have now decided not to include language in the bill that would direct funding for projects inside Tibet after consultations with Lodi Gyari. I am sure this was the prudent decision, as this bill will definitely attract attention in Beijing. We must not jeopardize the efficacy or continuation of even small efforts in Tibet. The future prospects for my people in their homeland are growing dire, and projects that provide economic empowerment or health and educational services to Tibetans are desperately needed. Therefore, I ask that you please continue to be supportive of the work of the Bridge Fund through some other means than this bill.

China has been very public about its intention to accelerate the development of Tibet under what it calls its "Western Development Plan." Of course, Tibetans are terribly poor, and I would like to encourage and support any and all economic progress in Tibet. But China's methods, like building, railroads to move Chinese settlers in and Tibet's precious resources out, and other development plans underway, are not the answer for my people's needs and can bring more harm than benefit. That is why I was so pleased to see the inclusion of the so-called "Tibet Principles" in the bill.

As you know, I have accepted an invitation to provide the commencement address at the Johns Hopkins School of Advanced International Studies on May 24. I hope my Washington visit might provide us an opportunity to meet.

The Dalai Lama began a liaison with Colin Powell in 2001, as:

"...for your commitment at to be aggressively engaged on the issue of Tibet. An early indication commitment is the appointment of the new Special Coordinator for Tibetan issues Under Secretary Dobriansky.

If you know, I had a useful and friendly meeting with President Bush who, indicated, offered genuine concern for the situation facing the Tibetan people. He also assured me of the support of his administration and that he would raise the issue of Tibet with President Jiang Zemin at the APEC summit. I asked that he convey to President Jiang my continued commitment not to seek independence but rather to achieve a mutually agreeable solution to the situation in Tibet through negotiations.

After our meeting I also had the opportunity to have an in depth discussion with Deputy Secretary Armitage and other senior officials. I shared with Deputy Secretary Armitage my assessment on the current impasse and the difficult situation in Tibet. He provided me a useful overview of your foreign policy, particularly with regard to Asia. I commend your determination to engage China in a matter that neglects your principles. In the long run this approach will be fruitful for the United States and beneficial to the whole region.

I also support the holistic approach this administration is pursuing towards Asia. Unfortunately, in the past many American policymakers focused their sight almost exclusively on the Pacific Rim. But to ignore the rest of Asia is counter productive and may be one reason why policies towards the region have not always been effective. A holistic approach is particularly crucial because Tibet is strategically located between these two nations and has a long and complex historical ties to them both, stability in the region will be difficult to achieve until the Tibet issue is resolved.

I also welcome the recent warming of relations between the United States and India. As the champion of democracy I consider it natural that the U.S. has closer ties with the world's largest democracy, India.

Gross violation of human rights in Tibet and the real threat of extinction of the Tibetan identity have always surfaced as the most urgent and immediate issues with regard to Tibet. Thus I am very grateful that successive American administrations have taken an interest in being proactive on human rights and have been involved in helping to preserve our identity both inside and outside Tibet. But these concerns are symptoms of a far greater problem. Accordingly, my middle way approach focuses on developing a lasting solution in Tibet through negotiations with the Chinese leadership. I firmly believe that this approach takes into account not only the well-being of the six million Tibetan people but also seeks to help bring stability and unity to the People's Republic of China and create the possibility of genuine and lasting cordial relations between India and China."

There was a meeting between Dalai Lama and Colin Powell in June 2001. He briefed him about his meeting with the Chinese leaders, as,

"I was pleased to have an opportunity to discuss with you our commitment to save Tibetans' unique cultural, religious, and linguistic legacy.

I wanted to respond to your letter after having met with senior leaders in Beijing. Assistant Secretary Craner and I had many productive meetings and I believe you will be heartened to know that we reached an agreement with the Chinese to rcsume human rights dialogue. We will continue to urge the Chinese to promote religious freedom in Tibet and to cease human rights violations there. In my meetings, I also encouraged the Chinese government to engage in substantive negotiations with Your Holiness or your representatives. I look forward to hearing opinions from you or your representatives as we prepare for bilateral human rights dialogue and for the President's visit to China in late October.

Thank you for our session in May. It helped me greatly in planning for my trip to China. I have taken the liberty of using a photograph from our meeting."

When President George Bush was to meet President Jiang Zemin in Shanghai, the Dalai Lama took the opportunity to remind him to talk to the latter, as,

"Our purpose in seeking a dialogue with the Chinese leadership is to find a mutually agreeable solution to the situation inside Tibet and nothing else. However, the Chinese continue to insist that I am calling for Tibet's independence despite my consistent statements that I am seeking genuine autonomy, which is actually guaranteed by the Chinese Constitution. I believe that at such a solution would help to remove Chinese fears of the Tibetans seceding from China and for the Tibetans it would guarantee the preservation of their unique cultural identity with its own way of life. It is time that the repeated Chinese excuse that I am seeking independence is put to rest. One therefore hopes that you and your delegation can strongly press President Jiang Zemin to move beyond this and agree to begin a dialogue with us.

I am pleased to learn from my Special Envoy, Lodi Gyari, that you will be visiting Shanghai for the Asia Pacific Economic Conference (APEC) and that you will have the opportunity to engage in bilateral discussions with President Jiang Zemin. I was further pleased to learn that Tibet will be on your agenda, as you had earlier indicated to me, and that Under Secretary Paula Dobriansky, Special Coordinator for Tibet, will be on your delegation. Her presence alone will illustrate the United States continued commitment to the issue of Tibet."

Soon after 9/11 terror attack on America, the Dalai Lama was quick to respond with a donation of $50,000 and sounded caution against a violent reaction as:

Your Excellency,

It may seem presumptuous on my part, but I personally believe we need to think seriously whether a violent reaction is the right thing to do and in the greater interest of the nation and people in the long run. I believe violencc will only increase the cycle of violence. But how do we deal with hatred and anger which are often the root causes of such senseless violence? This is a very difficult question, especially when it concerns a nation and we have certain fixed conceptions of how to deal with such attacks.

The tragic September 11th terrorist attack of the World Trade Centre in New York and the Pentagon in Washington D.C. and the uncertain world situation following these attacks reinforces my conviction for solving problems through non-violence and dialogue. I am grateful to my people for patiently listening to my reasoning for non-violence and peaceful means in our struggled, hope that the international community realises the importance of giving genuine support for just causes striving to address the issue through non-violence and dialogue.

George Bush acknowledged as,

"On behalf of the American people, I am grateful to you for your kind expressions of condolence and concern in the wake of the terrorist attacks on September 11, 2001. These savage deeds were attacks against freedom and serve as a warning to all civilized people.

Americans are grateful for the expressions of friendship and support from the Tibetan community following these devastating events. I am personally grateful for your heartfelt condolences.

On September 11, 2001, freedom was attacked, but freedom will be defended. The shared values and determinations of our peoples are crucial to rooting out terrorism across the globe. The struggle may be a long one, but we draw strength and resolve from your solidarity and support."

The Dalai Lama was invited to address the European parliament on October 24, 2001. Subsequently the Dalai Lama wrote to Jens-Peter Bonde, a member of the European Parliament. He requested him, as,

"I am extremely happy at the opportunity of meeting and discussing the issue of Tibet and its present situation with many members of the European Parliament. Your personal concern and interest is particularly encouraging. I am hopeful that Mr. Kelsang Gyaltsen will be able to follow up on the tremendous enthusiasm in the European Parliament for the cause of Tibet.

I would like to appeal to you once again about the appointment by the European Parliament of a Special Representative for Tibetan Affairs. I believe that such an appointment will ensure that the European Parliament members are regularly kept informed of the Tibetan situation and that the support we receive from the European Parliament is better channelled and becomes more effective. It will also send the right signal to the Chinese authorities about the serious commitment of the European Parliament towards the preservation of the Tibetan cultural identity and the violations of human rights inside Tibet."

It is a frequent occurrence that such meetings bring statesmen to Dharmshala even on informal visits. Anna Karamanou, a Member of the European Parliament, did so soon after the above event. She had an inimitable proposition to a temporary peace when she wrote to the Dalai Lama on 8 October, 2001, as,

"The Dharmashala trip was a unique experience for me and I would like to express my warmest thanks and gratitude for your kindness and warm hospitality you offered us, making this trip unforgettable and most rewarding.

Privileged moment was to come to know you personally. Our encounter and the exchange of views that followed were very enlightening as to the philosophy of the peaceful and unique culture supported by Tibet. Your ongoing efforts to acquire a legal status that protects Tibet as a true spiritual centre, is of worldwide importance. Tibetan involvement in the world's politics invokes the principles of non-violence and dialogue, desperately needed now-a-days in our troubled world.

During our conversation, you may remember, I mentioned the initiatives undertaken by Greek Foreign Minister Mr. George Papandreou, to revive the ancient custom of "Olympic Truce" during the Olympic games of 2004, which will take place in Athens. According to the ancient practice, during the games, all states refrained from any conflict. It is an ancient example how to create opportunities to promote dialogue and peaceful existence.

I think the Olympic Games of 2004 can give us a great chance to promote and solve, in the best possible way, the conflict between Tibet and China and most of all, to convince China that a peaceful solution will benefit both sides and will contribute to the universal effort to promote respect of cultural diversity, human rights and peace."

While engaging in serious concerns, most occasions important to others were attended by the Dalai Lama. Even than he combined his uncanny wisdom to connect the history and touched emotional cords as he wrote to Mary Harney TD, Ireland on July 17, 2002, as:

"Although belated, I would like to convey to you my warmest felicitations on your being re-elected as the Deputy Prime Minister of Ireland.

I take special pleasure in doing this because of the long-standing support that Ireland has given to the Tibetan struggle for freedom ever since 1959. It was a time when there was very little support for Tibet because many countries did not know anything about the tragic situation of Tibet or were enchanted with China and its experiment with Communism. In spite of this, there is still much need for more international support for the just cause of the Tibetan people, at least in the fields of human rights, freedom of religious belief, protection of the Tibetan cultural heritage and the protection of the delicate environment of Tibet. I must therefore appeal for the continued support from Ireland, especially when you hold the Presidency of the European Union in 2004."

And he repeated once again,

"November 24, 2004

As Ireland's President for a second term and take this opportunity to congratulate you for winning the Presidential election.

....cherish the important role that Ireland played when in 1960 it successfully co-sponsored with Malaysia a resolution on Tibet in the United Nations. Ireland also joined six other countries in 1965 in sponsoring another resolution on Tibet ...your country has continued to show its concern for the situation in Tibet and the plight of my unfortunate people.

....express our gratitude for the funding received from your Development Cooperation Ireland ...has allowed London-based Tibet House Trust to support the project: Sustainable Livelihood Programme for Tibetans in North-East India."

The Dalai Lama is in close circuits all the time with other Nobel Peace Laureates. He even suggested to the President Nelson Mandela, the Mandela Foundation, to form a group of peace keepers on November 7, 2004, as,

"I would like to express my deep appreciation and gratitude for your taking the time to see me on November 5 despite some difficulties. I hope this did not cause you too much inconvenience. As I expressed during our meeting, I have great admiration and respect for you and for the pivotal role you played in South Africa's non-violent freedom struggle.

I would also like to remind Your Excellency about my proposal to form a group that in the future can play an active role in preventing the outbreak of violence in possible areas of conflict and in times of crisis. As I related during our conversation, after the recent outbreaks of violence in Kosovo and Iraq, I strongly felt that there was a need for such a group. This group, comprised some Nobel Peace Laureates, respected statesmen like former President Vaclav Havel of the Czech Republic, famous scientists and thinkers, etc. who have no personal interest or hidden agenda in the crisis, could visit these areas and meet with the concerned parties to try and bring about a solution that would avoid violence and bloodshed."

Apart from the history making landmark dialogue that is narrated above, there were several contacts that mattered. That also makes interesting reading. For instance,

On November 19, 2001, congratulating John Howard on his election as the Prime Minister of Australia for an historic third term, the Dalai Lama made a reference that his people have been very patient for a very long time.

On July 17.2002, he wrote to Borut Pahor, President of the National Assembly, Slovenia:

"You have expressed interest in forming a Parliamentary Group for Tibet. As I mentioned during our conversation, I think the establishment of such a group will send a positive signal to Beijing that the people of Slovenia are concerned about the Tibetan issue."

Antonio J. Fas Alzamora President, Commonwealth of Puerto Rico Senate wrote, quoting Mahatma Gnadhi, on June 17, 2004, as,

"The High Body I am honoured to preside expresses its adherence to the issues. Your Excellency defends so vehemently the respect of human rights, the denunciation of the erosion of our environment, the striving towards finding the solution to the multiple armed international conflict, and the achievement of world peace.

Mahatma Gandhi once said, speaking about peace: "There is no path to peace, peace itself is the path". I acknowledge the fact that Your Holiness has long walked along that harsh path, creating consciousness among the world's diverse social sectors about the urgent need of cease. Puerto Rico has followed your trajectory, and considers your efforts to be of transcendental importance for fill of us who repudiate egotism and indifference to other's pain and suffering."

On a similar occasion, Pat Cox on his being elected as the President of the European Parliament, wrote to the Dalai Lama, on 25th April, 2002, as,

"The issue of Tibet is of great concern to me, as indeed to all Members of the European Parliament."

Following the upheaval in Eastern Europe, Dalai Lama at his very first meeting with Vaclav Havel, the poet President of Czech Republic had established a tremendous rapport. Both of them identified themselves as reluctant politicians. This had resulted in a lasting bond of friendship."

The Dalai Lama after meeting him once again in July 2002 wrote as follows:

"It was very kind of you to invite me to visit Prague soon after your assuming the Presidency in 1990 and to have had the opportunity of meeting and knowing you. Ever since I have had much admiration for you because of the principles you uphold. You were kind enough to invite me to Prague on three more occasions, thus giving me the opportunity to know you more and more. Your friendship has, therefore, meant something special to me and I will always cherish it.

I strongly believe that even after your retirement in January from the Office of the President, you still have an important role to play in promoting human rights and moral values in the world. Your commitment to promoting dialogue amongst people and the major religions of the world is needed more than ever."

Addressing the Dalai Lama as Your Holiness, 'dear friend', Havell wrote back as follows:

"I would like to thank you once again for your participation in the discussion on the role and responsibility of world religions, which was held on 3 July.

The considerable interest in the discussed issues on the side of public as well as media strengthened my opinion, that it is essential and meaningful to conduct and develop this kind of dialogue. I agree with you that mutual understanding and respect among diverse religions are necessary in order to maintain peace and reconciliation in the world."

Taking a pause from the diplomatic initiative and its results; there is an important event to insert here. Vaclav Havel passed away on 16th December, 2011 soon after the Dalai Lama visited Czeck Republic on his invitation. The Dalai Lama expressed his sadness immediately and conveyed his heartfelt condolences to the late leader's family members. He said, "Vaclav Havel on many occasions raised his voice over Human Rights violations in Tibet and expressed his support for Tibetans and Middle-way approach to solve the issue of Tibet.

In his death the world has lost a great statesman whose steadfast and unflinching determination played a key role in bringing freedom and democracy to the then Czechoslovakia."

For me personally, I will miss my dear friend for whom I always had the greatest admiration and respect. He was an unassuming and a courageous leader.

I first had the privilege of meeting President Václav Havel in February 1990 — months after he became President following the Velvet Revolution, which he led with an extraordinary display of people power. Over the ensuing two decades I had the opportunity to meet with him regularly, most recently in Prague on December 10 — the anniversary of the Universal Declaration of Human Rights.

"Perhaps the best tribute we could honour and remember him is to work as best we can towards building a more peaceful, open and just world."

Reverting back to the initiative, a breakthrough came about in October 2002. The Tibetan Policy Act was passed to authorize the State Department in matters of Tibet and was signed into Law by President George Bush. Senator Dianne Feinstein informed the Dalai Lama, as,

"As you know, I share your commitment to promoting greater understanding and dialogue between the Tibetan and Chinese people, and to safeguarding the cultural and religious autonomy of Tibet and its people. I believe that the Tibetan Policy Act represents an important statement of United States commitment and support for the welfare of the Tibetan people and a negotiated solution for Tibet, and I hope this legislation will help make a modest contribution towards attaining the legitimate aspirations of the Tibetan people."

A further landmark was made when the Dalai Lama wrote a detailed letter on September 10, 2003, explaining to President George Bush the purpose of his US visit, as,

"I have come to Washington to convey appropriately the deep gratitude of the Tibetan people to the U.S. Government for accepting the responsibility of promoting human rights, especially religious freedom, in Tibet and for its strong support for my efforts to achieve a negotiated settlement with the People's Republic of China. Since my last visit to Washington in May 2001, my envoys have made two trips to China and Tibet, in September of last year and in May and June of 2003. Therefore, I can say that China has responded positively to international encouragement to take steps to begin a dialogue.

"Our talks are still in the preliminary stage of confidence building, and my envoys report an overall positive attitude from their Chinese counterparts. Yet, there are many complex and difficult issues to resolve.

"I am encouraged by the renewed contact with China after such a prolonged impasse. From the Tibetan side, we are doing everything we can to signal our eagerness to begin earnest discussions. Our elected Tibetan leadership has appealed to the Tibetan people and our supporters to cease demonstrations and show no ill-will to Chinese officials touring abroad. My envoys have been accommodating in every aspect of our outreach. We are sincerely committed to the process and are making many efforts while the Chinese have made no comparative gesture and the situation on the ground in Tibet has not improved. Even in the small matter of banning my photos, China is creating tremendous resentment among my people and splitting the Tibetans and Chinese further apart.

"Therefore, I must ask for your help. I would like you to stay on course with direct and personal support for the process of dialogue. Specifically, I ask that you request President Hu Jintao for his assurance of China's commitment to continue with the present process until a mutually beneficial conclusion is reached. Such a commitment would help me to do all I can, including making a personal visit to China, if that would further help. I have already conveyed to the Chinese this offer and my intention to send envoys back to China, I have never asked for support for Tibet at the expense of good relations with China. Ultimately, I believe a solution in Tibet will benefit the Chinese people and add to stability and security in that region, which is also of great importance to the United States.

"The talks leading to such a solution will necessarily take time. In the meanwhile, there are urgent concerns for the situation in Tibet that cannot wait until a political solution is reached. If some of these concerns are not addressed in the near term, the very purpose of trying to reach a negotiated solution becomes meaningless. These immediate concerns are:

- Population transfer,
- Economic marginalization,
- Development and environmental degradation.

"Although Tibetans are in dire need of economic and development assistance, China's development policies are, instead, creating opportunity and prosperity for new Chinese settlers and further marginalizing the Tibetan people. Therefore, the Tibetan people require protection against inappropriate migration of non-Tibetans into Tibet, just as Hong Kong's Basic Law gives those people powers to determine the number of Chinese from the mainland who can enter into their territory for the purpose of settlement. Having seen the fate of the Mongols and Manchurians, you will appreciate that in our case, the real threat to our distinct identity comes from this unchecked migration. I have expressed these concerns both in my Five-Point Peace Plan and Strasbourg Proposal, in which I formally declared my intention to seek a solution for Tibet within the People's Republic of China.

"In the early 1980s, then Communist Party Secretary Hu Yaobang saw the urgent need for the Chinese government to rectify its wrong policies in Tibet and formulated principles to ensure comparative economic, employment and educational advantages to Tibetans, including that positions of influence held by Chinese should be replaced by Tibetans. I share this with you in the hope that among the new Chinese leadership there may be people who can be encouraged to recognize and act on such a precedent for Tibet.

"The Chinese government knows that I am seeking a Middle Way solution that would provide genuine autonomy for the Tibetan people within the People's Republic of China. I am not seeking independence. The autonomous system of governance I envision would guarantee the Tibetan people the determining voice in matters that exclusively affect them, specifically the preservation of our distinct cultural, religious and linguistic identity. Therefore, this system must allow the freedom of expression, belief and association, and respect for the rule of law. And, it must involve the right of the people freely to determine their own economic future, which means that Tibetans would control Tibetan resources, protect their environment, arid determine how Tibet would be developed.

"Presently, Chinese development schemes for Tibet remove precious resources, degrade local conditions, and deliver material benefit principally outside Tibet. While the Chinese loudly proclaim how much they contribute materially to Tibet, they make little acknowledgement of the tremendous resources taken away. Efforts by the Chinese government to develop Tibet in a way that genuinely benefits Tibetans will be welcomed. This was a consideration that influenced my decision to commit to Tibetan autonomy within the People's Republic of China because I thought that Tibet could benefit materially from such an arrangement.

"I had a good meeting with Secretary Powell. I was able to brief him on other issues relating to the welfare of the Tibetan people, both inside Tibet and those in exile, and I sought your Administration's support. I have also shared with both the Senate and the House leadership my concerns as well as our needs. It is such a great encouragement not only to have strong bipartisan support but also that both the Administration and the Congress share a common viewpoint on our issue.

"Mr. President, in conclusion may I once again draw your attention to the specific issues of immediate concern that I have raised and seek your help in trying to address this concerns. Equally important is your help in trying to get a clear commitment from the Chinese leadership of its willingness to continue with the process of dialogue that will lead to a mutually beneficial conclusion.

"I commend you for appointing Under Secretary Dobriansky as the Special Coordinator for Tibetan Issues. No one is more suited than she at this critical stage for the Tibetan people. Lodi Gyari will continue to work closely with her and other members of your administration."

By now, USA support was firmly established. On September 17, 2003, Colin Powell had informed the Dalai Lama about exploring the ways for a continued dialogue with China, as,

"It was a pleasure to see you again during your recent visit to Washington. I appreciate your insight about the current situation in Tibet and welcome your desire to engage China in a dialogue on Tibet's future as to seek ways to encourage China to continue the dialogue on a substantive basis with you and your representatives."

China responded by openness for further dialogue. They needed appeasement of world leaders: they held the trump card to finally stick to their position that they have been holding since 1959! This we will see in later chapters.

Senator Patrick Leahy wrote from Washington on October 1, 2003, as,

"I was pleased to hear that China has responded favourably to your appeals for a dialogue and that the initial results have been positive.

"Please know that I will continue to work with the U.S. Special Coordinator for Tibetan Issues and other Members of Congress to try to protect Tibetan culture and human rights. I will also continue to support funding for programmes that assist Tibetans inside Tibet as well as the Tibetan exile community."

This put the Chinese Government under pressure, and, at long last, it accepted to negotiate. However true to their style, they have already extracted a major concession. He must give up the demand for the independence of Tibet. True to his style of honesty, sincerity and transparency, the Dalai Lama did not indulge in bartering and conceded that he shall be happy with the status of an autonomous region for Tibet, though this almost amounted to putting the cart before the horse.

While US has been proactive in diplomacy, the support from the European Union has grown. The World Bank was about to sanction a huge loan to China that got aborted because of the intervention by the Union in 2000. In the same year, EU passed a strong resolution threatening to even recognize the Government in Exile. If this were to happen, a new corridor of diplomacy will be wide open.

Apart from the detailed correspondence narrated, one exemplary quote is reproduced:

Senator Feinstein to Jiang Zemin, 1991

....Please understand. Most of us are Americans today because our parents or grandparents, or great grandparents fled to another land to avoid oppression. In my case, my mother fled Russia and my grandfather, alone, at 14, fled Poland out of depression. I deeply believe that we are our brothers' keepers, that the right of people to speak out and to just and fair treatment knows no borders. It is internal affair of any government but the responsibility of us, wherever we find ourselves, to speak out against oppression.

For many years, the plight of the Tibetan people was unknown to people, but today the Tibetan situation is well known worldwide, as documentary evidence of and brutality toward the Tibetans is played on screens and reported by respected organizations such as Asia Watch and Amnesty International.

In September 2003, The Dalai Lama congratulated Hillary Clinton on her being elected as a Senator. He was quick to brief her about the Tibet situation. On the occasion of the conference of Rights of Women in Beijing, Hillary Rodham Clinton also spoke about universal human rights and civil liberties. China managed just a few protestors and small demonstrations.

George Bush on December 26, 2003 almost sounded like a Tibetan envoy to Beijing when he wrote to the Dalai Lama:

"When we met on September 10, 2003, I indicated to you that I would pursue the issues related to your dialogue with China. During my recent meeting with Premier Wen Jiabao in Washington, I shared my hope that the people of China would be able to practice their religious beliefs. We both agreed that this issue was important to China. I also conveyed to him the importance that I attach to continued visits by, and a dialogue with, your representatives. Your dedication to promoting peace and preserving the culture of Tibet should be recognized."

In early 2004, Vice- President Dick Cheney on his Beijing visit, insisted that what he said be broadcast live and unedited, conveyed a message as if it was from the pundits of political science:

"If people can be trusted to invest and manage material assets, they will eventually ask why they cannot be trusted with decisions over what to say and what to believe... Economic growth is important in allowing individuals to lead lives of comfort and dignity, but material goods alone cannot satisfy the deepest yearnings of the human heart; that can only come with full freedom of religion, speech, assembly, and conscience."

The Dalai Lama was deeply moved by US gestures. He wrote to Colin Powell, US Secretary of State on November 23, 2004:

"Your thoughtful engagement on the Tibet issue and concern for my people is something that I value... your decision to appoint Under Secretary Paula Dobriansky as Special Coordinator for Tibetan Issues."

While the awareness about Tibet is universal in 2011, the position has not changed from what it was. The Chinese have just yielded to negotiations that have not produced anything concrete so far. By one estimate, they will not in the future too; they are just waiting for the Dalai Lama's demise. Without stretching even a hand, they have got everything that they wanted. It was certain in 1950-1965 that nobody is going to send an army to Tibet, as Nehru publicly said. It is certain now that no influential nation will go to severe trade and commerce with China for the sake of Tibet. And, the population transfer is going on so that Tibetans will be difficult to spot in Tibet. And as seen by Jimmy Carter, The Chinese are able to convey a message of "Tibetan expansionism" when the Dalai Lama talks of *Cholka Sum* (U-tsang, Amdo and Kham regions).

The Chinese have not succeeded in marginalizing the Tibet question to that of the return of the Dalai Lama to Tibet. Whether the Dalai Lama returns or stays indefinitely in India, it cannot help resolve the impasse. Emergence of civil liberties in the mainland China can only bring the aspirations of people to surface. That such liberties wrecked havoc on the erstwhile U.S.S.R. is not lost to the Chinese.

Neither the Dalai Lama nor the Chinese leadership nor the enlightened

Western concerns at the present are the monitors of history any more. Only resurgent idealism of the youth — Tibetan as well as modernized Hans Chinese and other minorities — will have to take the future in the palm of their hands, look face to face with alternatives that bifurcation paths hold for them and decide what is their choice of destiny. Only they can give it a destination, then.

What is a loss for Tibet has been a gain for humanity at large. Self-contained and contented Tibet is now wide open culturally to the world. Its immortal software systems that probe the human mind and the mysteries of existence, generate wisdom and peace, to be available all over the world.

REFERENCES

1. Paul Ingram, *Tibet, the Facts*, London, 1990. p. 266.
2. This partly applies to us too. We were drawn to the Dalai Lama searching for a scientific explanation to the phenomenon of consciousness in 1987. Human consideration soon superseded metaphysical and that has brought about a personal, political commitment that has seen us marching through the streets with our grandchildren. (ref. Changing Course of Brahmaputra, 1992).
3. Tom Gromfeld, *The Making of Modern Tibet*, 1987.
4. John Rawls, *A Theory of Justice*, London, 1972.
5. Henry Sidgwick, *Classical Doctrine, The Methods of Ethics*, London, 1907.
6. For diplomatic reasons, a meeting with the Vice-President Al Gore was set up. It was said that Bill Clinton, the President happens to pass by and dropped in by chance!
7. It appears India seems to have had advance knowledge of this peace offensive. Usually an official of Foreign Ministry accompanies the Dalai Lama on his travels. At this time the practice was not followed. However, India had no comments to make.
8. Dawa Norbu, Pandit Hridayanath Kunzru Memorial Lecture on International Affairs delivered on 22 March, 1990 at Jawaharlal Nehru University City Centre, New Delhi.
9. The Report on Tibet Support Groups, Conferences held, first in 1990 at Dharamshala, second in 1996 at Bonn, and third at Berlin in 2000. At the last conference, 282 participants from 52 countries attended. (Friedrich Naumann-Stiftung, New Delhi, 2001).
10. Tibet: The Position in International Law, 1994, p. 143.
11. Embassy of the People's Republic of China, 14th December, 1992, Tibet: The Position in International Law, 1994, p. 155.
12. Tibet: The Position in International Law, Report of the Conference of International Lawyers, London, 1994.
13. Half jokingly and half sincerely, the Dalai Lama has told us a few times that he enjoys the dubious distinction of a guest that has stayed longest ever!

8
Indo-Tibet Situation

We asked the Dalai Lama about his dialogues with various Prime Ministers. It is an obvious fact that he has not been able to break ice with any of them. He has repeatedly reminded Indians that India should wake up to the realization of its giant stature. He also told us that the very essence of democracy is in the ability of the citizens to influence the policies of their Government. If the Government of India were hesitant to correct their past mistakes, the citizens should exercise their democratic right to persuade them to do so.

Alas! Today most of the Indians are ignorant about the status of Tibet. Even though in the archetypal religiosity of Indian masses, Kailas and Mansarovar are intrinsically rooted the average Indian pilgrim to these places has no qualms of conscientious for applying for a Chinese visa to visit these holy places. The Dalai Lama half in joke and half in anguish told us once, "Tibet would rather be a part of India and welcome the pilgrims without any document whatsoever rather than to be a part of China."

India owes its democratic tradition to a very great extent to Pandit Nehru. This statesman was a giant amongst giants of his era. The Indian masses dotted on him to the extent that in the guise of an anonymous reader, he himself penned a letter to a leading newspaper cautioning about spoiling Pandit Nehru with admiration and affection least he may become a dictator. It is no exaggeration, however, that Pandit Nehru was a *de facto* dictator of independent democratic socialist republic of India and, he had the last word. While the stalwarts like M.V. Kamath, Lohia and other socialists challenged him in parliament, there was a tremendous *bonne homie* between him and socialists. In fact the socialists' faction within the Congress party, Congress Socialist Party came into being at his behest.

Nehru shaped the future of Tibet as much as he did that of India. Nehru had imbibed socialism right from his young days and had interacted with giant socialist intellectuals of his time. Had he so wished, India may have been a socialist country with various shades of red. Mahatma Gandhi's moderation was a dampener and the stalwarts like Sardar Patel whose contribution to the independence struggle was as great, if not more than Pandit Nehru's, opposed communism. Sardar Patel had gone to the extent of saying that there are 84 types of Brahmins in the Indian caste system and, only the socialists outnumbered them in the division[1]. Nehru ridiculed Sardar Patel on his rustic down to the earth bearings and remarked in private that his only culture was agriculture. But antagonism between two giants meant well for India. Nehru succeeded in conniving with Mahatma to supersede Sardar as the Prime Minister; he did not succeed into converting Congress to any shade of socialism.

There is enough on record about Nehru's mind on Tibet. Certainly he ignored Sardar Patel at a cabinet meeting and, turned a deaf ear to his warning about the dangers from communist China. However, Sardar asserted and made his point through a statesmanlike letter (Appendix I).

Certain distinct features of Nehru's personality make his attitude regarding Tibet clear. Apart from his socialism, he had no track with any religion or religiosity. In fact the present day confusion in India about what does the concept secularism means has its origin to Nehru's bias against all religions. Mao said: religion is the opium of masses, but he did deal with the Buddhist Dalai Lama. Nehru practiced what Mao said. In his vision of independent India religiosity had nothing to do with the affairs of the state.

Having seen the bad days of imperialistic exploitation and studied the aristocracy in England it is easy to understand that Nehru would abhor the exploitation or the peasantry by the feudal landlords and monastery institutions in Tibet.

He was a historian and as a paradox was conscious of what his role would be in the history yet to be written. He wanted to be the tallest statesman in Asia and in national terms with Chinese and China. At the Bandung Conference, he adopted a patronizing elder-brotherly approach even to Chou En-lai. Observers say that Chou En-lai silently at that point of time resolved to teach Pandit Nehru a lesson.

With this backdrop when the issue of Tibet first come up before the United Nations in 1950, instead of going by historical facts, India pleaded on behalf of communist China. India argued that the Dalai Lama himself has adopted the 17-point Agreement. United Nations need not do anything in the matter.

In 1954 Nehru went to China. There he signed 5-point Agreement with China that came to be known as Panchsheel. One of the points of the treaty was that there shall be no interference in the internal affairs by each other. And the treaty formally acknowledged that Tibet was a part of China. What could have been Nehru's motivation to engage into this kind of understanding? While the Tibet had undergone PLA invasion, Tibet-India border along the McMohan line was quiet. There was no significant political or social cultural compulsion to proclaim these high-sounding principles. There were numerous Chinese living peacefully in India during this time; in fact the profession of dentistry was largely practiced by the Chinese doctors. China apart from the large number of cadres in people's liberation army was not a military power of any significance. This is best illustrated by the fact that for conveying Chinese leaders to Bandung Conference China did not have a good enough aircraft. They had requisitioned a plane from the Indian Government Kashmir Princess to carry Chou En-lai. (The plane crashed and all the passengers died but vilely Chou En-lai had decided not to travel by that plane. Was there a conspiracy and if so, who planted it, has not come out and shall probably never.)

In retrospect, rather than a strategic compulsion, Nehru's motivation to sign Panchsheel appears to have its origin in his megalomania to go in the history as one of the great statesmen of his times. Tibetans do not speak of this betrayal openly but only recently the Dalai Lama has spoken critically of Nehru. The history of Tibet has been shaped by the betrayal of this historian statesman scholar who probably did not give much credence to his own discipline when it came to the history of China's past.

Venkatesaran, a Former Foreign Secretary acknowledged the mistake about Panchsheel. He said it imposed restrictions as per international law; so that if India would have wanted to change its stance, it could be done only by fighting a war with China. But India did fight a war with China in 1962. Catastrophic it was in the sense of ignominious defeat of Indian forces. Only a little while before the war, Pandit Nehru had indulged himself into rhetoric, "throw them out" before he went to Sri Lanka. This turned out to be hollow bravado totally isolated from the realities of ground situation. Pandit Nehru will go down in the history as a statesman not only with unclear wisdom, almost as a blind man. A few years earlier, he had gone to defend the Chinese invasion of Ladakh with the remark, "not a blade of grass grows over there".

The Chinese betrayal of his trust was to crush Pandit Nehru physically, so that he died within a couple of years. But here again was an opportunity for India to standby defiant in defeat and proclaim a mistake that was made *vis-à-vis* Tibet.

Chinese proved to be cleverer, more sharp witted and more defence oriented when they decided to unilaterally withdraw. They have taught

India a lesson. They did not want to over stretch their supply lines from the mainland China and would now onwards deal with India with a superior stance. The Dalai Lama puts the matter on record in his biography but did he also miss an opportunity to impress upon Pandit Nehru and other leaders? Only a few years back, the Dalai Lama had been admonished by Nehru. This was the time to cultivate Nehru and abrogate the Panchsheel treaty. It is not in the personality of the Dalai Lama. Once rebuffed, twice shy: He did not re-approach Vajpayee after a cold response from the latter as we shall see. Smarting under the defeat, India did not dare and could not do so even today. Rather than correcting the historical blunders, India looks forward to better economic and trade prospects than can accrue by resolving pending border issues with China.

It is customary for the Dalai Lama to pay a courtesy-call to every Prime Minister of India following his election. Vajpayee's stand was very clear before he became the Prime Minister. He has been categorical that India was historically, morally and strategically in its own national interest should change its position *vis-à-vis* Tibet. On 27th April, 1989, he stated in the Parliament that Nehru had made a Himalayan blunder when he accepted Tibet as a part of China. He had even argued that even if Tibet was never independent nation before it has a natural right to demand independence afresh. He also questioned the autonomous status on Tibet region in the Chinese Republic. He had praised the moderation in the Dalai Lama's demand and argued that this was a reason to persuade Chinese[2].

Encouraged by their earlier statements of Janata Party leaders and particularly of Atal Bihari Vajpayee, the Dalai Lama took the lead to approach the latter when he became the Foreign Minister in Morarji Desai government in 1977. Vajpayee seemed suddenly to grow cold when reminded about his publicly stated support of Tibet. The Dalai Lama was so taken aback that subsequently when Vajpayee became the Prime Minister in the year 1999, he did not think it worthwhile to ask him again. Though Vajpayee's term lasted for full five years there was no visible change in the foreign policy. Vajpayee's tenure was riddled with many contradictions in the matters of foreign policy. Picking up the friendship of one of the old time comrades of George Fernandes, we wrote to him at least to declassify the documents which are more than 50 years old. Fernandes was very prompt to answer in a sympathetic cord that he shall do everything within his capacity to de-classify documents. We sent a few reminders to George Fernandes. The documents still remain unclassified and non-available for public scrutiny; probably the Government of India has much to hide.

Soon after the arrival of the Dalai Lama in exile, in April 1959, George Fernandes organized a massive rally in Mumbai. He was further to organize international convention on Tibet in August 1989 at New Delhi. The main agenda for the conference was to bring the Tibet issue in the centre stage of political stage. Considering that the freedom of Tibet is *sine qua non* for Indian security, he wanted the Indian masses to be aware of Tibet question. Even if the whole world were to support Tibet it would make little difference if India were not to be involved. He even floated an idea of international *satyagraha.*

George Fernandes explained his inability to effectively change the policy of Indian Government during his tenure as Cabinet Minister. He said that unless the people of India become aware of the issue, the politicians are unlikely to take notice of it. However, he will keep on fighting all the time for the cause of Tibet.

History seems to be of least importance to the present generation, whose primarily concerned is consumerization. The efforts by the Tibetan Government in exile to impress upon Indian masses about Tibetan recent history are also too meagre to make any impact. So much so that many eminent citizens of the country who may have sought blessings of the Dalai Lama, describe Tibet as part of China. When their attention is drawn to the complexity of political situation, the pre-emptory response generally is that they are concerned with the spirituality of the Dalai Lama and not with politics! On the other hand the stories from the pilgrims who have been to Mansarovar and Kailas do turn out soul-stirring at times. Dr. Usha Mody described her own experience along the way to Kailas. She saw some of the ruins what would have been monasteries also along the way she saw several places strewn with human bones and she had experienced an eerie silence that not only saddened her but frightened her too as if the spirits were still hovering round the place, she experienced them with the profound sorrow. A few years has passed since her return from the pilgrim but the illness that she brought from Tibet in her guts has still not left her.

Reverting back to the polity, on 7th December, 1950, Pandit Nehru said in the Indian Parliament, "It is inappropriate that any country tries to establish his sovereignty beyond its boundary. It is absolutely up to the people of Tibet to decide their fate. This is regardless of the fact as to whether Tibetans are capable of exercising such a choice. It is not pertinent for India or any other nation to advice or exercise such a choice for Tibetans. I have no difficulty in telling the Chinese Government that the question of sovereignty or suzerainty has to be decided only according to the wishes of the Tibetan people and not according to any legality or on constitutional forms."[3]

Pandit Nehru on 27th April, 1959 after the Dalai Lama came into exile and, was granted asylum, said, "I have been assured by the Chinese Prime

Minister, Chou En-lai that they are sincerely willing to discuss the matter of Tibet on a wide scale. He had indicated to me that though historically Tibet has been a part of China at certain times he himself does not believe Tibet to be a Chinese province. Tibet is radically different China and Tibetans should have genuine autonomy. He further went to say that it will be senseless to imagine that China is going to impose communism on Tibet."[4]

When the Indian Government granted asylum, there were two differing opinions. While a majority supported that it is in tune with the age old traditions of India, and a refuge should be granted on the humanitarian ground, a minority opinion felt that it compromised national interest. It was bound to affect the relationship with China. This certainly happened. When the Dalai Lama set up Government in Exile. India played a double game. While it did not obstruct the formation, it did not give it a formal recognition. The dichotomy continues even today. Apart from considering the Dalai Lama as a State guest, protocols are that of a Head of a State. Chinese demands that Chief Ministers or the Ministers of Central Government should not attend public functions where the Dalai Lama is present are just ignored.

During a decade and a few years more after being exiled, Dalai Lama's focus was to work for the welfare and settlement of the Tibetan refugees. Here he was in footsteps of Mahatma Gandhi. Mahatma Gandhi had an uncanny sense of timing his movements. There were times during the independence struggle when agitations were absent. When asked what the freedom-fighters should do during this time, his response was that there is a tremendous lot of social work and reform to be done with the masses. When questioned whether this would have any impact on the struggle for the independence, he was categorically sure. Not only the social action provided the opportunities for mass contact but it also raised the level of social awareness and whatever good that came out of social and constructive work would make India more resilient in struggle for the independence.

Always conscious of his status as a Buddhist monk the Dalai Lama has considered it to be enjoined upon him to give religious teachings. Little would have himself known that these teachings were to provide him with a worldwide platform to espouse the Tibetan cause.

While the overall attitude of the Indian masses is that of apathy and ignorance about Tibet – we have problems enough of our own – and most Indians do not see Tibet as different from China, there are a selected few who are even annoyed by the Tibetan presence in India. First to experience the discomfort were the villagers of Dharmashala region. With the pouring in of Western tourists to Dharmashala, and envying the lifestyle of some of the "affluent", the living standard has gone up. The prices have soared. Scanty meat has become scantier since Tibetans are non-vegetarian. This has brought the local population in conflict with the exiled Tibetans. While the ordinary taxi-driver is aware that his livelihood is very much dependent on the influx of the tourists because of presence of the Dalai Lama, he is more worried about the market prices. They are often heard to remark non-chalantly that the Dalai Lama should go back to Tibet and fight his battle out over there.

This simmering hostility emerged into large scale violence. Some shops were burnt. There were slogans against the Dalai Lama. Deeply disturbed by these events in 2001, the Dalai Lama wrote to the Government of India that he will shift to New Delhi. This he said publicly too. It had an immediate cooling down of the tensions. The officials of the district administration saw the Dalai Lama to personally request him to reverse his decision. There afterwards, the Government of Himachal Pradesh also actively participates in cultural events of the exiled community.

Looking from the side lines, instances galore when Tibetan presence in India rakes up controversies. The Dalai Lama has been remarkably open to all kinds of suggestions and people from all walks of life. Openness invites creative inputs: it may also bring in trouble. And to weed out the wheat from the chaff may not be easy till the trouble arises. In August 2001, at Akhil Bharat Ratnatmak Samaj in Chennai, the Dalai Lama was approached by the Hurriyat leaders from Kashmir. They wanted an audience with him to discuss Kashmir issue and true to his inimitable style he invited them to Dharamshala for a dialogue. *Hindustan Times* published the news on the front page under the heading, "Dalai rakes up J and K again". The critics of the Government of India tried to draw mileage out of this.

The Government of India took up the issue immediately with the Dalai Lama. And he clarified his stand that he has been misquoted. "I have always accepted the fact that the state of Jammu and Kashmir is an integral part of India. I have never considered the issue of Tibet and Kashmir to be similar." He said that his main concern in the matter was that the bad feelings should end and the issue should be resolved through negotiations.

There is sharp criticism from a small scholarly minority too. China has also utilized lobbying with them. This was evident when N. Ram, Editor of *The Hindu* wrote a supplement full of 36 pages following his visit to China. The arguments of such scholars are based on pure materialist logic: they have no need to dabble in morals or virtues. They argue that the most outstanding irritant in India-China relationship today is the Dalai Lama and the Tibetan Government in exile. Ram advocates that India should expel the Central Tibetan Administration from Indian soil and this single step will be a leap forward for a grand alliance between India and China.

Chinese policy has been to invite such foreigners that would carry out the Chinese propaganda on their behalf because, "when they do so for us that is more powerful than if we do it." The long term aim is to uproot the Government in Exile at Dharmashala and, Tibetan Buddhism from the minds of Tibetans.

There is no doubt that the synergy between India and China has immense potential. When Nehru signed the Panchsheel Treaty, he was probably guided by such a grandiose vision. It may be said that he was ahead of his times and did not see the stark difference of China-India mindset and systems. Today, in a radically different world where the economy of communist China is also driven by free market forces, the equations have changed. Thomas Fredman, the author of *The World Is Flat: a brief history of 21st century,* writes:

"When I was growing up my parents used to say to me, 'Tom, finish your dinner – people in China are starving'. But I am now telling my daughters, 'girls finish your homework – people in China and India are striving for your jobs'." He goes on to further predict that in cooperation between India and China, there lies a tale of technology and geo-economics that is fundamentally reshaping our lives much more quickly that many people realized. Historically according to him this is the new era of globalization III. The first era started in Fifteenth century, the second began with the industrial revolution. The comparison itself is significant.

"The new equation is the omission of or between China and India. It is not even the addition of hyphenation between China-India. A new reality which is much more in terms of economics rather than politics has emerged. That is CHINDIA. If these two Asian giants were to leave aside their political differences the synergies in terms of economy, even Bill Gates feels a threat. He said, "When I compare our high school to what I see abroad I am terrified for our workforce for tomorrow. In 2001, India graduated almost a million more students than the US did. China graduates twice as many students with bachelor's degree as the US. And they have six times as many graduates in engineering. In the international competition to have the biggest and the best supply of knowledge workers, America is falling behind."

In 1991 when Li Peng visited India, before his arrival, hundreds of Tibetan youths were rounded up in New Delhi. The Dalai Lama had to appeal to TYC workers for peace. And the Government of India took the discourteous step of asking the Dalai Lama too, as if his very presence in New Delhi would pollute the air. In a short span of less than 15 years the drastic change in equations is evident by the fact that in 2005 the Chinese Premier, Jiabao, flew straight to Bangalore rather than New Delhi! President Clinton did the same.

The emergence of a possibility of synergy between the two most populous nations of the world is creating apprehension in the Western minds. That is why Lee Kuan Yew the Former Prime Minister of Singapore has predicted that CHINDIA will spread renaissance across Asia. They will shake the world.

Bottom line for Tibetans is that they are grateful to India for asylum. They know that solution to Tibet situation is not through Indian corridors.

REFERENCES

1. Personal letter to Rohit Mehta.
2. Sankarsaran, *Atal Bihari Vajpayee in Indian Parliament*, DIIR, Dharamshala, 2000.
3. Vijay Kranti, *Bharat Aur Tibet, Tibet Desh*, Special Issue, 2000, p. 92.
4. Vijay Kranti, *Bharat Aur Tibet*, Special Issue 2000, p. 92.

9
In Gandhi's Footsteps

Analogy studied with respect to Religiosity, Vegetarianism, Celibacy and Himalayan Blunder.

Indo-Tibetan situation gets further poignant when the Dalai Lama talks about Mahatma Gandhi. Amongst several mistakes that Tibetans made as he considers, not meeting Mahatma Gandhi is one of the biggest. Both of them are classic case studies about how to influence people and win friends. He has no hesitation to say that he is following Gandhi's footsteps. Let us have an overview of collaterals between the two.

The twentieth century witnessed the emergence of two charismatic personalities in South-East Asia. On the Indian scene Mahatma Gandhi overshadowed everyone else and through his innate masterminding skills, he virtually became the benevolent dictator of India. He held no office, was not even an ordinary member of Indian National Congress and yet his authority was supreme. This is ascribed to his thorough identification with the common men all across India. He spoke common man's language. He spoke it with humility, generally looking down and in simple short sentences devoid of any rhetoric. He wore the poor man's dress. His sandals[1] were also of the kind that a poor man can just afford. And so was his food. The anatomy of his dictatorial power was rooted in charisma and connection with his people. However, his own interpretation has been that he would not wish to impose his will on anyone; such an act will also amount to a form of violence. He only practiced what he thought as truth through non-violent means. Magical charisma of this poor man is a guiding light-post for the Dalai Lama as we shall see.

During the same period China saw the emergence of communist rule under the leadership of Mao tse-Tung. At that point in history, with the backdrop of imperialist exploitation, and monarchy that was only a form of anarchy, the lot of the common men in China was so hopeless that it provided the most fertile ground for communism to sprout. A common Chinese peasant would understand nothing about the high sounding communist ideology. However, the ideology meant dictatorship of the proletariat and a dictator was required as the leader to implement it. Chairman Mao provided such a leadership that his word was the first and the last word for the Chinese masses. Mao tse-Tung also did influence the Dalai Lama. He felt a charisma about him to the extent that Mao's hands appeared to be emitting a lot of warmth during handshakes[2]. The Dalai Lama is mystic about them; he says, such charismatic personalities do not just happen. This is just what Tibetans say about the Dalai Lama[3].

The canvass of the multi-faceted personality of Mahatma Gandhi was rolled out in widespread experiments with truth. The pursuit of truth for Gandhi was a matter of personal evolution. However, he utilized the results towards one aim and that was the goal of independence of India.

We shall just explore three of Gandhi's footprints that the Dalai Lama is following apart from truth and non-violence. The latter are reflected all through out the book. These footprints are personal but contribute overwhelming to their personality. They are: (1) Religiosity, (2) Vegetarianism, and (3) Celibacy.

A deeply religious man who died with the name of the God in his mouth at the penultimate moment before his death, Gandhi's religiosity was a matter of personal experience devoid of any rituals except prayer. He died just before he was going to evening prayers. Even this simple ritual he had utilized for the education of the congregation.

Before returning from Britain, Gandhi had a short interlude with theosophy. The theosophists are said to derive their wisdom, occult knowledge and secret power from Tibetan masters in Tibet. They incorporate a circle within, Esoteric Society, that is quite ritualistic. It is presided by masters who are said to be perennially alive.

Gandhi had no religious initiation of any formal kind when he first heard Annie Besant speak about how she became a theosophist. Her talk concluded when she said that she would be satisfied to have an epitaph written after her that she lived for truth and died for the same. Gandhi was left with an indelible print of this event when he recalled it three decades later as, "I had from my childhood an instinctive fascination with truth. The way she spoke those words have captivated me ever since."[4]

Gandhi's meeting with Annie Besant came through his British friends, Bertrand and Archibald Keightley. They were reading *Bhagvad Gita* with Gandhi. Gandhi felt ashamed as he had not read the divine poem either in Sanskrit or in Gujarati[5]. This was Gandhi's first initiation to Hindu scriptures. His readings of the theosophical literature were to further convince him about the fundamental validity of Hindu precepts. At the same time, he could wash off the brain-washing that he had through Christian missionaries about Hinduism being a religion of superstition.

However, Gandhi's flirtation with theosophy ended with its precepts of brotherhood and search of the truth. But Gandhi cultivated relationships on the theosophical basis in Africa. This earned him the friendship of many Europeans, the most notable among them being Herman Kallenvach and Henry Polak[6]. Even when Gandhi made his distaste of occultism clear to them, he tactfully utilized their friendship towards the Indian cause. In fact, theosophy provided a generative ground to harness English collaborators. The Europeans looked at Gandhi as an authority on Hinduism. This made Gandhi study Hinduism and Hindu culture more deeply.

How Gandhi and Annie Besant collaborated and then came to a conflict later on in India is of little relevance here since there is no such parallel Tibetan landscape. The relevance *vis-à-vis* the Dalai Lama is two-fold:

(1) The importance of religion and spirituality in their respective lives and how both of them have successfully amalgamated them in their temporal spheres.
(2) How both of them have found it instrumental to utilize the religion in the service of the national cause.

So, Gandhi had practically no understanding of Hinduism leave apart any initiation till he was in Britain. It was his inquiring mind and openness to the quest of perennial wisdom that prompted Gandhi to study Hinduism through *Bhagvad Gita* with British friends. However, he had no truck with occultism. Though he became a formal member of the Blavatsky Lodge in London, he let it slip on his return to India.

Though Gandhi thus abdicated from the occult practices and left theosophy, he had found his bearings in Hinduism when he went to Africa. Without subscribing to any dogma, his search for a religious identity led him to several religious persons most of whom were vegetarians too. These contacts led him to be an agent for the Esoteric Christian Union and he almost came to a formal affiliation with Christianity. Such rendezvous made Gandhi to believe firmly that the spiritual East will heal the material West. Apart from the maturity of his religious belief and flowering of his spirituality, Gandhi's uniqueness lies in his being able to translate these values in actual life.

Mahatma Gandhi was a statesman who never held any office in the State. However, his political activities can be described as statesmanship of spirituality. The collateral isomorphism is immense in this context. Regardless as to how both of them came to acquire authority/sovereignty, both have renounced/abdicated power of their own choice.

He had an uncanny sense of timing his movements. There were times during the independence struggle when agitations were absent. When asked what the freedom-fighters should do during this time, he said that there is a tremendous lot of social work and reform to be done with the masses. When questioned whether this would have any impact on the struggle for the independence, he was categorically sure. Not only the social action provided the opportunities for mass contact but it also raised the level of social awareness and whatever good that came out of social and constructive work would make India more resilient in struggle for the independence.

During a decade and a few years more after the escape in 1959, the Dalai Lama's focus was to work for the welfare and settlement of the Tibetan refugees. And always conscious of his status as a Buddhist monk he has considered it to be enjoined upon him to give religious teachings. Little would he himself have known that these teachings were to provide him with a worldwide platform to espouse the Tibetan cause.

Spiritual teachings took the Dalai Lama practically all across the globe (he tells us that he very much regrets not to have made much contact with Islamic world and would want to do so if there was an opportunity). There was a time when almost every Western leader shunned dialogue with the Dalai Lama. If they do not as much as care to meet him how was he to influence them?

The first spiritual teaching to make a large impact was in 1987, arranged by Robert Thurman in USA. He was granted a visa as a religious head. We have seen (Chapter 7) how this provided an opportunity to address US Congress and unfold his plan about Tibet as a zone of *ahimsa*. There afterwards, year after year, the Dalai Lama goes round the globe, talks about ethics, values and human quest for happiness. His recipe is very simple. Buddhism has no god and it refuses to be a dogma when he recalls the Buddha's saying, "accept only those of my teachings which appeal to your intelligence, do not believe in anything because it is said by Buddha."

Discussing the eternal values, he elaborates on the Buddhist principles of harmony with the environment. He asserts that no internal harmony in the heart is possible without seeking harmony with Mother Nature. His environmentalist appeal is strongly respected by the Western sensibilities, and when they know that the nuclear debris is dumped in Tibet, their hearts go for Tibet.

He talks about respecting each and every individual to the extent of respecting the enemy. This trail easily follows to universal human rights.

The rights were enshrined in the Charter of United Nations. Probably this did not have as much impact on the Western sensibilities as the Dalai Lama's plain and simple advocacy of human rights even for an enemy.

While proclaiming that the Dalai Lama does not want anything for himself, he argues that every citizen of the world has a duty towards Tibet. This is because the Tibetan culture has an invaluable treasure of spiritual traditions and techniques for the betterment of the mankind. To work towards the Tibetan cause is to contribute to the preservation of a precious heritage of mankind.

In the form of Tibetan refugees spread world over, the silent revolution is taking shape in all these monasteries where they teach Tibetan meditation and Vajrayana techniques. The Ministry of Religious Affairs at Dharmashala details such monasteries in the various regions of the world. The list is amazing. If any Government were to conduct so many embassies and consulates, we wonder what it would entail!

China claims that the success of the Dalai Lama's campaign comes from his wealthy and influential friends in the West. What problems Gandhi has perceived as of materialist West have further multiplied and more and more Westerners seek answers to their existential questions through esoteric Buddhism. Little would the Dalai Lama have thought that his Buddhist teachings would provide him such a spring board for the advocacy of the Tibetan cause. After two decades of groping with the difficulties of hundred thousand refugees, an opening came to him through an invitation to address an American University on Buddhism. And in all the 29 subsequent visits to USA, he has ardently utilized his religious status to serve Tibet politically too. This has made him earn the title of "A Wolf in The Monk's Robe" from the Chinese.

But the Dalai Lama is born in religiosity. He would not accept that he has utilized religion in the service of diplomacy. Once we suggested that he should pay tribute to Mahatma Gandhi on 2nd October every year since that will attract media coverage. He scolded us that selfish interest does not justify motivation for even correct actions; a correct action is one that is right. But thereafter, whenever he is in New Delhi on 2nd October, he pays a visit to Mahatma Gandhi's *Samadhi*.

His very existence is based on the dogma in Tibetan Buddhism. From the day of his identification as the reincarnation of 13th Dalai Lama, his entire tutelage lies in training as a Buddhist Lama. The principle precept of Mahayana Tibetan Buddhism is compassion for all the sentient beings and its practice is engineered through the empowerment by *Vajrayana*. *Vajrayana* is study and practice of the occult. Even though, classically it is ordained that its study and knowledge were only to be imparted through initiation, the Dalai Lama has demystified *Vajrayana.* He has published the full text of various initiations including the most secret *kalachakra*[7].

Now, it is elementary to appreciate the deep rooted belief of the Dalai Lama in Tibetan *tantra.* Even in the midst of the eye of the storm as in March 2005, the Dalai Lama spent more than three weeks in religious teachings and initiation of various kinds. Maybe this is towards a spiritual empowerment that makes him cope with the enormous stress. Maybe this is a mature/immature defence of the self that helps him not to crack against the severe criticism from his own people. However, his Achilles Heel became visible through the eruption of the Shukden Affair.

During his visit to UK in 1995, he was faced with the demonstrations by the followers of Dorje Shukden. We were astonished. Our calls to the Tibet Office as well as to the Office of the Bodhi Society in London, who had organized his UK visit, did not yield any satisfactory explanation. The Chinese had an opportunity to show how obscurantist the Dalai Lama and Tibetans can be.

The belief is explained by Samdong Rinpoche and the Dalai Lama himself. The institution of the Dalai Lama rests on an elaborate ritual. The 5th Dalai Lama, in Seventeenth century, tried to unify various sects and traditions. The monasteries of the Ge-lug tradition and Nying-ma tradition had conflicted ever since.

Dorje Shukden was a high lama of Ge-lug tradition during the times of 5th Dalai Lama. He opposed the efforts of the 5th Dalai Lama to unify diverse traditions. According to the Buddhist tradition, his spirit, even after his death, has been opposing such a move. The 14th Dalai Lama has taken recourse and inspiration from the 5th Dalai Lama; and now that Tibet is united under one leader, Shukden, therefore, is opposed to 14th Dalai Lama and, through the worship of his followers, is trying to cause harm. The story smacks of utter superstition in the eyes of most modern scientific men.

The belief is fundamental to human existence. Such phenomena are observed and there is much scienticism about them today. It is irrelevant to discuss science of belief systems here. But thc matter is obviously based on belief system. The Dalai Lama explains that what is not understood by science today may, some day, be proved true according to the advanced understanding by science[8]. Be that as it may, the Dalai Lama seriously believes that Shukden worshippers can do him physical harm through their worship. Since this appears to be witchcraft, the Chinese have made full use of it to malign the Dalai Lama as superstitious and gullible before the Western audiences.

While Mahatma Gandhi had practically nothing to do with occultism/mysticism he did believe about the voice of wise man within. Several of his decisions were based on pure hunch. He had no truck with obscurantism though. However following four deaths in a short period of time in 1942, he did waver a bit. As narrated to us by Narayan Desai (son of Mahadev Desai, personal secretary to Mahatma), this is reflected in the following two incidents:

Following the death of Mahadev Desai, he gave the last bath himself. He wiped the dead body with a clean towel. Thereafter he took bath himself and wiped his body with the same towel. When dry, he neatly folded the towel and entrusted it to Sushila Nair, who was the youngest amongst the detainees with the instruction that she should pass it on to Narayan Desai.

He gave the pot containing the ashes of Mahadev Desai to Sushila Nair too. This was to be passed on to Durga Ben, Mahadev Desai's wife. Immersion of the ashes in holy waters is ritualistic in Hindu tradition.

While Gandhi's utilization of the religion had numerous facets that finally ended with the partition of India on the basis of religion, the Dalai Lama's sojourn to the internationalization of the Tibet issue has been a success story through the corridor of religious teachings. During sixties and early seventies the situation appeared very dark since no country was willing to take any cognizance of the Dalai Lama or the issue of Tibet. However, hundred thousand refugees in 1959 and, subsequent ever flowing stream of them ever since, has resulted in Tibetan diasporas being dispersed world over. As such, Buddhism is a worldwide religion and it is emerging as the religion of Twenty-first century. And, all Buddhists recognize the Dalai Lama as a high spiritual master.

The tenor of the political campaign in the West has also changed during last three decades. The popular concern has focalized on moral issues like the rights of nationalities, human rights, environment and nuclear issues. The Tibetans could mobilize the Western popular support on these issues and, simultaneously could highlight the damage to their 2000 year old civilization. The evidence was not lacking.

The temporal and spiritual aspects are generally seen as contradictory. Such artificial generalization has brought about misconceptions and dichotomy in everyday dealings. People hide their God and spirituality in some unknown corner of their life. They believe that these aspects have nothing to do with what they do in performance of their worldly actions. Essentially, the spirituality should percolate in action through the body, mind and soul. Then it will exude through each and every temporal action of a cultured individual. The particular situation of the Dalai Lama as the temporal leader and the spiritual master of the Tibetan people, in such difficult times when the Tibetan people have been subjected to genocide and their civilization has been trampled upon, provide a good example for evaluation of the above premise. Elaboration on these concepts will carry us to obvious proximity of the Mahatma and the Dalai Lama.

An intellectual wonders at the exploration of marvelous vistas through philosophic pursuit. Such exposition of the concepts and ideas provides him with parameters that he calls values. These values then provide a meaning to his life. The values evolve into the guiding principles by which he navigates through the stormy seas of life. Endeavour of many such giant intellectuals and spiritual masters generates a protocol for the society. Adoption of the protocol, either with the understanding and acceptance of the meanings attached, or, may be in a ritualistic method, gives rise to the culture of that society. When the culture gets ingrained and enriched by further inputs of values and meaning over a long period, there comes about a civilization. This is the ultimate culmination of search for values. It also is the beautification of researched and rehearsed values that may span even millennia.

The values then percolate through the lives of common men so that they are enriched by aesthetic sense, joy and, even, fulfilment. In the least sense, these values provide a blue print in navigation through conflicts in relations and, to a great extent, even for cultural collisions[9]. Buddha, Mahavir and Mahatma Gandhi have not only preached non-violence, they have provided exemplary protocol for its practice. The ideals of Mahavir and Buddha have culminated into practice of religions that are about 2500 years old. The fruition of the non-violent efforts by Mahatma Gandhi, Martin Luther King and such others in the last century provided impetus to the non-violent action, but Twenty-first century has yet to bring out any such shining example. Would the toils of the Dalai Lama bear such a fruit? Or, shall he have to remain content with right means being the correct end?

In the world given to war in the present times — there has always been war in some part of the world. Mahatma Gandhi's practice of non-violent action is put to severe test. Most of the influential countries seem to act only by what is the guiding principle in the foreign policy, the so called enlightened self-interest. However, the self-interest is seen as the commercial advantage and strategic reward; there is hardly any place for the lofty ideals like just and moral action. The entire process and practice of violent action is so masterly crafted through the precise steps of deductive logic and, unveil such meticulous data that it justifies nuclear bombs! The world goes on functioning on validity of such assumptions, in spite of all the probabilities of them being wrong!

On the other hand, common man looks towards philosophy with a sense of derision. Accustomed as he is, to be happy to move along a grooved path, he considers it futile to speculate about the probabilities concerning the ultimate reality or the final truth. No wonder, Radhakrishnan was once asked, whether philosophers are not the real ailment that world suffered from! His answer[10] was: not the philosophy but non-practice of the philosophy in everyday life is the root cause of various maladies that have afflicted the world civilization.

This leads us to simple surmise that the precepts are worthless without practice. It is daily living through the precepts generated out of philosophical postulation that is meaningful. Life derives its meaning out of its outward expression; living through the precepts that have been thoroughly imbibed into the entire being becomes a beautiful flowering. Such a life comes to be an experiment with the truth.

Mahatma Gandhi is not considered to be a philosopher in the academic circles. He had difficulty in understanding the Classical Indian thought and had to ask Vinoba Bhave to explain him the finer nuances of *Gita*. But he made his life an open book, where he tried to practice time honoured values of. Philosophy to him became a real yardstick to measure any action: all actions were just if they measured up to the value-system of his religious philosophical tradition, irrespective of apparent gain or loss. Alternately, any action in contradiction to the values was futile, even if that was seen as immediately beneficial. Thus, the means became the ends for him. He could do so, because he not only pondered over the philosophical precepts through the dialectical dissection of a barrister, but also internalized the values as the very essence of his being. Philosopher he may not be called, but he culminated into a spiritual giant. And the propensity of his action was such that not only it shook up the Empire; it elevated the consciousness of the entire mass of people and is doing so even now at the worldwide scale.

The Dalai Lama draws parallel with Mahatma Gandhi here. He was ordained as a lama at the age of three and has imbibed the Buddhist doctrine since then. Little would he have known the vagaries of the wicked world, nor could it be expected that the adolescent lama as a sovereign or, the helpless fugitive that he was in 1959, would have the wisdom and vision to guide his own conduct or that of his people. We asked the Dalai Lama that a diplomat is one who *lies* abroad for the sake of his country. How could the Dalai Lama conduct his foreign affairs without taking recourse to lies? The Dalai Lama said that he does not see any need to lie. Moreover, lies are unlikely to carry weight for long in modern interconnected world.

Buddhist tradition is unique in combining the merits of dialectical wisdom as well as intuitive insight. The Dalai Lama's day begins early in the morning at 3.30 a.m. — (so it did for the Mahatma too) — when he starts his prostrations to Buddha. Then he meditates on the *kalachakra.* In *kalachakra* meditation there is centring over the empowering qualities of 928 deities. This experiential happening may be described in the Dalai Lama's own words as, "those qualities of human spirit such as love and compassion, patience, tolerance, forgiveness, contentment, a sense of responsibility, a sense of harmony — which brings happiness to both self and others."

This intuitive revelation would find validation through the Buddhist doctrine of dependent origination. With dialectical discussion the *karmic connection,* or the principle of causality and change, mutual dependence between a part and the whole, interconnectedness and impermanence would lead us to the pathways as mentioned above. Such dealing would automatically accept that one should re-orient from pre-occupation with only "self-interest" and recognize the right of the others to happiness as much as our own. In fact such preoccupation with "self-interest" is seen as selfishness that is doing harm to self.

Buddha had proclaimed that nobody should accept any saying of Buddha as truth simply because Buddha had said so. The entire gamut of the Buddhist thought, therefore, rests on the rationalism and dialectical training has important role in Buddhist learning. The Dalai Lama puts great emphasis on keeping the perception clear. As a consequence, he is free from various faulty projections or neurotic defences.

Tibet has suffered from the Communist regime that is anti-religion. Buddhists consider religion as the basic appetite of the soul. Mao told the Dalai Lama to be wary of religion; it is the opium of the masses! And we can carry on the list of contradictions between communist ideology and Buddhist philosophy in the field of fundamental human rights, ideas about nationalities, and, above all the methodology of putting ideology into practice: one might therefore expect the Dalai Lama to condemn communism outright. But his objectivity is clear. He sees that the communist ideology has its origin in essential humanism. And he is candid to admit that religion has done immense harm, especially to Tibet.

The future of Tibet, as of now, appears uncertain. The chances for independence are bleak. The hope generated by the events in Europe in eighties and Russia in nineties has faded. The Tienanmen Square events have not culminated in any democratic upsurge. And the astrological predictions of a significant change by the year 1995, 1997 and 2000 have also proved to be one of the many fallacies. This could bring about a sense of nervous breakdown: even Mahatma Gandhi suffered from it on the eve of partition of India.

However, religiosity of the Dalai Lama compensates him through the principle of karmic connection. Irrespective of no actual gains for Tibet, he has stood firm by non-violent way. However, a theory is judged by the results that it yields. Inspired by the Gandhi Way[11], Aldous Huxley advocated a non-violent defence force in the last century through his philosophical masterpiece, *The Ends and Means*. He exulted in the nobility of non-violent means and was sure that the practice of such a doctrine will invite the sympathy of the rest of the humanity to bring about a just end. Alas, sympathy of the rest of the humanity is with Tibet now, but no just happening is in sight!

Can it be said so finally? After 1959, the world thought of Tibet as a lost case. Through sheer perseverance and determination along the Buddhist philosophy, the Dalai Lama has brought the cause of Tibet to the attention of the entire world. When there is enough reason for righteous indignation, he has been humble, has avoided bitterness and has shown willingness to negotiate. There is no room for alternative of retaliation. On the contrary, he had called off an armed rebellion by the Khampas. There is voluminous evidence to prove a distinct nationality for Tibet, which is denied by the Chinese altogether. Even then, going by the doctrine of *Madhyampratipada*, the Dalai Lama has conceded that Tibet may remain a part of China, as an autonomous state. Mahatma Gandhi was offered such a choice through Cripps Commission; had he compromised, maybe India would not have been partitioned.

The Dalai Lama himself is not so difficult to approach. His charismatic personality has drawn numerous people to him. Conducting himself with a sense of universal responsibility while advocating the Tibetan cause, he has made himself a leader of the mankind. No wonder that the Nobel Peace Prize has been conferred on him. Sometimes, an award distinguishes the person. When the first Mahavir-Mahatma award was conferred on the Dalai Lama in 2004, the award itself got elevated to an alternative Peace Prize.

The empirical data about his statesmanship spanning over half a century can be voluminous. But his motivations and actions arising out of a spring bed of Buddhist thought can just be illustrated by his wish for the coming birth that he may take. He says it is for the Tibetans to decide whether they would want to have a 15th Dalai Lama or not; He being an incarnation of the Lord Avalokiteswara, would not seek *nirvana*, but shall be reborn to help all sentient beings.

But vegetarianism is a mixed bag for the Dalai Lama as compared to Gandhi. Vegetarianism was natural to Mahatma Gandhi. By birth he was born in a religious Hindu family. His mother was a Vaishnavite. His first encounter with non-vegetarian food is interesting since that was the last. During his school days, some of his peers could convince him that a strong body is necessary to fight the foreigners. They argued that erstwhile rulers of India, Muslims and British, were able to rule India because they were mightier due to non-vegetarian food. Thus persuaded, Gandhi went with them to a non-vegetarian joint and ate goats' meat.[12]

Gandhi could not sleep at night. He felt that the goat was crying in his abdomen and wanted to come out. Thus unable to bear the anguish, Gandhi remained vegetarian for the rest of his life. This was to earn him many friends and followers in his struggle for Indian independence.

Here the Dalai Lama is a parallel only at the end. To begin with, he was borne in a non-vegetarian peasant family. After being initiated as a Lama he learnt the virtue of compassion for all sentient beings. While overlooking the windows of the Potala palace, when the young boy Dalai Lama would see the herds of the cattle being driven to slaughter house, he would pay for the cattle and get them released[13]. The net result was only an increase in the price of meat. He himself continued to be a non-vegetarian!

Late in his life, in exile in India, the contradiction became clear to him. He became a vegetarian by choice. However, this was not easy and when he had an attack of jaundice in early eighties, his Tibetan doctors reverted him back to non-vegetarian food. But he changed once again. This dichotomy is characteristic of the Dalai Lama's mindset. Change is the very crux of human life. And the Dalai Lama once again changed when he realized that continued good health following an attack of jaundice has nothing to do with non-vegetarian diet. Perhaps, it has much more relevance to compassion and he is vegetarian for good. So that during *kalachakra* initiation at Amravati in January 2006, the entire city went vegetarian!

Vegetarianism, as it is rooted in compassion, is fundamental to Buddhism. The Dalai Lama gets invited to large gatherings on this ground. To what extent these collaborations help the Tibetan cause is uncertain. When questioned, the Dalai Lama argues that his actions are based on pure motivation. What is good and worthwhile should be pursued because it is good and worthwhile to pursue it and not because it is likely to yield a particular political mileage. Thus it becomes a matter of means, regardless of their service to the ends.

Let us now review celibacy. The Dalai Lama is born to be celibate. As a value that has been a constant pursuit of Mahatma Gandhi. Mahatma Gandhi was married early and produced a large family. Eric Erickson[14], a Freudian psycho-analyst attributed Gandhi's obsession with truth to the guilt feeling that he embedded in his subconscious mind. Gandhi has confessed in his autobiography that at the time of his father's death, he was having sex. Gandhi admits a great sense of shame and guilt.

Psycho-analytic truths are so relative that it is impossible to prove them false. Life is so chaotic and random that it is most unlikely that a single event will dominate the gigantic lifespan of a magnetic personality like Mahatma Gandhi. Be that it may be, a fact remains that sex was one of Gandhi's personal obsession for lifetime. He considered celibacy as a value. He took the vows of *brahmacharya* twice, once before sailing to England and later at the early age of 37. He said that the manner in which celibacy came to him irresistibly, he saw every woman as the mother. She became too sacred for sexual love.

He had, however, his distractions. His grandson, Raj Mohan Gandhi[15], researching on this topic scooped out a story that he had an affair with Sarla Devi, the niece of Ravindranath Tagore. However, Gandhi was quick to put a stop. In his own words, "If I was sexually attracted towards a woman, I have courage enough to become a polygamist. I do not believe in free love – secret or open. Secret love besides, is cowardly."

However, the experiments with celibacy did become a matter of public controversy in the last phase of Mahatma[16]. Gandhiji replied to this question by a series of articles in his mouthpiece, *Harijan*. On June 8, 1947, he explained, "*How did I begin it?*" In the following week he was to explain his way of avoiding sexual arousal under the title, *"Walls of Protection"*. This he connected to God and God realization in subsequent weeks. However, *A Perplexity Remained* (*Harijan*, July 6, 1947) till the last. Mahatma Gandhi wanted to lie down naked in bed at night with a naked young woman to experiment as to whether he has succeeded in rooting out total desire. Of course, everyone shuddered and no woman dared. His followers suppressed the design of the experiment till such time that he was a martyr.

For the Dalai Lama the story is altogether different. Repeatedly he has maintained that celibacy is very much an internal environment for a lama. He admitted to us that he had some kind of sexual thoughts during adolescence. But according to him the Buddhist tradition has well laid out pathways to celibate life and there are standard meditations to sublimate sexual energy. The mere thought, "I am a lama", is enough to evaporate sexual feelings. However, he has been repeatedly teased on the topic. In 2004, at an interview with the *Readers Digest*, he was asked what he has missed so far in his life. He may have wanted to sound comical in his inimical style, when he grotesquely pointed his fingers to his loin! But to the journalist this was not funny at all and he blew it up not only in the interview but also in the promotional advertisements by the magazine! Within a few months, *Newsweek* interview also focused on the issue of the Dalai Lama having ideas/dreams regarding sexuality. The Dalai Lama in his childlike innocence had only said that such ideas may arise but the Buddhist practices are an effective way of ridding them. We had asked him whether any woman had fallen in love with him as he is the most eligible bachelor. We had a long laugh when he pointed to his shaven head and Buddhist's robes, and asked, "Me and an eligible bachelor?"

Thus, the Dalai Lama has drawn many friends and collaborators in the Tibetan cause through his religiosity, and such other spiritual traits, just as Gandhi did. But their action plans differ. Mahatma Gandhi was a man of masses. He utilized one non-violent mighty weapon in the form of *padyatra*. It appears that he had derived this method from Jain Saints in *Kathiawad*. Mahatma Gandhi had publicly acknowledged indebtedness to a Jain saint Rajchandraji. Whatever the religious basis of tradition may be, it had its own merits of mass-contacts at grassroots levels. At dusk, the Jain saints will stop and spend the night at any of the villages. The villagers will assemble to pay their respects to the saints. This provided ample opportunity for story-telling and spreading the message of the religion.

Historically, Mahatma Gandhi was the first one to have utilized this method to generate awareness through mass-contact, resulting in mass-support of unforeseen strength. When he floated the idea the Indians were skeptical and the British were full of ridicule. The method was strange and the cause to which it was applied appeared to be too simple. Almost everyone wondered as to what can come out of such an effort by a select group of about 75, strolling across the unpaved dusty roads for a small amount of tax on manufacturing cheap of the cheapest commodity like salt. What came out is a matter of history. At the end of the day Gandhi would hold roadside meetings with the small group of villagers, evening after evening for 42 days. These meetings were nationally reported and it became a movement. As it gathered further momentum, he had the entire collective consciousness of the Indian people focused upon him. This was the culmination of realization by the British of the might of non-violent means.

The movement snowballed into various parts of India and more than hundred thousand people courted the arrest in the cause of a mere grain of salt. We shall only mention just one instance of the demonstration of non-violent might. At a salt factory in Valsad, Gujarat, there is a small village named Dharasana. Gandhi's followers decided to picket the factory and not let it function. The agitation had Gandhi's blessings and it was plain that there will be no violent demonstration. The picketers marched into groups of four up to the gates of the salt factory where baton wielding soldiers waited to beat them up. Not one of them raised an arm either in protest or in defence! The women volunteers were standing by to carry off the fallen comrades. One of the freedom-fighters died. This elevated the moral heights of the entire nation while the British were put to shame before the international community through coverage by the Western media.

Of course, after this historic march there are numerous examples of similar kind in modern history. In China Mao tse-Tung led the mammoth march of the Peoples' Liberation Army to force Chiang Kai-shek away to Formosa. In United States, Martin Luther King led the mammoth rallies to arouse blacks.

Samdong Rinpoche, Ex-Kalon Tripa had thought of such a march that may extend all the way to Tibet. It would have invited immense displeasure of the Government of India. It is argued by the policy-makers in New Delhi that the route to the freedom of Tibet does not pass through Indian corridor.

The Dalai Lama has constantly thanked the Government of India for granting him asylum as well as the unique status of a guest who has stayed over for the longest duration of time. He would not want to embarrass. However, now it is a matter of survival. If the Government of India is displeased, he may simply to ask to pardon him since the time is short. The utmost that the Government of India can do in the matter would be to prevent such a march. There cannot be any question of putting any one to prison since India is a free democratic country and the fundamental human rights are enjoyed by the refugees too. If the Government of India on this account asks the government in Exile to move elsewhere, it shall be at their own discomfiture. The predicament will turn out favourable to Tibet.

We talked to Samdong Rinpoche about the issue. We tried to impress upon him that such consideration is unwarranted when the Tibetans are fighting a battle for their independence. We had offered that in case of such a march we shall be happy volunteers to join. And the Indians will far outnumber the Tibetans. At a mini-march in New Delhi in December 2004, by Tibetan protestors, the Former Defence Minister of India, Mr. George Fernandes walked side-by-side. At a small march in the year 2002 we feel ourselves privileged to have led such a march of Tibetan youths through the main roads of our city and, the Tibetans had the support of two tiny Indian girls/two tiny Indian boys, of 7 and 4 years old, our granddaughters and grandsons, who held the Tibetan flag with full understanding as to what does independence mean.

Such a move may be considered reckless by the prudes as was thought about Gandhi. In the Indian ethos most sacred thing is to have a feminine form. A struggle for independence, a movement, a revolution or idealism or any such kind of activism, is the worship of a divine deity in the form of a Devi. The nation is motherland. The Chinese also call the Chinese nation so. The worship of the mother deity is certainly with the flowers and perfumes of idealism and truth. But the deity is not appeased by mere aesthetics. She demands sacrifice. Entering Tibet unconditionally would be a return to the Mother's lap. A lot of sufferings and tremendous hardships may ensue. More often than not, in freedom struggle, the sacrifice has been written in red bold letters of blood of the very best youth. In 1985, the Chinese had prepared 500 Tibetan officers to welcome the Dalai Lama, should that event were to come about. Now, at the worst, they will put him to some kind of confinement as the Burmese have done to Aung San Sua Kyi. Would a confinement in the motherland not be better now than hankering for the Mother's lap in Exile?

On the demise of the Mahatma Gandhi, Albert Einstein paid an unusual tribute to say that the generations to come may not believe that there walked a man like Gandhi on this very earth. More than half a century later at this point of time, Einstein seems to be vindicated, because of overwhelming consumerism where, most individuals are preoccupied in the service of their ego. But if this were to be a general trend, there are shining illustrations to the contrary. People respect, regard, appreciate, pay tribute and join hands with good and truth even when, it amounts to sacrificing their personal interests. Maybe the majority of the human kind does get propelled by the herd instinct. But a creative minority — just about 2 per cent—, refuse to confirm to the narrow confines of self-centred interests and go out of their way to step into the whirlpool of strife and struggle in service of altruism. Tibetan youths shall not be found wanting of the virtue of sacrifice. And they can trust history that they will find fellow travellers, as Mahatma Gandhi did, from nowhere!

On April 6, 1930, after having marched 241 miles on foot from Ahmedabad to the sea, Salt satyagraha was immensely successful in peaceful way, in spite of British brutality at Dharasana. When police post was set on fire and a few police men were burnt alive Gandhi called off the entire Satyagraha and apologized for his "Himalayan Blunder"; he had mistakenly believed that his followers truly understood non-violence. Since then, the phrase 'Himalayan Blunder' has gained currency in India. When the Dalai Lama has given concessions to the Chinese, it was felt that there is no middle way if the other party does not move half way. It may lead to capitulation.

While there is no collateral about the agitation or putting reins on TYC etc. it is a possibility that the middle way may prove to be a Himalayan Blunder for Tibet[17].

The future of Tibet, as of now, appears dark. The chances for independence are bleak. The hope generated by the events in Europe in eighties and Russia in nineties has faded. The Tienanmen Square events have not culminated in any democratic upsurge. And the astrological predictions of a significant change by the year 1995, 1997 and 2000 have also proved to be one of the many fallacies. This could bring about a sense of nervous breakdown; even Mahatma Gandhi suffered from it on the eve of partition of India.

However, religiosity of the Dalai Lama compensates him through the principle of *karmic connection*. Irrespective of no actual gains for Tibet, he has stood firm by non-violent way. However, a theory is judged by the results that it yields. Inspired by the Gandhian Way, Aldous Huxley advocated a non-violent defence force in the last century through his philosophical masterpiece, *The Ends and Means.* He exulted in the nobility of non-violent means and was sure that the practice of such a doctrine will invite the sympathy of the rest of the humanity to bring about a just end. Alas, sympathy of the rest of the humanity is with Tibet now, but no just happening is in sight!

Can it be said so finally? After 1959, the world thought of Tibet as a lost case. Through sheer perseverance and determination along the Buddhist philosophy, the Dalai Lama has brought the cause of Tibet to the attention of the entire world. When there is enough reason for righteous indignation, he has been humble, has avoided bitterness and has shown willingness to negotiate. There is no room for alternative of retaliation. On the contrary, he had called off an armed rebellion by the Khampas. There is voluminous evidence to prove a distinct nationality for Tibet, which is denied by the Chinese altogether.

Conducting himself with a sense of universal responsibility while advocating the Tibetan cause, he has made himself a leader of the mankind. No wonder that the Nobel Peace Prize has been conferred on him. Some times, an award distinguishes the person. When the first Mahavir-Mahatma award was conferred on the Dalai Lama in 2004, the award itself got elevated to an alternative Peace Prize.

The Dalai Lama's sojourn to the internationalization of the Tibet issue has been a success story through the corridor of religious teachings. During sixties and early seventies the situation appeared very dark since no country was willing to take any cognizance of the Dalai Lama or the issue of Tibet. However, hundred thousand refugees in 1959 and, subsequent ever flowing stream of them ever since, has resulted in Tibetan diaspora being dispersed world over. As such, Buddhism is a worldwide religion and it is emerging as the religion of Twenty-first century.

The tenor of the political campaign in the West has also changed during last three decades. The popular concern has focalized on moral issues like the rights of nationalities, human rights, environment and nuclear issues. The Tibetans could mobilize the Western popular support on these issues and, simultaneously could highlight the damage to their 2000 years old civilization. The evidence was not lacking.

The temporal and spiritual aspects are generally seen as contradictory. Such artificial generalization has brought about misconceptions and dichotomy in everyday dealings. People hide their God and spirituality in some unknown corner of their life. They believe that these aspects have nothing to do with what they do in performance of their worldly actions. Essentially, the spirituality should percolate in action through the body, mind and soul. Then it will exude through each and every temporal action, as is the case with the Dalai Lama.

The particular situation of the Dalai Lama as the temporal leader and the spiritual master of the Tibetan people, in such difficult times when the Tibetan people have been subjected to genocide and their civilization has been trampled upon, provide a good example for evaluation of the above premise. Elaboration on these concepts will carry us to obvious proximity of the Mahatma Gandhi and the Dalai Lama.

An intellectual wonders at the exploration of marvelous vistas through philosophic pursuit. Such exposition of the concepts and ideas provides him with parameters that he calls values. These values then provide a meaning to his life. The values evolve into the guiding principles by which he navigates through the stormy seas of life. Endeavour of many such giant intellectuals and spiritual masters generates a protocol for the society. Adoption of the protocol, either with the understanding and acceptance of the meanings attached, or, may be in a ritualistic method, gives rise to the culture of that society. When the culture gets ingrained and enriched by further inputs of values and meaning over a long period, there comes about a civilization. This is the ultimate culmination of search for values. It is also the beautification of researched and rehearsed values that may span even millennia. The Dalai Lama has provided a shining example. Let us hope George Bush is there to see!

The values then percolate through the lives of common men so that they are enriched by aesthetic sense, joy and, even, fulfilment. In the least sense, these values provide a blue print in navigation through conflicts in relations and, to a great extent, even for cultural collisions. Buddha, Mahavir and Mahatma Gandhi have not only preached non-violence, they have provided exemplary protocol for its practice. The ideals of Mahavir and Buddha have culminated into practice of religions that are about 2500 years old. The fruition of the non-violent efforts by Mahatma Gandhi, Martin Luther King and such others in the last century provided impetus to the non-violent action, but twenty-first century has yet to bring out any such shining example. Would the toils of the Dalai Lama bear such a fruit? Or, shall he have to remain content with right means being the correct end?

Going by the doctrine of *Madhyampratipada,* the Dalai Lama has conceded that Tibet may remain a part of China, as an autonomous state. Mahatma Gandhi was offered such a choice through Cripps Commission: had he compromised, maybe India would not have been partitioned. However, the middle way appraoch of the Dalai Lama seems to be a choice out of compulsion and may indeed be a step to follow Mahatma Gandhi in parody: it may prove to be the Himalayan Blunder! The Chinese has not moved an inch. The Middle Way then, in reality, is only like Xeno's paradox, whereby the Tibetans may walk right upto the jaws of the Dragon!

If not that, now in 2012, it has at least ended in an impasse!

REFERENCES

1. The Dalai Lama emulates Mahatma even here; he wore the Hawaian sandals, a poor man's foot wear, when he met Bill Clinton.
2. The Dalai Lama, *The Freedom in Exile*, London, 1992.
3. The present Dalai Lama is Fourteenth in a lineage that began with Lord Avalokiteshwara, Buddha of compassion. His wisdom is supposed to transmigrate to the Dalai Lamas as he is reincarnated.
4. Patil, V.T., *Studies on Gandhi*, Bangalore, 1985.
5. M.K.Gandhi, *My Experiments with Truth*, Ahmedabad, p. 57.
6. *The Collected Works of Mahatma Gandhi*, Vol. 11, Delhi, 1958, p. 65.
7. However, the reading does not empower. Initiation is a must.
8. The Dalai Lama, *Freedom in Exile, The Autobiography of The Dalai Lama of Tibet*, London, 1990, p. 237.
9. Bhaskar Vyas and Rajni Vyas, *The Collision of Cultures*, New Delhi, 2000.
10. S. Radhakrishan, *An Idealist View of Life*, London, 1949.
11. Bhaskar Vyas, *The Gandhi Way*, Glasgow, 1996.
12. M.K. Gandhi. *The Experiments with Truth*, Ahmedabad, 2002.
13. The Dalai Lama, *Freedom in Exile*, London, 1992.
14. Eric Erickson, *Gandhi's Truth*, New York, 1991.
15. Raj Mohan Gandhi, *Gandhi, the Boat Man*, New Delhi, 1990.
16. Pyarelal, *The Last Phase*, Ahmedabad, 1951.
17. *The Times of India*, 10th March, 2006.

The Dalai Lama (in centre). Escape to India, 1959

The Dalai Lama at Gandhi Centenary Celebrations with Khan Abul Gafar Khan, V. V. Giri, Indira Gandhi and others, 2 October 1969

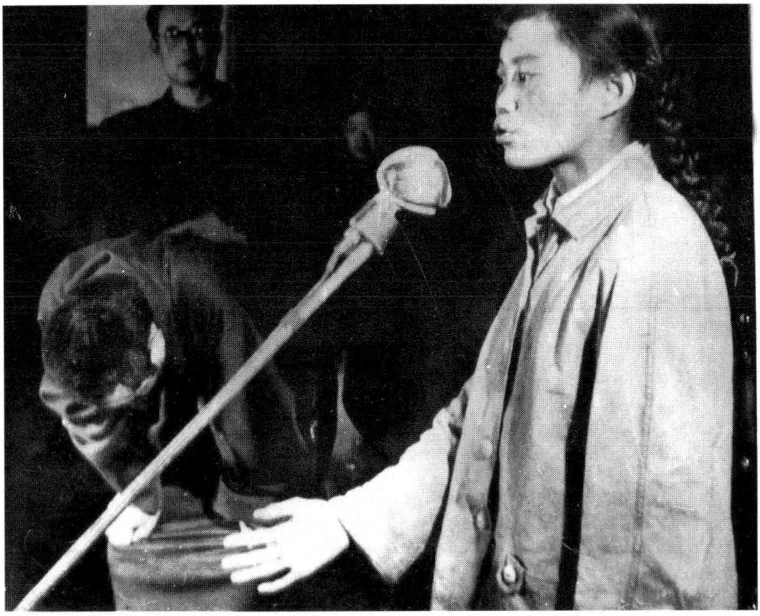

Panchen Rimpoche Undergoing Struggle Sessions

Tibet Delegates Visit Lhasa, 1979

The Dalai Lama at US Congress, 1987

The Dalai Lama being received by King Olav V of Norway after the award of Nobel Peace Prize

Demonstration in Lhasa, 1988

The Dalai Lama with George W. Bush Sr.

The Dalai Lama with John Major and Archbishop of Canterbury

The Dalai Lama is welcomed by Aruna Mehta, President, Medical Care Center Trust. Bhaskar Vyas is on the right. Driven by compassion, the Dalai Lama came in hot summer, 4th May 1989 to Baroda. He had heat stroke.

Protest 1989

The Dalai Lama with Taiwanese Monks

The Dalai Lama at Strassburg at European Parliament, 1996

Bhaskar Vyas with his grand children at March by
Tibetan Youth Congress in Baroda

The Dalai Lama with A.B. Vajpayee, Prime Minister of India

Tenzin Tsundue Protesting from the Balcony of Indian Institute of Science, Bangalore, 2005 against Wen Jiabao

The Dalai Lama with President George Bush

Regional Tibetan Youth Congress Volunteers on a Protest March on Human Rights Day in Baroda

The Dalai Lama with the author, Rajni Vyas

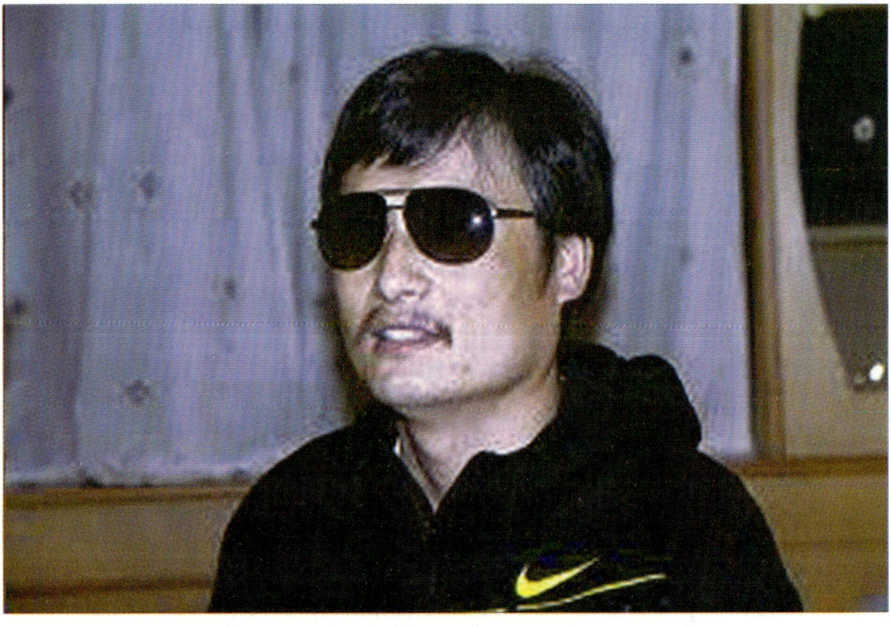

Blind Chinese Dissident: Chen Guangchen

The Dalai Lama with President Obama

Leader Tiananmen square era: Died in asylum in USA

Lobsang Sangáy being blessed by the Dalai Lama on assuming office as Kalon Tripa

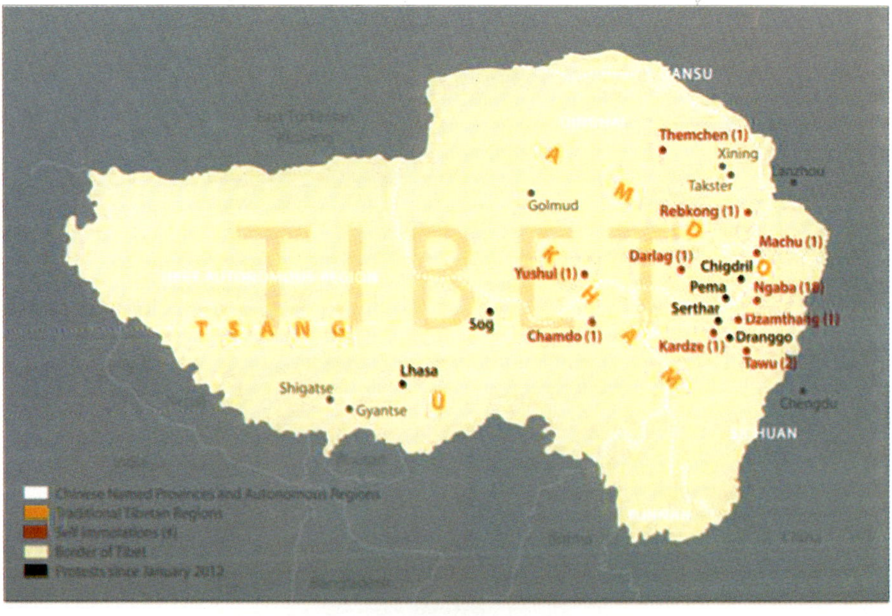

Tibet-Map Immolations Protests

10
How to Win Friends and Influence People

Chinese attribute the influence of the Dalai Lama with the Western governments to his influential friends. But why should wealthy and influential people do not just eat, drink and be happy, than to step by the side of the Dalai Lama? The Western model of hierarchy of motivation cannot explain this. If one goes by the Freudian assumption that each individual's actions are finally to be understood as the service unto himself in some overt or covert form, it will be a gross mistake. The world then appears to be a place where people are scrambling to get as much a piece of a cake as they possibly can. Even a cursory look at the nature of activities of the creative minority shows how false that concept can be. Altruism, love of truth and care for one's fellow-beings are not the ideals found in the religious text of monasteries and ashrams only.

In every period in the history of all people and nations, there are shining examples of illustrious relationships between people, in pursuit of an ideal way of life. Gandhi's life was full of such friends and collaborators in his experiments with truth. We take just one example of his friendship with Charles Andrews. Andrews was a Cambridge educated Englishman. He was as much an anti-imperialist as Gandhi and that was the basis for their idealist friendship rooted in deep conviction of an idealist way of life. This idealism did not step in the personal conduct of their individual lives only. It went far beyond; Charles Andrews donated his life's earnings of three hundred pounds to the cause of fighting for the suffering from an intolerable wrong that Gandhi was involved in.

In the analysis of the motivation for such actions not only Freud comes out wrong but even the refined psychologists like Maslow, seem to be inadequate. There certainly appears a spirit prevalent, at least in such creative people, which bind and blend them to the world around. Mahatma Gandhi and the Dalai Lama are such persons. So, while they are engaged in countering what they are convinced as evil doings of their opponents, hatred is alien to them. Instead, their actions are rooted in the firm conviction that the enemy is not a heartless person and would understand and subscribe to basic decency and values.

Innumerable people from across the globe are drawn to the Dalai Lama. His openness and readiness to welcome everybody does land him into a hotspot at times. Let us illustrate one such experiment that misfired. In 2001 while the Dalai Lama was in New Delhi, Huriyat leaders from Kashmir approached him *vis-à-vis* Kashmir problems. He readily invited them to Dharmashala for discussion. Before that could happen, the Indian press led by *Hindustan Times* was agog with the news that the Dalai Lama sympathizes and sees an identical and similar situation between Kashmir and Tibet! In consternation, the Government of India took up the issue with the Dalai Lama. Numerous explanatory statements at various levels had to be made to explain that it was a mere welcome. It cannot be interpreted as a policy statement on issues of vital importance like Kashmir. The Dalai Lama had to repeatedly clarify that Kashmir is integral part of India. The meeting with the Huriyat leaders had to be cancelled.

It is a matter of chance as to how much good or harm can come out of openness. The crux of the matter is that those who have nothing to hide, do not mind being vulnerable. And that is how they win friends and influence people.

The glimpse of the illustrious friends of the Dalai Lama can be had by glancing at the names of the people who signed for his nomination for the Nobel Peace Prize (Appendix IV). But taking a cue from the British friends of Gandhi, we review the contributions made by the Britishers first to the cause of Tibetan freedom.

Lord Ennals, an MP has been a crusader for Tibet. He took leadership in pioneering efforts for the nomination of Nobel Peace Prize. He was the Chairman of the Conference of International Lawyers on the issues relating to self-determination and independence for Tibet. The right of self-determination of people is a cause of many bloody conflicts. His appreciation for the Dalai Lama springs from the assertion by Tibet that the Tibetan issue is one that can be settled peacefully and in accordance with the international law through non-violent means.

Justice Michael Curby supports the Tibetan cause and, that is based on the optimism that in the solution of the Tibetan cause, there may not only be a resurgence and resurrection of the United Nations; such a solution may even bring about a new world order.

While the Chinese continue to deride the Dalai Lama as "splittist", "a wolf" and derogatory usage of his name, "Dalai", the Dalai Lama means well for the Chinese even when he is seeking a solution of Tibet Question in "mutual interests". It is noteworthy that in Mahatma Gandhi's political consciousness also there were several grades of such notions that made him serve the masters. He had fought on the British side during Boer war in South Africa. During Zulu rebellion also he had helped British. He justified these actions by the argument that it was the duty of every civilian to help the ruling government. Such actions made him earn three medals from the British. It was a long while before he returned them when he was no more enamoured with British. After his return to India, his policy was to discuss and debate so as to persuade in a spirit of trust. For Mahatma Gandhi also, it took a long time to realize that the antagonist talked nicely only in the service of their selfish motive and, clichés like the "white man's burden[1]" that the Fabians coined, were only meant to be neurotic defences of exploitation. Only in 1942 did he give the unconditional call for the British to quit India. The friends and collaborators in the Tibetan cause are more clearheaded than the Fabians.

The story on the American side is also equally interesting. The Americans are known for their trait of wonder, excitement, travels and the powers of the Fourth estate. They are also known for the existential problems. Some identify them as most affluent and unhappy people! Rooted in a tradition of barely 200 years only, an average American is not worried about what the world is like till such time that he is faced with problems. And there is a significant creative minority who are chiseled at the high centres of learning that impart education to be world leaders of future. Many Americans approach the Dalai Lama to find meaning to their lives. Many more are in quest of peace and swarm not only at the teachings of the Dalai Lama but at the Buddhist monasteries spread around Dharmashala. The Buddhist monasteries from Leh to Darjeeling are crowded with Americans of all hues. So much so that quite a few of them are either in search of instant *nirvana* or want to know all about Tibetan *tantra* in two days!

Tibetan Lamas have well-recognized this trend and when the Dalai Lama referred us to his Guru, Ling Rimpoche, for learning *Vajrayana,* the first question he had asked was "Would you like to know all about *Vajrayana* in a few hours"? Needless to say that people who have approached Buddhist monasteries or lamas with this kind of motivation, and benefited for a life time, would have been permanently indebted not only to Buddhism but to the cause of compassion in the service of Tibet, as well as to all, who are suffering and need help.

Our personal history stands out as a lucid testimony to the above. When we approached the Dalai Lama in 1987, we were intensely occupied with the study of consciousness. While reading about the recent discoveries of endorphins in Adyar library at the Theosophical Society, Chennai, we got a flash of insight to approach the most knowledgeable living person in the field and, the bond has been getting stronger-and-stronger year-after-year. So the Dalai Lama at the last visit told us half-jokingly and half-seriously that there must be a *karmic* connection extending to previous life or lives.

Coming back to the friends that became collaborators to the cause, let us reflect on a few instances.

- Richard Gere is internationally famous as an actor, film producer and director from Hollywood. It is said that following his contact with the Dalai Lama, he turned to Buddhism. A few years later his movie Kundun[2] won all the academy awards in 1999. It surpassed many records of the box-office collection not only in USA but other Western countries too. Here was an ambassador at large spreading appeal to help this nation in trouble through the medium of entertainment with his powerful brand-name. Tenzing Geyche once jocularly told us that the best bet for someone to shake hands with Richard Gere would be to lounge about the slopes of Dharmashala where one is most likely to bump into this celebrity who frequents Dharmashala of and on. He has been a source of funding for several publications on Buddhism too.
  Time magazine brought out a special issue. *The Time*, that chronicled the lives and ideas of the world's 100 most influential people. Six of them were featured on the cover page. The Dalai Lama, as an icon, was waving large amongst them. Richard Gere wrote about him: "The Dalai Lama does not belong solely to the Tibetans, he belongs to us all. He has emerged over the past half-century as one of the very few universally respected beings on our planet. His appeal lies in his utter simplicity and honesty, the uncluttered clarity of mind, his infectious laughter and his uncanny ability to explain the most complex Buddhist concepts to anyone." However, the magazine ran out of its memory when it described him as an advocate for Tibet for more than 25 years!
  Gere Foundation has funded some publications too[3].
- Apart from people who are in quest of meaning or spirituality, the powerful fourth estate is again-and-again lured to Dharmashala and Tibetan refugee camps as well as to places like Lhasa in Tibet. John Avedon came to Dharmashala as an enlightened journalist. Probably he may have never realized that he would end into extensive travels for four years with the Dalai Lama. The culmination of his journalistic pursuit was best selling book, "*In*

Exile from the Land of Snows" first published in 1979. The book has seen many editions thereafter. This brought John Avedon in contact with Buddhists both from East and West, like Shanghai Samdup a Swiss monk and Yeshi Khadup a monk residing in New York. The stint brought him in contact with Western doctors practicing Tibetan medicines like, Gerald Goldstein and Donald Baker at the University of Virginia. If one glances at the list of the acknowledgement in his book, we also came across Professor Jeffery Hopkins, who has been one of the most eminent Western scholar on Tibet.

- The Tibetan mysticism is also one of the ways people have been drawn to Dharmashala. Herbert Benson, a professor of medicine at Boston was drawn initially by a lecture by the Dalai Lama at Boston. He dropped a letter to the Dalai Lama and, almost forgot about it till he received an appointment to meet him.
  He finds the Dalai Lama open minded to scientific investigation. And the Dalai Lama made all arrangements for Benson to investigate "*G-tummo-yoga*". Benson's experiments reveal that the Tibetan monks were able to raise their body temperature at will by several degrees. This explained their relative comfort in frozen climate of the Himalayas with their barren backs. Benson also investigated levitation. That could not be proved. And Benson was free to publish what he discovered in the form of a best-seller, "*The Relaxation Response*". It is more than a quarter century since Benson published his book. The book has been a notable contribution in establishing mind-body relationship. It became a guide-book to learn relaxation strategies for the stressed Western society.
- Rajiv Malhotra, anchor with popular channels and journalist, turned Buddhist when he publicly acknowledged the Dalai Lama as his *guru.* He edited an erudite book on the Dalai Lama with contributors spread over the globe. Arnav Goswami followed.
  An exhaustive list of friends and collaborators is beyond narration. Religious discourses, scientific symposia and peace conferences have won the Dalai Lama more and more friends. We just catalogue as to who all attended a business community symposium with him in 1990 at Amsterdam. It was a dialogue between internationally distinguished representatives of the arts, science, spirituality, and economics and top managers. Some of the messages that were generated are:

- P. Fenterer van Vlissingen, President and Chief Executive Officer of SHV Holdings NV said, "Short-term thinking, in which profits are central, is giving way to long-term vision. The managers of the 1990s will have to change. To understand the world they will have to open their minds."
- Dr. J.R.M. van den Brink, former Minister of Economic Affairs and Chairman of the Board of Directors of AMRO-Bank: "An economy such as ours, that is rapidly changing from a product industry to a service industry, needs investment in 'human capital'. If drastic changes are taking shape within the cultural pillars of art, science and spirituality, a service industry should not fail to make a thorough enquiry into them. It is these changes that determine the direction of growth processes in the market economy, and the future of business activities. The forecast of the outcome is: We are moving from a 'competitive society' to a more 'compassionate society'."

Participants included:

- Robert Rauschenberg (Artist): I believe very strongly that artists could be negotiators for peace. Everybody else who is negotiating for peace is elected and therefore has to make certain compromises.
- David Bohm (Scientist): The first step in economics is to see that the earth is one household. It is wrong to say the environment is just surrounding us, because that would be like the brain regarding the stomach as part of the environment.
- Stanisiav Menshikov (Economist): The world is in a process of great change. Of course, everybody is looking at the Soviet Union and Eastern Europe, but my view is that the planet is changing in all parts, including Western Europe. A new society is emerging.
- Lawrence Weiner (Artist): One of the nicest things about being an artist is that hierarchy does not exist, it sounds romantic but it is the truth.
- Rupert Sheldrake (Scientist): We should not just think three or five years ahead but a hundred or two hundred years ahead. When we do that, I think, we would see a very different way of planning what we do.
- Sogyal Rinpoche (Spiritualist): If you simply make more short sighted profits, then on the long term there will be more suffering. We have to have economists who have a far reaching vision.
- Jean-Maxim Leveque (Economist): I am the one who first

pronounced the word "denationalisation" in France. Now-a-days the French people are discovering what capitalism really is.

- Marina Abramovic (Artist): The Twenty-first century will be a world without sculptures, paintings or art installations. Artists will have such a strong mental state that they can transmit energy to other people without objects in between.
- Fritzof Capra (Scientist): We are in a state of global crisis. The characteristic of that crisis is that the major problems of our time are all interconnected. Ultimately it comes down to an outdated perception of the world.
- Raimon Pariikkar (Spiritualist): We have to strive to demonetize society. We succeeded in monetizing everything, now we have to demonetize culture.
- H.J. Witteveen (Economist): Under the surplus of difficulties there is a move in the direction of greater spiritual awareness.
- John Cage (Artist): You breathe better when your feelings are anarchy than you do when you are governed by a government.
- Ilya Prigogine (Nobel Laureate — Scientist): With this information revolution going on we may come closer to a society which will permit creativity to be more commonly distributed. It will have levels and ways of expressing which could never be reached before.
- Huston Smith (Spiritualist): The real religion of the modem world is science, because we look to science as the oracle of truth. It gives a different view of truth, because it emphasizes the material, whereas the religions have focused on the immaterial.
- J.C.J. van der Heyden: The brain can have any speed. I think what we need in the future is to work faster with information.
- Francisco Valera (Scientist): Behavioural processes on the basis of cooperation can be called love.
- Mother Teresa (Spiritualist): Times are dreadful. They call for tremendous heroism and self-sacrifice. The purpose of a religious community is to be a micro-cosm of what the world ought to look like.
- F. Wilhelm Christians (Economist): Communication has created another consciousness in the world. The leaders of China are afraid that through communication the changes going on in Europe will spread out. They better realize that they can't be isolated anymore.
- M. Pinheiro Me (Economist): We have had nearly fifty years of peace and try to learn how to continue living in peace.... countries, businesses, art, spirituality have advanced to such a state that it will be possible for the general people to live in peace.

And to enumerate a few more public figures:

- Brad Pitt who featured in Seven Years in Tibet as Henrich Harrar is to marry Angelina Jolie in a Buddhist ceremony in December 2005. His films are banned in China.
- Vijay Kranti was a media person with photographic talent. Through a long association of more than three decades and extensive travels with the Dalai Lama, he still remains a media person in service of Tibet. He published a photographic album of the Dalai Lama and now is the Editor of *Tibet Desh* (Hindi). He went to Tibet, did extensive photography and has created an exhibition.
- A Greek Princess (name withheld), deeply distressed in her life, discovered a historical connection between Greece and Tibet. She came to Dharmashala and found what she wanted.
- A famous "wealthy and influential" friend from US implored the Dalai Lama to intervene in the dispute with his girl friend! The Dalai Lama had time to do so. Then he wanted him to get them married soon!
- A famous European (name withheld) from Strasbourg wrote to the Dalai Lama on 23 October, 2001, to convey concrete suggestions about resolution of the issue of Tibet and, to declare that his family already belongs to Tibet, since, "...essential and urgent, to find new ways, with financial help to develop a solid, systematic educational system for the young expatriated Tibetans. Thus to create a new elite, of doctors, lawyers, business people, scientists, etc., yet with a deep sense of identity and a peaceful sense of mission, little would, with time, give the "Club Tibet de Strasbourg" a new, more realistic image and serve as an example to other minorities.

  My son-in-law is a Tibetan refugee, my wife and my daughter are Buddhists, as for me, I give eternity the benefit of doubt! Messages of peace are not enough; they have to be put in practice with efficiency.

  Destiny has to be given a destination!"

The universities across the world find peace conferences as education at its best and highest, inspiring and uplifting. University of Virginia organized a Nobel Peace Laureates Conference, chaired by Jeffrey Hopkins. The following attended: Jose Ramos-Horta (East Timor), Betty Williams (Northern Ireland), Dr. Rigoberta Menchu Tum (Guatemala), Archbishop Desmond Tutu (South Africa), President Oscar Arias Sanchez (Costa Rica),

Harn Yawnghwe for Aung San Suu Kyi (Burma), Bobby Muller (Co-founder, International Campaign to Ban Landmines), Jody Williams (United States).

- Activist across Europe, with the view to keep the issue of the Tibet alive by motivating parliamentarians, formed several friendship and support group. They continuously impress the parliamentarians that one way to get elected is to support Tibet! The Activist are Henning Gjellerod (Denmark), Shiela Finestone (Canada), Matt Robson (New Zealand), Zoltan Rockenbauer (Hungary), Jaques Lefevre (Belgium), Jan van Erps (Belgium), Cluaude Huriet (France), Uschi Eld (Germany), Zdenek Babka (Czech Republic), Andrius Kubilius (Lithuania).
- To make the long list short, let us just enumerate Nominators for Nobel Peace Prize as:

  Prince Sadruddin Aga Khan, The Lord Ardwick, The Lord Bellhaven, Sir Hugh Casson, Conor Cruse O'Brien, Brigadier M. Harbottle, OBE, The Earl of Longford, Sir Yehudi Menuhin, The Revd. Canon Paul Ostreicher, The Lord of Sainsbury, Secretary Eneritus, Smithsonian Institute, Dr. S. Dillon Ripley, Professor Luis O. Gomez (University of Michigan), Professor Jeffrey Hopkins (University of Virginia), Dr. J. M. Rae (Westminster School), Professor Ronald Oliver (University of London), The Charlie Rose (Congress of United States), Paul Moore, Jr. (Bishop of New York), Professor Olin C. Robison (President of Middlebury College, Vermont), Dr. Gary T. Whiteford (University of New Brunswick), Dr. Michael Aris (University of Oxford), Mrs. Shirley Williams (President, Social Democratic Party), Mr. John Templeton (Templeton Prize), John Driscoll (President, Lona College), The Countess Mountbatten of Burma, The Lord Bishop of Rochester, Prof. R.F. Gombrich (Balliol College, Oxford), Dr. Peter Fischer-Applet (President of Hamburg University), Mr. Jim Lester, MP, Sir Bernard Braine, MP, Prof. Bimilal Motilal, The Lord de Saumarez, Dr. Franz Alt, Germany, Dr. Carmen Blacker (University of Cambridge), The Earl of Harewood, Jeremy Thorpe, The Dean of Westminster, Prof. Sir Karl Popper (The London School of Economics and Political Science), The Baroness Ewart-Biggs (UK), Sir George Trevelyan, Jr., The Lord Ennals and Fredrick R. Hyde-Chambers.
- The nominations from U.S. leaders were:

Hon Charlie Rose, House of Representatives, Mel Levin, Washington, DC, House of Representatives, Benjamin Gilman, House of Representatives, Claiborne Pell, U.S. Senate, Jesse Helms, U.S. Senate, Christopher Dodd, U.S. Senate, Elliot Abrains, Assistant Secretary of State, Department of State, and Dante Fascell, House of Representatives.

- The religious leaders
  Bishop John O'Connor, Archdiocese of New York, Bishop Paul Moore, Cathedral of St. John, the Divine, New York, Pir Viliyat Khan, Head of the Sufi Order in the West, Rev. Richard Neuhaus, Director, Center on Religion and Society, New York.
- The Buddhist scholars
  Prof. Luis Gomez, University of Michigan, Prof. Alex Wayman, Columbia University, Prof. Jan Willis, Wesleyan University, Prof. Robert Thurman, Amherst College, Prof. Jeffrey Hopkins, University of Virginia, Prof. Donald Lopez, Jr., Middlebury College, Prof. Nathan Katz, University of Florida.
- Notable scholars
  Prof. Christopher Beckwith, Indiana University (History), Dr. Elliot Sperling, Indiana University (History), Brother John Driscoll, President, Lona College, Prof. Steven Rockefeller, Middlebury College (Religion), Prof. Gary Whiteford, New Brunswick (Geography), Dr. Daniel Boorsteen, Librarian, Library of Congress.
- Indian group of sponsors
  A coordinating group was set up in India under a former Indian permanent representative to the United Nations, Mr. Rikhi Jai Pal. The group included, General Secretary of the Janata Party, Venerable Kushok Bhaku, a former Minister of Jammu and Kashmir Government, Prof Rajni Kothari and a number of MPs of different parties.
- There were nominations from smaller countries too and some prominent religious leaders in Mongolia and the Soviet Union also joined to nominate.

The easy accessibility of the Dalai Lama and his willingness to help anyone whom he can, has drawn people from all over the world to Dharmashala. Let us see an illustration. A Western lady, in her early twenties, daughter to a divorced mother who has deserted her in teens, barely relating to her alcoholic father, unhappy with about half a dozen relationships, bereft of any meaning to life, goes to Dharmashala to learn *vipassyana* meditation. Incidentally, she happens to visit Tibetan Children

Village. In the face of the desolate ones, she sees the laughter and love. She is transformed into a volunteer for life in the cause of Tibet. This is a recurring scenario.

Most of them sympathize and pray, since that is what most of them can do. A few who dare to act, do so. Those who have acted have brought Tibet issue in global perspective. The spark has become a flame. But would prayers by many and just action by a few result in Rangzen? God sees the Truth; but waits.

REFERENCES

1. This is how the idealist Fabians of the imperialist Britain defended their occupation of India.
2. Kundun is the story of the boy king Dalai Lama, his growing up in monastic tradition and crushing off Tibet by the China.
3. The Dalai Lama, *The World of Tibetan Buddhism*, published in Boston, 1995.

11
Sino-Tibetan Dialogue: Clapping with One Hand

Historical Perspective

The Tibetans write to Chairman Mao in November1949; Freedom in Exile,1959; Let Hundred Flowers Bloom, 1957 and Cultural Revolution, 1966; Gyalo Dhundup in Peking, 1979; Fact finding delegations, 1979, 1980, 1981; Tumultuous welcome and emotional outbursts; second delegation expelled, 1980; Dialogue after Strasbourg Proposal, 1988; Marshal Law in Lhasa, 1988; the Dalai Lama writes to Deng,1992; Negotiations resume under Western pressure,1999-2001; Delegations of the Dalai Lama return empty handed, 2004-2011.

A civilization that is medieval and yet, has undergone modernization develops a distinct culture of its own. This is most evident for the Chinese. Mao tse-Tung was rooted in robust, rustic culture. Chau En-lai was a suave, modernized French educated vile Statesman. Subsequent Chinese rulers have followed the traditions laid down by them.

Tenzing Chogyal, younger brother of the Dalai Lama said, "No matter whether a cat is red or black, it shall kill the mice". This poignantly describes the China-Tibet relationship. Before it was overrun by the communists, even Koumingtan had described Tibet as China's territory. Take-over of Tibet by Communists was fully in unanimity with Koumingtan policy. Whatever maps Chiang Kai-shek Government had drawn showing Tibet as part of China were *ipso facto* retained by the communists.

The Marxists dream was for the workers of the world to unite. There was a dream of a world rule by communism as a single unit and China is and has been most populous region of the world. Chinese mind set has been expansionist and, remains so.

So it began with the expansionist design based on ideology and need. Manchuria was taken over. Mongolia was divided and the Inner Mongolia was also absorbed and, so was Tibet.

China's attitude to treaties is very simple. In 1912 at the proposed tripartite conference between British, India, Tibet and China they refused to participate. Britain was the biggest world power then. They understood the disadvantage of negotiating with a super power. Their non-participation has been used their huge advantage. On the other hand, India has not been able to hold on to its position as a successor to British Government. The treaty between Tibet and India meant a sovereign status for Tibet.

Writing in *The White House Years*, Henry Kissinger succinctly paraphrases Chinese style of negotiations. They manage to cajole with utmost courtesy. They seem to have infinite patience. A big Chinese trait in negotiations is their deliberate procrastination. As long as there is liberty to carry on the way they wish, why invite limitation by concluding any negotiations? They can pretend not to understand when told that a ball is likely to travel in the wrong direction if not controlled. They do not protest but give a cold stare! The delegations arc lavishly hosted, feasted and thrown parties around. Much of time is spent in sight-seeing. Appointments are not to be kept on time; arrive after tiring out the counterpart for hours of delay and then talk round about. Subterfuge is a part of diplomacy. Henry Kissinger writes that when he finally came face to face with Chinese negotiators, much time was spent on deciding whether the table ought to be a square or round one.

This is what exactly has happened when 17-Point Agreement was signed. The Tibetan delegation to Beijing peace negotiations in 1951, headed by Ngapoi Ngawang Jigme, better known now as simply Ngabo signed *the Seventeen-Point Agreement for the Peaceful Liberation of Tibet* with the Chinese Communist government, accepting Chinese sovereignty in exchange for guarantees of autonomy and religious freedom. The Tibetan delegation was unauthorized and the Chinese made fraudulent seals. The Dalai Lama says he came to know about it only when he hears the radio broadcast from Peking.

And even if a treaty were to be signed, the letter and the spirit can always mean two different things. If the semantics were to be carefully paraphrased then also the relevance of the matter changes from time to time. A treaty is valid at the time when it is signed. Why should it be perennially effective? Circumstances change with the time and the Chinese use this argument often.

Seventeen-Point Agreement guarantees autonomy and religious freedom; now Chinese have different connotations to the words, autonomy and religious freedom.

After all this, Chinese still have option that if they are found to be on the wrong foot, to err is human. Good decisions are taken by the highest leader and their poor execution is a bad outcome. If there was genocide in Tibet, it was very bad. But then was it not about 50 years before? If there was a cultural revolution in Mao's time, of course, there were many mistakes. The mistakes should be corrected and so let us negotiate how to correct the mistakes. And the Chinese way of negotiation is the same all the time. Delay, delay all the time and promise to keep on negotiating!

For numerous years Chinese even refused negotiation with the Dalai Lama. This continued till such time that there was a bamboo curtain. Reciprocal economic interests between the world and China caused the lifting of this curtain. And in the realm of trade and commerce what dictates a dialogue is whose need is greater.

When he was in India on the occasion of 2500 anniversary of Buddha, Dalai Lama had tried to seek favour with Pandit Nehru and pleaded for asylum. The Dalai Lama's choice was as much as that of a prisoner on parole. Simultaneously Chou En-lai had managed himself to be in New Delhi. Nehru had tried to broker peace. However, what came out was that Dalai Lama's discussions with Nehru got conveyed to Chou En-lai. In return, Chou En-lai, with his French polish could beguile Pandit Nehru into believing China's honesty. In his autobiography, *Freedom in Exile*, the Dalai Lama narrates the episode without any emotion as "Pandit Nehru regrets".

Obviously Pandit Nehru was the towering elder Statesman of India. Maybe, unsure of his conscience and, traditionally even consulting an oracle, the Dalai Lama listened to his advice and returned to Tibet. Through the cooperative actions, he hoped to make the best of the 17-Point Agreement. Obviously he hardly had a choice.

When the US policy was to counter communism and the cold war was really waging hot, why should Dalai Lama not have taken an alternative to seek asylum in USA ? The reason stated by him is the fact that at that time, United States was already engaged in a war in Korea. Tibet was a far off hostile land and it appeared to the Dalai Lama that it would be difficult to obtain any substantive support. Even if US because of its anti-communist policy were to extend support that would culminate into a war between US and China. And he felt such a war would be a protracted long drawn out affair.

This made him to choose to move to a comparatively southern place in Tibet. If there were to be a need it will be easier from there to escape to India.

With the above prologue as a backdrop to the entire Tibetan situation, let us first see a letter[1] by the *Kashag* addressed to Chairman Mao in November 1949. It said:

"Tibet is a unique country where the Buddhist religion is widely flourishing and which is predestined to be ruled by the living Buddha of Mercy or Chenresig, the Dalai Lama. As such Tibet has, from the earliest times up to now, been an independent country whose political administration has never been taken over by any foreign country; and Tibet also defended her own territories from foreign invasions and always remained a religious nation.

In view of the fact that Chinghai (Qinghai) and Sikiang (Xikang), are being situated on the borders of Tibet, we would like to have an assurance that no Chinese troops would cross the Tibetan frontier from the Sino-Tibetan border, or any such military action. Therefore, please issue strict orders to those civil and military officers stationed on the Sino-Tibetan in accordance with the above request, and kindly have an early reply so that we can be assured.

As regards those Tibetan territories annexed as part of Chinese territories some years back, the government of Tibet would desire to open negotiation after the settlement of the Chinese Civil War."

The British Agent as well as Indian diplomat Dayal, stationed in Lhasa considered the letter to be strongly worded and, advised caution to the Tibetan Administration. Nevertheless, the letter was dispatched. Instead of any formal answer, it brought troops in Eastern Tibet and then, there was deluge. Finally, the situation culminated into escape of the Dalai Lama to India.

After coming into Exile in 1959, the Dalai Lama happened to breathe freedom for the first time in his life. Paradoxically this freedom was at a moment when he had been most vulnerable. At Norbulingka palace, he would have been either captured or killed. This was probably a rare instance when the Chinese were caught on a wrong foot and the mouse could give the cat a slip. But contrary to the mouse burrowing itself in a hole, here the Dalai Lama was in the vast expanse of independent India within a whole new free world.

But it appears that good people see no evil. When we personally asked the Dalai Lama, way back in 1987 about the prevalence of bad and ugly in the present times, he brushed our question aside by asserting that the world to a major extent is governed by the good forces that are represented by in the kindness and the nobleness of the ordinary people. He said that the bad appears to be dominant over good because it is widely noticed as abnormal and so attracts wide media attention. Tibet dialogue is a good illustration.

In terms of sheer numbers, six million Tibetans are no match to a thousand million Hans Chinese. China has grown from might to mighty and Tibet has just managed to survive. However, its survival has emerged as its greatest intangible strength. The survival of the fittest — propounded by Charles Darwin — is no more valid. Tibet is an apt illustration that Nature so ordains its affairs that even the weakest finds ways to survive. The mainstay of Chinese policy has been to consider the Dalai Lama as an irritant that shall disappear with the passage of time.

It is frequently asked to the Dalai Lama as to what will happen to the institution of the Dalai Lama after him. His answer is that as long as there is misery on this earth and there is suffering, he shall be born again and again. As to the institution, he says it is up to the Tibetans to decide. He is sure that he will not be reincarnated in China and, goes to the extent of warning against such an attempt. The Chinese believe that with modernization and better standard of living, the Tibetans will be weaned away from religion and they will forget the Dalai Lama. Did not Mao say that the religion is the opium of masses?

After escape into India, the Dalai Lama's initial democratic efforts were with the footage that Tibet is and has been an independent nation. Writing in *The Wall Street Journal*, the Dalai Lama said on 8th November, 1979, that to claim that Tibet is a part of the Chinese nation is both distorted and hypocritical[2]. This was with the heavy burden of the illegal 17-Point Agreement and with the history of having spent considerable time in the Chinese mainland, having attended the proceedings of the Communist Party in official position as the Vice-President.

This can be answered, as the actions of a prisoner. Tibet is a poor nation. There was no prospect of lucrative trade and commerce. In contrast to Kuwait, there was no oil to explore. If any nation was to extend support to Tibet, they will do so only because of truth, justice and morality as Malaysia and Ireland did.

The main concern in the sixties was the resettlement of 100,000 refugees[3]. There was a hope that, following 1965 resolution by the UN and confirmation of genocide internationally, China would be put to shame. At least they will abide by the Seventeen-Point Agreement in true spirit and effectively implement genuine autonomy.

Though the UN resolutions did not materially change anything, China became aware that they have to deal with the issue. It went through the gigantic trauma of Mao's 'let hundred flowers bloom' brand of Cultural Revolution. In the process, Tibet had suffered once again. So when the reversal to restitution began, Tibet was a priority. For the first time the Chinese were making overtures for reconciliation. At the end of 1978 there was much congruence between Beijing and Dharmashala. The Chinese were confident that they have won over the Tibetans inside Tibet by overall prosperity. They had persuaded upper class Tibetans having some connection with the Dalai Lama to go to India and impress upon him to return to Tibet.

There was a veiled threat that relationships between India and China were on a path of improvement. Even BBC reported that a further improvement may make the Dalai Lama's stay in India difficult. The Chinese were constantly reminding India that the Dalai Lama's stay in Dharmashala with a Government in Exile, that India did not formally recognize but let it function, was not conducive to good neighbourly relationship.

In 1978, during the reversal of the Cultural Revolution, the Chinese began to release many of the imprisoned former Tibetan Government officials. Even a number of people who had been involved in the March 1959 uprising were also released and Panchen Rimpoche appeared in public. He was made a member of the Standing Committee of Chinese Peoples Political Consultative Committee. Though imprisoned for a long time, his courage was still strong. He told the Chinese that the leniency shown towards a few leaders would not mean that the things have changed unless there was a genuine rehabilitation of numerous people that have been persecuted. Panchen Rimpoche handed over the well known 70,000 character petition to Chou En-lai personally, even when advised not to do so by Ngabo and others. Chou was leaving for Formosa and had no time to read, but listened carefully when it was presented to an audience comprising high officials. This was to bring a tragic end. Panchen Lama was soon to be branded a reactionary, imprisoned and some time before his death when he appeared in public, had a broken hand. The pictures of his undergoing "sessions" are evidence of a tragic saga.

After being a party secretary, when Deng snatched the power from Hua Guofeng, a conservative, his control over the party became strong. He had different ideas about implementation of the ideology. Foreseeing the amalgamation of Hong Kong with the mainland, he coined a slogan "one country-two systems". Even during the Cultural Revolution Deng was of the opinion to keep the aristocratic Tibetans happy. They had approach to the Dalai Lama. Confident that he had won over the Tibetans by overall prosperity, Deng wanted to persuade the upper class Tibetans having some connection with the Dalai Lama to go to India and impress upon him to return to Tibet. Thus, Deng genuinely wanted to resolve what he called "an unsolved problem of Tibet". If the Dalai Lama were to return to China, it would improve China's international image. China was also wary that the Dalai Lama, in June 1979, had visited Soviet Union and Mongolia to attend the Asian Buddhist Conference organized by a Russian Buddhist

NGO. By now, the Chinese-Russian rift was wide open and Dalai Lama's closeness to Soviet Union did not go unnoticed by the Chinese.

Seeing that there was a softening in the Chinese leadership, in his annual statement to commemorate the 10th March Uprising, in 1978, the Dalai Lama said that the main issue was the welfare and ultimate happiness of six million Tibetans in Tibet.

Therefore, China made a major initiative towards reconciliation. Li Jusin, the official Chinese News Agency Xinhua's representative in Hong Kong, went up to Gyalo Dhundup. He suggested to him that the changed leaders in Beijing were keen to repair the damages done by the Gang of Four and the Cultural Revolution. The resolution of the problem of Tibet was on a priority for them and towards this end Gyalo Dhundup was invited to Tibet. This was a clever diplomacy on the part of China. While utilizing the Dalai Lama's brother as the prime negotiator, the Chinese thought that it will then focus that the Tibet issue is a matter of personal status of the Dalai Lama. And they will project to the international governments that kind of message. However, the Tibetans already had learnt a hard lesson. The Dalai Lama insisted that before his return can be thought of, the Chinese should meet the members from the Exile government.

The Dalai Lama utilized it to show that he is prepared to reconcile. China invited Gyalo Dhundup alone. He had no official status with the Government in Exile.This limited the scope of his visit to a mere visitor's status. On the other hand, he was the person who had spearheaded insurgency. Negotiating with him meant that China was prepared to forget the past. And, finally, he was Dalai Lama's elder brother. So he will be the closest to the Dalai Lama's ears.

On March 1, 1979, Gyalo Dhundup met the Chief Director, Ulanfu. He was in-charge of Tibet. Right at the onset, during the welcome speech only, Ulanfu admitted past mistakes. He attributed them to the Gang of Four. This gave earnestness and honesty to his desire to change the situation. This was highlighted a few days later when Gyalo Dhundup had a meeting with Deng Xioping, the Chinese paramount leader. This meant that Chinese were indeed quite serious to repair the relationship with the Tibetans. Deng went to the extent that so far as independence for the Tibet was not asked for, he was prepared to discuss all other matters. He asserted that these were not temporary commitments but would yield fundamental changes. When confronted with the past history that the Chinese were liable to make phony promises and revoke them on fake situations, Deng asked Gyalo Dhundup that the Dalai Lama can depute his teams to observe the situation in Tibet.

As suggested by Deng, in August 1979, the Tibetan delegation left New

Delhi silently without any formal announcement. The Chinese tried to create a favourable environment by conceding to some of the sensitive demands: they may visit all Tibetan inhibited areas including Kham and Amdo and, they will not travel on Chinese passport. The Tibetans considered granting of these two conditions as very sacrosanct but for the Chinese, particularly if there was going to be reconciliation, this one time concession did not matter.

They were received at Hong Kong. At the first meeting itself the Chinese displayed an utter lack of understanding of Tibetan sensibilities by welcoming the delegates as, "we are the great land of China and you are the minority people. You must understand that you have such a wonderful opportunity to see your homes and birthplace only because of the generosity of the communist party leadership."

The Tibetans gulped the bitter pill with patience and equanimity. However, they refused to return the toast in whatsoever manner. They were to learn in the course of their 20-week tour that this was a standard format of welcome. The cadres from the Beijing seem to have been given standard instructions to parrot it out.

The delegation was formally welcomed by thirty officials. They were the highest ranking members of the Nationalities Affairs Commission, and Mr. Kao, a senior member was to accompany them on the tour. The delegation was thus given due importance. On the other hand, they were surrounded by numerous cadres of PLA. They were even housed in a PLA guest house. Mr. Kao was polite and diplomatic. Every now and then, while discussing their itinerary, he would interpolate with informal remarks like 'Come back to live in the motherland'. On the other hand, he seemed not to realize that references to the Dalai Lama have to be in appropriate terms. He was only His Holiness to the delegation. Calling him Dalai was bound to hurt their inner roots.

It appears that the Chinese had totally misjudged the mood of the Tibetans. Apparently, they have been suppressed and even if they would have sounded them before no one would unnecessary venture prison. In a few isolated contacts, even in Peking, the delegates were told by young Tibetan students stories that Chinese would never have dreamt of. These students had never seen independent Tibet. They were transported to Beijing and were undergoing studies under the communist brainwash system. Yet they were very nationalistic and went on to say in privacy that the Chinese cannot be trusted. All Tibetans are united against them. A stunning revelation was that there are underground roots all over.

As the word about the delegation from the Dalai Lama spread there was a showdown at Tashikyil. A few kilometres away, they were told, that the road ahead is lined up by hundreds of Tibetans. The Chinese officials were stopped by a jeep from the opposite side of the road bringing them the news.

The delegation was told that there were thousands of people waiting for them ahead. Their safety was endangered. And it is the responsibility of the Chinese to see that they are safe so they should not open the windows of the cars, should not put out their hands and must not talk to the people. In a few minutes the vehicles were submerged into a sea of humanity. The people wanted to touch them, give them fruits, flowers and scarves. They climbed on the top of the cars and broke the windows.

This was beyond any Chinese imagination. Kao was terrified. This is the state of affair; he is reported to have said, with the delegation from the Dalai Lama. What will happen if he was to be here? We would not be able to control it.

Even when the delegation was taken to a PLA guest house, many Tibetans just refused to leave and camped before the gate. These people were in rags. Their poverty was apparent. They were forlorn and yet a strong bond of common nationality welded them together.

This was indeed something novel and full of promises. Deng has also made a big debut on the Western front and was pictured on the *Time* magazine's front cover as 'Man of the Year' in 1980.

In extending the open invitation to the Dalai Lama's delegation, Deng has counted heavily on the indoctrination that the younger Tibetan generation had undergone in the form of Tibetan Red-Guards. This section of the younger generation Tibetans who had taken to communism and were working towards that goal, was supposed to have even won over the people. Tibetan communist red-guards had joined in denouncing the religion and join in the destruction of temples and monarchies.

But the Chinese had totally misjudged the situation. Mao had better perception when he is said to have exclaimed: "We are lost", on being told about the Dalai Lama's escape in 1959. Reverence to the Dalai Lama is at the core of Tibetan hearts. Even after 20 years of the Chinese rule, the Tibetans hardly had any opportunity to voice any dissent. Since there was no dissent voiced, the Chinese thought that the people were won over. This was a great mistake.

What happened subsequently was totally unexpected. At every meeting point, the delegation was surrounded by thousands of Tibetans. They recounted the horrible account of their sufferings. There was a flash point. Form the crowd surrounding the delegation a woman shouted, "Tibet is independent". She was arrested and tortured. A confrontation ensued between the delegates and the Chinese. The Chinese accompanying the delegation even suggested that the remaining of the visit may be cancelled. But Ren Rong in Lhasa was confident that when the delegation will visit the Tibetan Autonomous Region the communist indoctrination there would make the situation totally different. This was a further misjudgment.

The second delegation also arrived in China. Tenzin Tethong[4], a Canadian immigrant of Tibetan origin, who was then a representative of the Dalai Lama in New York, led the delegation. During the next six months, wherever the delegation went, they had the same stupendous welcome. All earlier welcomes were surpassed on their arrival in Lhasa. Ren Rong was so confident that he had even allowed the media to be present. The press managed to mingle with the delegates and pandemonium ensued.

Meanwhile, the second delegation that has continued their visit came to the same result. At their visit to the Ganden monastery they were surrounded by more than 5000 people. In open defiance of the Chinese cadres the monks performed religious ceremonies and recited prayers for the long life of the Dalai Lama. Many shouted slogans for independent Tibet. On the next day the Chinese through a Tibetan spokesman of the Party, informed the delegates, thus, there was an abrupt painful end to the detente. On the other hand Ngabo was made the head of TAR indicating a Chinese desire to appease Tibetans. However, next year there was a further resumption in the dialogue through a three-member delegation. Instead of a fact finding delegation, this meant business. They had discussions with Xi Zhongxun, General Secretary of the Party, Ulanfu, head of Nationalities Affairs, and other high-ranking officials. Both the sides defined their positions. There was a wide variance and a natural stalemate. The Tibetans wanted TAR to mean the unification of Amdo, Kham, and U-tsang. This was to be granted a status that was defined for Taiwan in case of its integration. In addition, the Tibetans wanted far greater freedom than that envisaged for Taiwan.

The Chinese response was that the Tibetan "entreaty" cannot be entertained. There is no comparison to Taiwan since Tibet has been "liberated" long since. And it has been belligerent by cries of independence abusing China of imperialist aggression. This is not acceptable to the Chinese as well as to the Tibetans in Tibet.

Five months spent by the Tibetan delegation not only gave so much of information about the actual state of affairs of the ordinary Tibetans to the delegation, but also generated new insights for the Chinese. One of the delegates, who was the then TYC president, went on to make a speech. Chinese had miscalculated so much so that in spite adverse happenings in the interior, they planned an international press brief. For the Tibetans it was obvious that people in Tibet were abjectly poor, subjugated people. There was no question of freedom.

For the Chinese it was obvious that they had not understood the Tibetans. Even if their economic condition may have been better than 30 years before, their loyalty to the Dalai Lama was absolute. And the cry for independence was deep rooted in the Tibetan hearts. This is illustrated by what has come to be the case of a 56 years old woman, Tsering Lhamo. While the delegation was in Lhasa, she had turned emotional, and shouted, "Tibet is independent." She was immediately arrested and for three days she was publicly beaten. In spite of her apology, she was thrown in the prison for 20 years and given electric shocks. This brought about a breakdown on the pretext that the Tibetans had violated the conditions of not contacting the press. The Chinese expelled the delegation and cancelled all further visits.

The overall impression that the delegation gathered was that Tibet was an occupied territory. However, the Chinese wished to persist with delegation diplomacy and conveyed that they will make amends. The reasons for the Chinese solicitude may be either a genuine appreciation that the Tibet issue cannot be solved without the involvement of the Dalai Lama. Or, they may have been truly apprehensive of East and West diplomacy by him. In 1980, he had visited Mongolia, the then Soviet Union, Europe, and United States. The identification of the Dalai Lama with other minority nationalities in China could not have been lost sight of. This may also have made them to attempt in earnestness.

However, before the second delegation was expelled, the third one led by the Dalai Lama's sister Jetsun Pema had arrived. All throughout Tibet the delegation had tumultuous welcome. Moreover in Lhasa their visit became a focal point for a major Chinese demonstration. The third delegation's tour ended on a rough note. The Chinese officials beat up a crowd of 7000 Tibetans before the eyes of the delegates. Their defence was that the crowd had been unruly. Pema told them that they are so uncontrollable now because they have been repressed so long. 'Tibetans are peace-loving and you can see that in India where they are allowed all freedom'. With tears rolling down her eyes Pema cancelled the rest of the tour. She realized that going on with the tour would mean more trouble for the Tibetans.

Pema is a graceful old lady in-charge of the Tibetan children village. She has been a virtual mother to scores of orphaned children. Most of them had either lost both their parents or were left at the village since the single parent could not have supported them. The very site of Tibetan children village is idyllic. Situated on a mountain top, by the side of a natural lake, scores of Tibetan children find substitute paternal love in the fondling by Pema and, other caretakers and teachers. Their age ranges from toddlers to teenagers. While on a visit, beware of hugging a chubby child – it might be a natural impulse for the visitor but then most of them will crowd to ask the same favour.

Visits of the Pema delegation were filmed and were broadcast on Western television. This was a terrible setback for the Chinese. British Broadcasting Corporation prepared a documentary film about Tibet which depicted the destruction of Tibet's cultural heritage. It also included several clips from the film taken by the first delegation.

To summarize the gains by the Tibetan delegation:

(1) Tibetans were able to pass on the message of Bod Cholka-Sum-Greater Tibet comprising not only TAR but other three provinces;
(2) It also meant that Tibetans over these regions owed their alliance to the Dalai Lama and were devoted to him;
(3) Chinese acceptance of the delegation of 1982, which was entirely composed of men originating from outside of TAR, also made it implicit that the Dalai Lama represents Greater Tibet.

Had the Chinese succeeded in projecting that the Tibetan delegations were very much impressed with progress than the people of Hong Kong and Taiwan would have been also favourably impressed. Since this did not happen, the party leadership was made to reconsider their choice in a positive direction. Deng decided that further liberalization and more liberalization should be the choice.

This was evident when Deng reconstituted the party secretariat in the 1980s. He appointed Hu Yaobang, Party General Secretary. Hu was a person in favour of liberal reforms. With this sort of backdrop, Hu Yaobang decided to visit Lhasa on 22nd May, 1980. This was a carefully chosen date since that was the 29th anniversary of signing of the 17-Point Agreement. A symbolic message was also conveyed when he invited Sampho and Lha, Wu Tara the signatories to 1951 agreement to meet him. These two former dignitaries had already spent 20 years in labour camps. One of the accompanying persons with Hu Yaobang warmly held Sampho's hand trying to convey that there is a new beginning. The Tibetan trust of the Chinese promises is reflected in the subsequent action by Sampho. A short while afterwards he left for India.

Hu Yaobang's position was further strengthened as he was empowered to make policy decisions. They were really farsighted reforms. It was on this account that the Dalai Lama, in one of his letters to Hu Yaobang, mentioned that he is looking forward to meeting him. This was probably the closest ever that the Dharmashala-Beijing dialogue ever went.

A notable personality to work within a Five-Men Working Committee formed by Hu Yaobang was Ngabo Ngawang Jigme, who had signed the Seventeen-Point Agreement in 1950. A notable exception was the Panchen Rimpoche.

The group set out in right earnest as to how to rectify the perception of the Tibetan in view of the receptions that the Dalai Lama's delegation had. In fact, the Chinese leader is reported to have said to the Tibetan delegation that the Tibetans should forget the past and look towards the future[5]. The new leader was ready to accept that there were mistakes but they were matter of the past. They blamed it on the previous leadership of the Gang of Four and claimed that the Tibetans were not only the ones who had suffered at that time. It was now thought that if the living conditions were made to be better, and if there was cultural and religious freedom to a certain extent, the Tibetans can still be won over.

So, on 22nd May, 1980, at a meeting of communist party totalling over 4500 members and leaders, Hu Yaobang admitted that the party had failed in Tibet. He said, "We feel that our party has let the Tibetan people down. We feel bad. The sole purpose of communist party is to work for the happiness of the people, who do good things for them. We have worked nearly 30 years but the life of the Tibetan people has not improved. Rather we are to blame." He bluntly asked the Chinese party leaders who were in-charge of Tibet as to what had happened with the millions of yuans that the Beijing Government had allocated to TAR. Whether he was carried away by rhetoric or he was genuinely angry, but he went on to say that it appears that money was thrown into Tsangpo River. And taking a step further, he even said that the situation is as if Tibet has been colonized.

During the visit Hu Yaobang announced a special policy with liberal commitments for Tibet:

(1) There shall be full rights for regional autonomy,
(2) For 3 years Tibetans would be exempted from paying taxes and from certain levies,
(3) In implementing economic policy Tibetans' special condition would be taken into account,
(4) A great part of the subsidy would be utilized for agriculture and animal husbandry, and

(5) There should be development of Tibetan culture, language and education and the minority cadres within the party shall be so treated as to promote unity between the Chinese and Tibetan cadres.

In September 1981, China announced a Five-Point Proposal for unification of all Tibetan inhabited areas of Tibet called as Cholka-Sum (wider Tibet). This meant that, in addition to what was then the Tibetan Autonomous Region, the other areas of Kham, Amdo and U-Tsang were to be included as greater Tibet, to be administered as single political unit. The second proposal was that Tibet should get an equivalent status to Taiwan as detailed in Nine-Point Proposal for Taiwan.

True to their policy of infinite patience. Chinese waited almost a year for the lenient policy to be implemented and, only on July 28, 1981 Hu Yaobang met Gyalo Dhundup and handed him over a Five-Point Proposal. This proposal was a clever deployment to deflect the central issue of the right of Tibetan people to that of the status of Dalai Lama. The Five-Points were:

(1) the Dalai Lama should recognize that China has entered a new period,
(2) the history and repression following 1959 rebellion shall not be raised,
(3) should the Dalai Lama contribute to upholding Chinese unity, the Chinese Government welcomes the Dalai Lama to return to the motherland. But he should not live in Tibet nor will he have any position in the Tibetan administration,
(4) the Dalai Lama shall be given the same status as he had before 1959, and
(5) when the Dalai Lama returns he shall be received by a suitable Minister and is allowed to make press statements.

This proposal was kept secret and was released only in 1984 for the Chinese official press. Of course, they could not have been accepted.

A Chinese scholar, a political analyst, who on terms of anonymity told us that after the collapse of Berlin Wall, the Chinese authorities have taken to a whispering campaign, i.e. imperceptibility spread not only in Tibet but all-over the China. The campaign tells the people to look at the state of Soviet economy after its breakup. It impresses that China is emerging as an economic giant and all the nations of the world are eager to trade with it. The economy has been gradually opened up so that every Chinese

— of whatever nationality — has a chance to earn more than ever before. There is every chance for everybody to cut the corners to indulge in corruption and to utilize the party positions for personal gains as long as one realizes that the future of China lies in being the world leader one day, lies in everyone forgetting about the rights like freedom of speech, equality before law and such other Westernized norms. And so most Chinese deprived and unaware about the finesse of status of free citizens are busy trying to work to their economic betterment. It may amount to working for 12 hours a day of work shift in a multistoried factory-cum-housing where the rest of the 12 hours they live in the same building.

The Chinese concentrated on several administrative and legislative reforms instead. However, the Tibetans dismissed all such moves as, "Thunder that does not bring rain". Probably at the root of Chinese misconception lies the communist inability to perceive that freedom is the basic appetite of the soul. Man does not live by bread alone and even if the reforms were to bring positive results in terms of better economic situation in matter of liberty and freedom as well as in terms of spiritual terms are not easy to manipulate.

Hu Yaobang's liberalization was inconsiderate of the sensibilities of the Tibetan people. There was little appeasement to the Tibetans since this was only a surface attempt to undo the grievances. There was no advancement for the Tibetans either in the official positions or, particularly, in the army. No doubt this would have angered several of the communist party cadres who had been previously been eulogized as vanguards in hostile atmosphere working towards the unification of the motherland. The Chinese cadres were made unhappy by the harsh remarks like 'unhealthy tendencies amongst the Chinese cadres' and so on. The unhealthy tendencies were specifically identified as having taken advantage of the positions of power, wasting the State money and granting of gifts and banquets. It was also said that the Chinese party cadres should be glad to relinquish their hold over Tibet. The liberalization went to the extent that the Chinese did indeed search for a committed communist Tibetan to be in charge of the party secretaryship for Tibet.

Confident that the socio-economic reforms have succeeded, in February 1983, the Chinese allowed hundreds of Tibetans to travel to India to receive *Kalachakra* initiation. The purpose was to give favourable reports to the Dalai Lama. At the face of it, it seemed to have worked. In the course of his teachings the Dalai Lama unexpectedly surprised everybody with the announcement by saying that, "if the present trend of meeting the situation in Tibet were to continue, he hoped to visit Tibet in 1985."

There was a fourth delegation scheduled but it hardly took off. The Dalai Lama choose to take the alternative route of internationalizing the issue. Perceiving his speech at the US Congress as a conspiracy in tandem with demonstration in Lhasa, Marshall Law was imposed and the relationship worsened.

In early 1984 the Central Communist party convened the Second Work Forum in Tibet and numerous cadres of the party from Tibet attended. However, this time, Hu Yaobang opened deliberations with the remark that this time he had no surprises. There was merely going to be continuation of the liberalization and reforms in the form of opening of Tibet. But opening of Tibet meant sinister designs.

As a matter of fact, this turns out to be a very important advancement in further colonization of Tibet. The opening of Tibet meant that the restrictions on Chinese entry to Tibet were to go and it opened the floodgates for migrants from China to Tibet. The implications were clear in the minds of China's leadership. When some of the Tibetan cadres protested with some arguments, Hu Yaobang at one of the seven meetings of this Forum made a cryptic remark that it would be suicidal to keep Tibet closed any longer. Probably the Chinese now saw the solution of the Tibet problem in a different context. Apart from the efforts to brainwash and win over the Tibetans, they saw the possibility of flooding Tibet with Hans Chinese so that the very complexity of Tibetan identity may be washed out.

This measure is seen as a clear proof of China's colonization. It has created tremendous hostility from its very inception and it is even argued that there is some enforced immigration. This caused double backlash because those who were forced to migrate were handicapped by the inhospitable terrain and inclement weather.

By this shift the Government in Exile was startled. When the clarifications sought by them were not answered, the Dalai Lama once again sent a three-man delegation to Beijing in October 1984. The delegation failed to make any inroads and it was obvious that Chinese would not go beyond the Five-Point Proposals made in 1981. This time there was no contact with any of the higher echelons of the party and it was evident that Deng Xiaoping has disengaged.

Jiang Ping, the Deputy Director of the United Front in Beijing, indirectly reminded the Tibetan delegates that the later should concentrate on the question of "Tibetan happiness" as the Dalai Lama indicated in 1978 and 1979. Jiang was convinced that China had poured enough money and material into Tibet to improve Tibetan living standards and bring about all-round development in the region. Between 1952 and 1983, the Central Committee gave a total financial assistance of RMB 72,300,000,000 to

Tibet and, Jiang gave a detailed breakdown of this grant which included money given to industrial projects, transport and communication development, education and renovation of monasteries. "Like the other nationality areas, Tibet Autonomous Region too must move under the leadership of the Party Central Committee, on the socialist path of unity and mutual help. In other words, the Tibetans also must accept an ideological condition: Tibet's present socio-political system cannot be changed. Ping concluded with these remarks: "Since the door is wide open, you are welcome to return. But the lien lies with you, you must change your stand and attitude; otherwise, there won't be any agreement. The Chinese message is consistent, though expressed in different words by various spokesmen: The Dalai Lama is always welcome to negotiate with Peking but the terms and conditions must be set by the Chinese.

On 23 October, 1984, Jiang Ping conveyed to the Tibetan delegates the Chinese official views on what they considered legitimate issues: the Central Committee welcomes the Dalai Lama's return either to settle permanently, or as a visit to China. It acknowledged that Sino-Tibetan dialogue over the years has promoted mutual understanding. Although there are differences of opinion on certain issues, such differences will not be an obstacle to further visits and exchange of opinion. With regard to the Dalai Lama's status upon his return, Jiang reiterated Hu Yaobang's Five-Point Proposal made to GyaloThondup in 1981 and in a subsequent interview with a Japanese reporter. Hu stated that the Dalai Lama's status as a religious figure, as a member of the nobility and as a popular historical character of Tibet will be guaranteed; and if he proves himself to be a Chinese patriot, the Dalai Lama will enjoy equal or similar status as the Panchen Lama.

Jiang Ping went to great lengths to elaborate and "prove" that (1) Tibet has been an inseparable part of China since the Seventh century AD and that the Tibetan Exiles must accept that premise, (2) Due to the vastness of the area, there would be no benefits for economic and cultural developments if Kham and Amdo were united with the Tibet Autonomous Region. Unless the demand for a greater Tibetan autonomous region is dropped, "we cannot have negotiations."

On 24 October, 1984 the same Tibetan delegation conveyed their views on various subjects to Jiang Ping, Deputy Director of the CCP Central Committee, United Front Department in Peking. They referred to the Resolution of the First All-China Congress of Soviets on the Question of National Minorities (November 1931) to the effect that the Chinese Communist Party "categorically and unconditionally recognizes the right of national minorities to self-determination."

There could not have been a wider chasm between the perceptions of the two negotiating parties. This is illustrated by the fact that though Deng accepted the Tibetan suggestion that fifty Tibetan teachers (Buddhists[6]) from India would be permitted to teach in various parts of Tibet, it could not materialize since the Chinese insisted that they travel on Chinese passports.

The Chinese proposals simply reduced the question of Tibet to that of the personal status of the Dalai Lama. Should such bait be accepted by the Dalai Lama, there would be no hope for the Tibetans. However, misjudge as they did the personality of the Dalai Lama, they were right in believing that if they can win over the Dalai Lama, the Tibetans inside Tibet and in Exile would most certainly accept the solution.

It appears that a golden opportunity offered by Deng was missed. The approach of the Dalai Lama can be well-understood by the treacherous past of the communists. The Chinese saw the mistrust and, entrenched as they were in their secured position of occupation, they warned the Dalai Lama "to stop beating-around-the-bush and look for a better and better bargain". They rejected the Dalai Lama's offer of a visit in 1985. The golden period of hope or the silver-lining to the black clouds had vanished.

In the face of this impasse, strategic developments happened in Europe. The Berlin wall was broken down leading to the eventual reunification of the two Germanys. There was collapse of the Soviet Union and the smaller nations of the Eastern Europe underwent upheaval. The culminating event on the Chinese scene was the student demonstrations at Tiananmen Square.

The developments in the Chinese communist party were also alarming. The liberal leaders were losing their power and in January 1987, Hu Yaobang was removed as the Secretary General of the party. He made a speech admitting his mistakes and resigned thereafter. This was a well-rehearsed method for the dismissal of any functionary. Hu Yaobang was indeed dismissed. With this development the soft line towards the dialogue with the Dalai Lama ended. It can also be said that there was no other person interested in facing the problem of Tibet head-on.

Nothing of material consequence emerged from the proceedings of the Second Work Forum in 1984 for a Tibet dialogue. It spared those party cadres who had been responsible for various crimes during the Cultural Revolution. This gave a direct message to the party cadres that as long as they are loyal they can get away with anything. And so the new policy was interpreted in simple terms, "to get rich as soon as possible". However it opened the floodgates of population transfer. The Chinese government wanted tc open Tibet to be a showcase now and poured money in to build show pieces like a sports stadium and a five-star hotel. All this had dire consequences for the Tibetans.

At this time the Western culture had taken great fancy about moral and ethical concerns. The issues such as human rights, preserving the environment and ecological safeguards *vis-à-vis* developments, the rights of minority people as well as the fear of a global holocaust as a result of nuclear catastrophe were the popular concerns of the masses. Tibet, of course, had over 2000 years old civilization which stood for these values. And canvassing popular support from this platform for Tibet were the Dalai Lama's many "influential wealthy friends" as the Chinese described them.

Petra Kelly a popular Germany Green Party leader was the first one to ask a question in German parliament in 1987 to define position on the Tibetan issues. This generated further interest in the Tibetan cause in Germany. So, to counter that in July 1987, Chancellor Helmut Kohl was invited by China. Simultaneously, Chinese invited former US President Jimmy Carter. To counter the European Parliament, a delegation from European Union was also ferried around. There access was restricted and of course, they did lodge a protest. The visits did produce a tangible result. The Chinese reiterated that the Five-Point Proposal made in 1981 was still open.

As coincidentally it happened, September 1987 was the first time that we had our audience with the Dalai Lama. We had approached him to seek his guidance in studies on consciousness[7]. Our own sensibilities regarding Tibetan issue were not focused at that time. During our college days, as was the mood of the youth in the emergent India, we had viewed the communist overtake of Tibet as a step towards modernization. As little was known about the atrocities behind the bamboo curtain, we had perceived the displacing of the Lamaist State as a stop to the exploitation of the ignorant masses.

We met the Dalai Lama on 6th September, 1987. We were a bit surprised that during such an esoteric discussion the Dalai Lama spoke about himself, "simply as a Buddhist monk", "one of the main purpose of his life mission is to engage into ensuring welfare of the Tibetan people." He left Dharmashala on 7th September, 1987 for his proposed visit to the United States. There he was to make a historic announcement at the US Congress. This became a watershed.

From 1987 till 1989 there were sporadic but repeated anti Chinese demonstrations in Tibet. This culminated on 5th of March, 1989 into the largest anti-Chinese agitation since 1959. There were riots for three days and the police fought street battles with the Tibetans. During the three days about 75 to 750 Tibetans were killed.The Chinese imposed martial law throughout Tibet on March 8.

The Chinese have claimed that there has been a decrease in the political activity ever since and the number of the political prisoners is on decline. Interpreting the decline[8], as well as its short and long term implications, one must take into account diverse factors. One is the constraining effect of vigorous political and religious repression deployed; it reached a peak in 1995-96.

In February 1997, Deng Xiaoping died. He was succeeded by Jiang Zemin as the chief of the Communist Party. Li Peng became the Prime Minister. However, the latter is better known as the strong advocate of authoritarianism. He had ordered the roll over of tanks on the squatting students in Tiananmen Square. The hope that there may be a softer policy towards reconciliation with Tibet ended.

Chen Kuiyuan was appointed communist party leader of Tibet. The *New York Times* scooped out a confidential speech where in Chen Kuiyuan declared that separatist activities are rampant in Lhasa and some other parts of Tibet. "We must absolutely clean up those places and sweep out hostile elements. Chinese troops have occasionally fired on crowds of pro-independence demonstrators, but the use of force appears to have antagonized even some Tibetans who serve in the local government. Some local cadres can't tell right from wrong, and they are blind to hostile elements who use the cloak of religion to engage in counter revolutionary activities." Mr. Chen declared, "Some party members do not fully reveal their roles in the struggle against separatism. They stand against the party and the people. While purporting to be party members and cadres, they act as internal agents for the Dalai Lama clique. They harm our nation's unity and betray the people." While Mr. Chen did not specifically say that the United States of America were using the Dalai Lama to subvert China, he seemed to suggest as much when he warned against surrendering to imperialism. "Enemy forces will unceasingly infiltrate and attack us, using the Dalai Lama as a banner of separatism and, as a banner of anti-Communism and, anti-Socialism," Mr. Chen warned. "We can't avoid this reality. We can only respond blow for blow. If we retreat, then separatism will spread like a malignant tumor."

He called for a purge of those officials who do not take a tough stance against the Dalai Lama. There have been regular practices at re-education of the Tibetans. Anyone returning from abroad is suspect. In 1997, Tsultrim was arrested following his return from India when it was known that he had made a pilgrimage to Dharamshala and sought the blessings of the

Dalai Lama. When the pictures of the Dalai Lama and the Panchen Rinpoche were found in his possession as well as some other co-habitants, all of them were expelled from the monastery.

Prisoners began decreasing after 1996 as political re-education campaigns spread throughout Tibetan areas. A second factor is the deterrent posed by severe physical abuse, including beating and torture that included electric shocks, meted out to political detainees during investigation and ensuing years of imprisonment. The pace of economic change, particularly in non-farming activity, is the third influence. Officials advocate the pragmatism of pursuing better living standards rather than risking the crushing effects of protest. A fourth element could be the appeal to Tibetans of undertakings that bolster Tibetan language, culture, religion and self-identity.

Let us see what can call for political imprisonment. Even carrying a photograph of the Dalai Lama is treason. It calls for imprisonment for three years! Same is the fate of those who shout a slogan like Tibet is independent. Penpa Tsering, who called himself a political prisoner (we called him a freedom fighter), was our guest in December 2005. And this is what he has to tell:

"Of 1,900 cases of Tibetan political imprisonment since 1987, 41 have resulted in death as the direct consequence of severe maltreatment; political detention has proven fatal at the rate of 1 in 46. The most pronounced risk is at the TAR Prison Number One (Drapchi) where the rate of deaths for political prisoners has been one in 28. Female political prisoners at Drapchi have faced the highest level of threat — one in 24 has died. Extreme abuse has caused the death. Currently 105 political prisoners remaining at Drapchi have an average sentence of 11 years; one-third of their sentences have been extended for further political protest while imprisoned.

Drapchi prison is situated in wilderness. If a prisoner was to make escape, he is most likely to be eaten up by wild animals; unable to find a way, some of the escaped prisoners choose to return!"

Based on TIN (Tibet Information Network) data, 42 per cent of all Tibetan political detainees were sentenced by a court to imprisonment, generally for "counterrevolution" until 1997 and for "endangering state security" thereafter. Sixteen per cent were ordered to serve administrative detention. The portion of current political prisoners, serving judicial sentences, has risen to 73 per cent as long-serving inmates accumulate and fewer new political detentions occur. Five per cent of current prisoners are serving administrative sentences averaging two years ten months.

Political detention of Tibetans[9] has become more widely dispersed though the numbers have declined. In the period, 1987-1995, detentions of TAR residents (more than 1,300) accounted for 91 per cent of the total. Lhasa prefecture alone accounted for 71 per cent. Only nine per cent resided outside TAR. But from 1996-2001, even though there were fewer detentions altogether (more than 500), TAR portion fell to 64 per cent, Lhasa fell to 39 per cent, and non-TAR portion rose to 36 per cent.

The numbers of people executed worldwide make an interesting comparison. Capital punishment is considered not civilized by the European Union. Portugal, a country with a long history of dictatorial regime also abolished capital punishment and would not entertain a request from India for repatriation till the Indian Government gave an assurance that the underworld don would not be punished with capital execution.

The capital punishment figures for 2004 are:

China	3,400
Iran	159
Vietnam	64
US	59
Rest	215
Total	3,797

We requested information from the Chinese Embassy in New Delhi. The Chinese position as stated by Fan Mingxing, the secretary at the Chinese embassy in New Delhi, is that there has been a tremendous progress in human rights situation in Tibetan Autonomous Region of People's Republic of China. This is in comparison with what was the situation during the previous regime of the Dalai Lama. The reforms carried out in 1959 ended a feudal serf system.

He said that the chairman of the standing committee of the Tibet Autonomous Region Congress of the people as well as the Chairman of the TAR are both Tibetans and there are numerous Tibetans at various levels of hierarchy. This includes judiciary too. Crime and imprisonment rates in TAR are lower than the national average. Following liberation there are more than ten thousand literary figures and artists. Tibetan artists are encouraged to visit foreign countries including USA, England, France, Germany, etc. There is modernization of medical and health care. This is free for the working groups. The emphasis is on the care of women and children.

He argues that "the Dalai clique" is shouting loud about the extinction of Tibetan culture. Cultural development is an ongoing process dependent upon the modernization through social change. Tibetan culture was monopolized by few aristocrats and there was autocracy by the religious leaders. Without the extinction of such a culture there could not have been real emancipation of the serf. *It is appropriate that such culture should be made extinct* (Italics by the authors). The Dalai clique is unhappy because the modernization has eliminated their hold.

According to him there is tremendous difference between old Tibet and modern Tibet as far as human rights situation is concerned. During the rule of the Dalai Lama, human rights were wantonly trampled upon. There was a savage and cruel system. He said that the Dalai Lama is trying every means to fabricate sensational lies. Since a Buddhist should not lie, he is violating a fundamental commandment so as to split the motherland.

Mr. Fan Mingxing was categorical that the "ownership" of Tibet vested with the People's Republic of China. To support his assertion he had one quote, a telegram by the Dalai Lama to Mao Zedong: "On the basis of friendship, delegations of the two sides signed on 23rd May, 1951 the agreement on measures for peaceful liberation of Tibet. The Seventeen-Point Agreement is of great and unrivalled benefit to the cause of the Dalai and to Buddhism, politics, economy and other aspects of life in Tibet... the Tibetan local government as well as ecclesiastic and secular people unanimously support this agreement and under the leadership of Chairman Mao and the Central People's Government will actively assist PLA troupes in unification of the territory and the sovereignty of the motherland."

Detailing enormous inputs of capital through the 8th and the 10th Five-Year Programmes for the economic development of Tibet, he is confident that Tibet's relationship with other provinces and the Central Government are in the best of terms and no plot to split China will ever succeed.

The Dalai Lama is hamstrung by his commitment to a Code of Ethics. He is committed to what he has said. But he knows that he has already given a gigantic concession to the Chinese that is in contradiction with his earlier demands for total independence and he is also aware that the large section of the Tibetan youth want nothing short of independence.

Nothing short of a revolution can cause metamorphosis of colonized Tibet to independent Tibet. There is no fixed recipe for revolution. And, a silent revolution is a welcome change but it also happens. Throughout the history of struggles for independence, the freedom fighter is treading a path everyday, where he is on the edge of violating law. It is a plain and simple fact that freedom is not won by law suits in a court of law. Comparing to the freedom struggle of India, Gopal Krishna Gokhale and Bal Gangadhar Tilak had fought legal battles. Gandhi had realized the futility of this course and when charged with sedition because he was printing literatures against the British, he had said to the judge that if the judge cared for the tradition for patriotism and love for his own nation, then only he will appreciate Gandhi's stand. And then he would be compelled by his moral conscience rather to resign than punish.

What triggers off the mass upsurge in the collective consciousness of a people is unpredictable and difficult to decipher. What were the psychodynamics of the masses on 10th March, 1959, or the German people that gathered to break the Berlin wall, or all the Polish people who veered around Lech Varela, or Russian people who pulled down the statue of Lenin? What caused a massive across the nations upheaval that uprooted many dictators and caused change of regime in Arab countries in 2011? The collapse of the communists rule in China may not have a written recipe for a future revolution. But it may mimic memorable, noble examples of how revolutions happen.

It is not denied that behind such happenings there is a backdrop of strategic political engineering. Without the covert backing from the Polish Pope and his collusion with the American President Richard Nixon, Communist Government could not have been overthrown in Poland. Without the earnest and total commitment of Gorbachev to *Perestroika,* the monolithic Union of Soviet Socialist Republic could not have collapsed.

But when there is a wave of upsurge a leader is needed to ride over. When the Communist party bosses rolled the tanks in the streets of Moscow, it required a courageous leader like Yeltsin to run and mount over an armoured tank. Nelson Mandela spent over two decades in South African prison. Lech Valecha and Havell, the Czechoslovakian President, could have been killed during revolutions in their countries. They decided to take the risk and plunged.

The Dalai Lama has no carrot to wield. However, there is an alternative course to make the goat move. Wielding of the stick is not a non-violent tool. Therefore, there is no question that the Dalai Lama would support a terrorists' squad as Bin Laden did. But some of the Tibetans have already started defying him. And when he is no more, can the Chinese rest assured that there shall never be a terrorist attack on the Hall of People in Beijing.

However, Chinese politicians remark that there is no need to negotiate. The Dalai Lama is already old and at the most will last 10-30 more years. With his demise will disappear "the Dalai clique" and all their supporters.

Twenty-first century is a unipolar world. Number one concern of the United States is to remain number one in the world. Consumerism is the ideology of the affluent American society. Liberty, equality and fraternity are the echoes of the Twentieth century. The imperialism is threatened to disappear from the world map. President Roosevelt's idealism and sympathy for the independence of all the nations was a matter of idealist peak in the post Second World War time. Today a large mass of Western intelligentsia is keenly aware about fundamental human rights. Which politician in the world would subscribe to the enforcement of these rights forcefully at global scale? China's retort is clear. They say "human rights situation in Tibet is the same as all-over China. Which country would put up with subversive activities that can split the motherland? And again, if you wish to negotiate, let us negotiate" (and negotiate endlessly!).

Not only in Tibet but all-over world history, the time to the succession of the supreme authority has always been a period of turbulence and turmoil with tragic consequences. Even China is no exception. The Dalai Lama at the present juncture has already laid a solid foundation by relinquishing his sovereignty and handing over the reins to a democratic system. China, bent upon counting the remaining years of the Dalai Lama's life has declared that they will decide the next Dalai Lama! It sure is in consonance with political wisdom and astute statesmanship except that communists should answer as to when did they come to believe in the superstition of reincarnation?

Going back to the Dalai Lama, there is always a scope for a non-violent stick. Mahatma Gandhi used it in the form of Dandi March in 1930. In a different way Jinnah used it in 1944 by extorting the people in the streets of Calcutta for Direct Action. Mahatma Gandhi too believed in trusting the adversary till he got tired of their contrivances to divide and rule, so that finally he had to give a call in 1942 for Quit India movement. No such option is available for the Dalai Lama.

Apart from the local population at Dharmashala[10], there is sharp criticism from small scholarly minority in India. China has also utilized lobbying with them. This was evident when N. Ram, the Editor of *Hindu* wrote a supplement of full 36 pages following his visit to China. The arguments of such scholars are based on pure materialist logic· they have no need to dabble in morals or virtues. They argue that the most outstanding irritant in India-China relationship today is the Dalai Lama and the Tibetan Government in Exile. Ram advocates that India should expel the Central Tibetan Administration from Indian soil and this single step will be a leap forward for a grand alliance between India and China.

There was a lull in negotiations. Chinese shut the shutters till, under pressure from the world opinion, there was resumption of the dialogue. The seventh round of talks was held on 1 and 2 July, 2008. And, the eighth followed within months raising hopes. Tibetan delegations have so far been discreet; secrecy in the diplomatic parleys was observed. Their press notes made vague statements like "Positive talks" etc. On their side, Chinese true to their inimical style of doing what suits their interests best, have been issuing public statements with thorough distortion of negotiations. This has beguiled even Western statesmen. Tibetans learnt, at last. Not only they gave a written submission, they made it public too. Salient points of the memorandum were:

Tibet Demands are within the Constituion of PRC

Of late, the Chinese policy has been to invite such foreigners who would carry out the Chinese propaganda on their behalf because, "when they do so for us that is more powerful than if we do it."

So, it appears that with failure of the 9th round of negotiation also, options to negotiate are exhausted. Both sides accept a dead lock in 2011. This was evident from the statement by Lodi Gyari as:

I see it more as a spiritual practice than an exercise in diplomacy. Let me explain this.

I remember very vividly that in 1987, when His Holiness first presented the "Middle Way Approach" in a formal document, he consulted a few people outside of the Tibetan leadership. One of them was former President Carter. His Holiness has a lot of respect for President Carter, not because he had been the US President, but because His Holiness believes he is very wise and religious minded.

There is no doubt that the synergy between India and China has immense potential. When Nehru signed the Panchsheel Treaty, about 50 years ago, he was probably guided by such a grandiose vision. It may be said that he was ahead of his times and did not see the stark difference of China-India mindset and systems. Today, in a radically different world where the economy of communist China is also driven by free market forces, the equations have changed. Thomas Fredman, the author of *The World Is Flat: A brief history of 21st century,* writes:

> "When I was growing up my parents used to say to me, 'Tom, finish your dinner – people in China are starving'. But I am now telling my daughters, 'Girls finish your homework – people in China and India are starving for your jobs'."

He goes on to further predict that in co-operation between India and China, there lies a tale of technology and geo-economics that is fundamentally reshaping our lives much more quickly than many people realized. Historically, according to him, this is the new era of third globalization. The first era started in Fifteenth century, the second began with the industrial revolution. The comparison itself is significant.

The new equation is the omission of "or" between China and India. It is not even the addition of hyphenation between China and India. A new reality which is much more in terms of economics rather than politics has emerged. That is CHINDIA. If these two Asian giants were to leave aside their political differences the synergies in terms of economy will so emerge that even Bill Gates feels a threat. He said, "When I compare our high school to what I see abroad I am terrified for our workforce for tomorrow. In 2001, India graduated almost a million more students than the US did. China graduates twice as many students with bachelor's degree as the US. And they have six times as many graduates in engineering. In the international competition to have the biggest and the best supply of knowledge workers, America is falling behind."

In 1991 when Li Peng visited India, hundreds of Tibetan youths were rounded up in New Delhi before his arrival. The Dalai Lama had to appeal to TYC workers for peace. And the Government of India took the discourteous step of asking the Dalai Lama too, to leave New Delhi, as if his very presence in New Delhi would pollute the air. In a short span of less than 15 years the drastic change in equations is evident by the fact that in 2005 the Chinese Premier, Wen Jiabao, flew straight to Bangalore rather than New Delhi! Did not the President Clinton do the same? However, one feature remained constant. In Bangalore, it was a single Tenzin Tsundue who managed to protest!

The emergence of a possibility of synergy between the two most populous nations of the world is creating apprehension in the Western minds. That is why Lee Kuan Yew the former Prime Minister of Singapore has predicted that CHINDIA will spread renaissance across Asia. They will shake the world.

The Dalai Lama has said again and again: "If the six million Tibetans in Tibet are really happy and prosperous as never before, there is no reason for us to argue otherwise."[4] He has explained that "the main reason why we are in exile is the welfare of the six million Tibetans."

He had interacted with several Chinese to say, "Chinese students have given me great hope for the future of China and Tibet. I feel that their movement follows the tradition of Mahatma Gandhi's *ahimsa* or non-violence which has deeply inspired me ever since I was a small boy. The eventual success of all people seeking a more tolerant atmosphere must derive from a commitment to counter hatred and violence with patience. We must seek change through dialogue and trust. It is my heartfelt prayer that Tibet's plight may be resolved in such a manner and that once again my country, the Roof of the World, may serve as a sanctuary of peace and a resource of spiritual inspiration at the heart of Asia."

Reverting back to the process of dialogue, the year 2008 has been critical. Olympics were held. There were widespread violence in Tibet. They should be called mini-revolts in fact. Question about the wisdom in pursuing the middle way were being raised. The Dalai Lama on 10th March, 2008, referring to the failure of negotiations said that there has been a brutal crackdown on the Tibetan protests that have shaken the whole of Tibet since March last year. Therefore, as to what future course of action we should take, the Special Meeting of Tibetan exiles was convened in November 2008. (This was a referendum without labelling it so). Efforts were made to collect suggestions, as far as possible, from the Tibetans in Tibet as well. The outcome of this whole process was that a majority of Tibetans strongly supported the continuation of the Middle-Way policy.

Pursuing this policy explicitly, at the Eighth round of negotiations, Tibetan aspirations were catalogued as:

- Decision-making and on the operation of the system of autonomy.
- Scientific development happens without the people losing their Tibetan identity, culture and core values and without putting the distinct and fragile environment at risk.
- The Central Government to recognise and fully respect the integrity of the Tibetan nationality and its right to exercise genuine autonomy within the PRC.
- Subject Matters of Self-government would be
    1. Language
    2. Culture
    3. Religion
    4. Education
    5. Environmental Protection
    6. Utilisation of Natural Resources
    7. Economic Development and Trade
    8. Public Health
    9. Public Security
    10. Regulation on Population Migration
    11. Cultural, educational and religious exchanges with other countries.

- The integrity of the Tibetan nationality must be respected. The entire community, comprising all the areas currently designated by the PRC as Tibetan autonomous areas, should be under one single administrative entity fragmentation and disregards the spirit of autonomy.
- The right of Tibetans to create their own regional government and government institutions and processes.

This was in complete consonance with various remarks by Lodi Gyaltsen Gyari. At the Brookings Institution, Washington, D.C on November 14, 2006 titled Seeking Unity Through Equality. Gyari has dwelved on the theme time. And again as[11]: His Holiness has made the offer to go personally to China on a pilgrimage. This has met with considerable opposition from Tibetans, both inside and outside Tibet, as well as from friends in **March 2007** — Mr. Gyari said that if there is political will, we have an opportunity to finally resolve this issue." **May 8, 2008** — Chinese President and Party Secretary Hu Jintao said "our attitude towards contacts and consultation with the Dalai Lama is serious". In **June 2008**:'While the Chinese side finally seems to have realized that their allegations against His Holiness for instigating the recent events in Tibet and in sabotaging the Olympics Games have become untenable, they are now urging His Holiness not to support violence, terrorism, and sabotaging the Olympics. While the Tibetan Youth Congress does not support the Middle Way Approach and stands for independence of Tibet, we categorically rejected the Chinese attempt to label it as a violent and terrorist organization.

Tibet was in focus world over by now. An opinion poll of people from several countries revealed.

Poll of Western and Asian Publics Finds Criticism of Chinese Policy on Tibet

After a lapse of 15 months a three-point message was conveyed to the Chinese leadership at the Ninth Round. By this time, Tibetans have understood the virtue of brevity and clarity through dots. They said:

Firstly, the seven points in the Note include respecting sovereignty and territorial integrity of the PRC, respecting the Constitution of the PRC, respecting the "Three Adherences," respecting the hierarchy and authority of the Chinese Central Government.

It was suggested that through consultation if some of the issues in the Memorandum that are easier to be implemented are taken up in stages, it would certainly help in the gradual implementation of the basic issues.

Secondly, ...sole concern is the wellbeing of the six million Tibetans in Tibet....no personal issues of His Holiness the Dalai Lama or the welfare of the few people around him. Our perception is that most of the Tibetans are in a situation where they face limitless suffering and where they do not have a satisfactory religious, political, economic, language and culture, and social situation.

The Chinese response was that Tibetans are happy and in satisfactory situation, and there is no Tibetan issue.

Thirdly, we had rejected the allegation that His Holiness the Dalai Lama and the leadership in exile have instigated the demonstrations throughout the Tibetan areas since March 10. The Central Government should rectify and halt the levelling of these allegations.

We will be studying the proceedings of the Fifth Tibet Work Forum and the "Four Not to Indulge In" points.

Obviously the talks have yielded all that the Chinese may have wanted: probably even more. Chinese have played according to the rules of diplomacy[12]: lies and counter lies. When it comes to any kind of deal, where one is involved in exchange of any kind of goods or value, caution of necessity comes in. Since Plutonian times ruse, greed, cheating, treachery, deceit and such other craft to beguile the adversary is as common in the world as the air that surrounds us.

There was no barter: complete transparency, honesty, earnestness and vulnerability are obvious on Tibetan side. Walking more than half way, almost up to the feet of the Chinese, they have yielded on most positions that were preciously held. Chinese have not conceded on a single point; not even to implement 17-Point Agreement in letter and spirit.

Would virtues win? In that case, only Gods would have ruled on the earth. However, if Naure has so designed that even the Weakest should survive, there is all the hope for Tibet.

China's Policy on Tibet

Critics of China say that it should allow Tibet to have autonomy, to preserve its traditional culture and to allow the Dalai Lama to return to Tibet.

China says that Tibet has long been part of China, that Tibet has benefited from modernization, and that the Dalai Lama should not be allowed to return because he aims to split Tibet from China.

Is your view closer to the critcs' view or China's view?

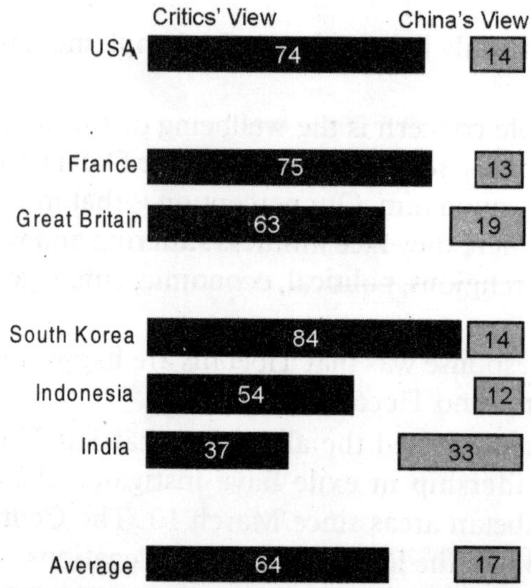

Fig. 11.1: Anniversary of the Tibetan National Uprising Day, Nations, Central Tibetan Administration, Dharmashala. and Prospects. Policy Studies No. 12, East-West Center, USA; Fourth Work Forum on Tibet in 2001 "that rapprochement region of the India subcontinent.

REFERENCES

1. British Foreign Office No. 371-76317.
2. Shiromany, A.A., *The Political Philosophy of His Holiness the XIV Dalai Lama*, New Delhi, 1998.
3. Apart from the main settlement in India, several Western nations accepted a few of them. They and their children through modern education were to turn ambassadors and activists of the twenty-first century. Tsering Shakya, British historian and Lhadun Tethong, Canadian activist are visible examples. The Chinese were surprised that the second delegation in 1980 composed of Westernized Tibetans in their thirties; and yet they had profound faith in religion. The displaced lamas established monasteries that dispensed effective prescriptions for enduring and alleviating stress.
4. Soon after the Dalai Lama's escape from Tibet, Tenzin Tethong had come across a Canadian school teacher in India. Afterwards, the couple migrated with their children to Canada. Lhadun Tethong is an activist daughter in the service of Tibet at Students for Free Tibet.
5. *Tibet Bulletin*, Vol. 12, p. 8, 1980.
6. This was welcomed even by the Pope since he believed that the religious influence will generate further goodwill.
7. Cf. with Marxist concept of consciousness in the Ch. Happenngs.
8. "The exercise by citizens of the People's Republic of China of their freedoms and rights may not infringe upon the interests of the state..." Constitution of the People's Republic of China, Article 51. "We must deal with hostile elements

with the iron fist of the people's democratic dictatorship" — an unnamed Party official speaking on Lhasa TV on the eve of the lifting of Martial Law in Lhasa (30 April 1990).

9. According to TIN data the number of current Tibetan political prisoners, (February 2002) has declined to 188. Prisoners being released after completing their sentences outnumber by a wide margin instances of new political detention. The current level is in comparison to nearly 700 then — reported in *Cutting Off the Serpent's Head* in 1996 (TIN and Human Rights Watch Asia), 538 listed in *Hostile Elements* in 1999 and 266 in *Suppressing Dissent* in 2001. Buddhist monks and nuns make up 74 per cent of prisoners.
10. There are a select few who are annoyed by the Tibetan presence in India. First to experience the discomfort were the villagers of Dharmashala region. With the pouring in of Western tourists to Dharmashala, and envying the lifestyle of some of the "affluent", the living standard has gone up. The prices have soared. Scanty meat has become scantier since Tibetans are non-vegetarian. This has brought the local population in conflict with the Exiled Tibetans. While the ordinary taxi-driver is aware that his livelihood is very much dependent on the influx of the tourists because of the presence of the Dalai Lama, he is more worried about the market prices.
    This simmering hostility emerged into large scale violence. Some shops were burnt, There were slogans against the Dalai Lama. Deeply disturbed by these events, in 2001, the Dalai Lama wrote to the Government of India that he will shift to New Delhi. This he said publicly too. It had an immediate cooling down of the tensions. The officials of the district administration met the Dalai Lama to personally request him to reverse his decision. There afterwards, the Government of Himachal Pradesh also actively participates in cultural events of the Exiled community.
11. *The Statement of His Holiness the Dalai Lama on the 47th Anniversary of the Tibetan National Uprising Day,* March 10, 2006, Department of Information & International Relations, Central Tibetan Administration, Dharamshala.
    Rabgye, Sharlho. *Sino-Tibetan Dialogue in the Post-Mao Era: Lessons and Prospects.* Policy Studies No. 12, East-West Center, USA; 2004. p. 29. It refers to Beijing University academics' presentation at the Fourth Work Forum on Tibet in 2001 "that rapprochement with the Dalai Lama would reduce China's strategic risks in the volatile region of the Indian subcontinent."
12. "A diplomat is one who *lies* for the sake of his country..."

12
Sino-Tibet Pugnacious Situations

I. Panchen Lama: Punishment without Crime

The Dalai Lamas has spiritual as well as temporal authority over Tibet. There are two other reincarnated spiritual authorities who have no political power. However, the religious influence of all three is equally great and originated from their respective monasteries. Three of them are the three jewels in the Tibetan National Flag. Traditionally, however, Panchen Lama is respected as being the *guru* of the Dalai Lama.

It is elementary justice that nobody can be punished for a particular crime twice. But the Chinese have a different code of justice. If we describe the Chinese treatment of Tibetans as punishment without crime, and if we subscribe to reincarnation, Panchen Lama is punished twice without any crime. Dostoevsky will have another novel to write! The cruelty of the punishment is aptly portrayed by the picture of the Panchen Lama undergoing struggle sessions and, by viewing the innocence of the youngest political — the kidnapped child — that is still in Chinese possession.

While the Dalai Lama escaped to India, Panchen Rinpoche continued to be in China. During Cultural Revolution, he was purged of his position and imprisoned. Before this happened he has been campaigning about Tibetan interests with the Chinese. However in order that brutal action can be justified in the eyes of the Tibetans, the communists were aware that he has to be discredited and humiliated in the eyes of the people. He had a harrowing experience from then onwards till his death.

Initially, Panchen Rinpoche also tried to co-operate with the Chinese. After the escape of the Dalai Lama, he declared his loyalty and, was promoted to the party position that the Dalai Lama occupied. Several speeches and actions of the Panchen Lama point that he tried hard to remain loyal. How much of this was motivated from the personal rivalry between the two monasteries. Whether it was Panchen Lama's personal ambition or his own helplessness and compulsions of a captive, shall never be known. It is a matter of history that subsequently Panchen Lama was publicly humiliated, beaten and had a broken arm at his last public appearance. He unfurled a portrait of the Dalai Lama that time.

When the Tibetans continued to suffer in various campaigns to change their mindset to communism, in 1962, much against the advice of others including Ngabo, Panchen Rinpoche submitted 70,000 character petition to Chou En-lai. This we have seen before. He used strong language and did not mince words to describe Chinese atrocities. He became a pariah thereafter and was kept away from the party activities till he was labelled as a reactionary, was accused of planning a rebellion and imprisoned. He was released in March 1978 and was restored to his position.

If any of the events in Tibet had to be judged, what happened to Panchen Lama should be kept in mind. Maybe, such a possibility weighed heavily and had a bearing on the actions of the Dalai Lama and his troupe that planned his escape. One would be thankful for that diplomatic manoeuvre that bought precious time. This tact has gifted the mankind with the repertoire of half a century of experiments with truth and non-violence that shall enrich the Twenty-first century civilization so that, we compare the happenings in Kuwait, Iran and Iraq with what is happening in Tibet.

Panchen Lama spent all his life in Tibet and China. There have been minimal contacts between him and the Dalai Lama after his Exile. On the other hand the tragic history about his seventy thousand character petition, the trial sessions, his imprisonment, subsequent public appearance with a broken arm and, his final unfurling of a *thanka* bearing the portrait of the Dalai Lama and, wishing him long life a few days before his death, would all have largely influenced the actions of the Dalai Lama. They surely have influenced the unwillingness of Tibetans in Exile as well as the Dalai Lama's own reluctance to deal directly and trust Chinese.

Panchen Lama's life is indeed a tragic experiment in terms of sincerity and earnestness to co-operate so that the interests and the welfare of the Tibetans may be looked after. It is also illustrative of the fact that the Middle Way approach in dealing with well determined oppressors does not succeed. To cap the sad story with melancholy, there is the story of the youngest political prisoner, reincarnated Panchen Lama.

Panchen Lama died in 1989. The Tibetan tradition required the identification and authentication of his reincarnation at Tashilhunpo Monastery. The Chinese very much needed a figure head that can be identified with Tibetans and yet be under their command. No sooner the funeral ceremonies for the deceased Panchen Lama were over, Chinese Premier, Li Peng announced that the selection of the new Panchen Lama is the Chinese prerogative. When he said that outsiders will not be allowed to meddle in it, he meant to convey that there was no role for the Dalai Lama.

This is a classical illustration of Chinese double-talk. The Marxism considers religion as the opium of the masses. It also sees its tremendous influence and so it wants to subvert the religion in such a way that their own wish is carried out. In 1989 there were massive anti-Chinese demonstrations in Lhasa and Martial law had to be enforced. It was argued that the Dalai Lama and the Government in Exile was behind the subversive activities. If any role is allowed by the Dalai Lama on the ground of spiritual tradition, it will also amount to giving him credibility. Therefore, the Chinese took the sole possession of search for the next Panchen Rinpoche. The contradiction is self-evident.

The monks at Tashilhunpo monastery were forced to accept a Middle Way approach much against their wish. They had also a face saving device to satisfy themselves that the Chinese Buddhist Association would be in-charge of the process without day-to-day interference. Chatral Rinpoche, who was thought to be under Chinese influence because he had studied in Beijing, was appointed as the head for the search party.

The Tibetan Buddhist tradition has an axiomatic role of the Dalai Lama in identifying reincarnated Panchen Lama. If he is excluded, the procedure would be null and void *ipso facto*. The high lamas from various provinces of China at a meeting in 1991 conveyed to Chatral Rinpoche that no candidate can be given final approval unless the Dalai Lama cleared the matter. Even if there was no agreement about the political status of the Dalai Lama, it was beyond any doubt that in matters of religion he has the last word. If this was not to be, how would the common Tibetan accept the new find?

When the tensions between Dharmashala and Beijing eased in 1993, Gyalo Dhundup visited China. The agenda included Panchen Lama too. Chatral Rinpoche officially met Gyalo Dhundup and gave him information regarding the search. So that the new find will have the approval of lamas from all parts of Tibet, Chatral Rinpoche announced that the Dalai Lama has been informed.

However, the controversy did not ease. The Chinese wanted the Dalai Lama to accede to their final authority and only endorse the proposal. The tradition vested final authority with the Dalai Lama. So the Dalai Lama unilaterally, exercising his religious authority, declared his choice. Once again, one wonders, did the Dalai Lama not anticipate what would happen?

For the Chinese to have accepted the Dalai Lama's verdict would have meant acceptance of his authority. It was alleged that there were secret contacts between the search party and Dharmashala. On the next day of announcement by the Dalai Lama, the boy Panchen Lama disappeared. His parents were also not to be found. For more than a year while the whole world believed that they must be in Chinese custody, there was no trace of them. Finally, the Chinese admitted to have kidnapped them.

The Chinese with the support of a few lamas conducted a further selection procedure. And in November 1995, they named a new boy as Panchen Lama who is now in Beijing under the Chinese eyes.

The Dalai Lama canvassed for the support of several leaders in Europe and in United States. Whether any of them believed in reincarnation and the religious procedures to identify, it was absurd by any civilized standards that such a young child and his parents can be in detention. There was strong pressure on China. A Child Committee was formed by European Union and they also intervened on behalf of the child.

So after a long silence, the Religious Affairs Office spokesman for China pointed out that "Dalai Lama violated traditional practice in reporting the reincarnation of the Panchen Lama abroad. That is illegal. As for the whereabouts of this boy, I would like to tell all of you here that due to the fact that there are some separatists and, the boy's parents consider that the boy is under some threat, therefore, the parents requested the government to ensure the protection of this boy.

"The government has acted in conformity with the request of the parents of this boy and given protection. I can tell all of you here that the boy lives with his parents and is in good condition."

The media were very tough and they expressed very strongly. They were not allowed to see the boy or meet his parents or relatives.

In the mean while, the matter gathered momentum in Europe. At Geneva, from 28th-30th May, 1996, the Twelfth session of the UN Committee on the Rights of the Child called the Chinese Government in connection with Chinese initial report on the child and, to answer 40 questions given to them by the Committee in January. The UN Committee was composed of 10 members from Egypt, Burkina Faso, Philippines, Sweden, Israel, Russian Federation, Barbados, Zimbabwe, Portugal and Brazil.

Chinese delegation of 14 members was lead by Wu Jianmin, Ambassador of China, and permanent mission in Geneva. The main question was about the controversy relating to recognition of the Panchen Lama. This was lengthily discussed during the meeting on 28th-29th May, 1996. The Chinese were asked to explain the controversy and provide information.

The Chinese Ambassador had this story to tell the Committee members for the Child at Geneva. "The titles of the Dalai Lama and Panchen Lama in Tibetan Buddhism were actually granted by Central Government in the Qing dynasty. The confirmation of Dalai Lama and Panchen Lama has always been subjected to the approval of Central Government. Since 200 years there has been the religious convention of drawing lots from Golden Urn. A search team is to find several candidates. and then in front of statue of Buddha, final candidate will be confirmed by drawing lots from a Golden Urn and, the selection must be confirmed by the Central Government. In the Urn there are various lots with names of boys, after spinning the urn one lot would fall. That lot carries the name of the boy who carries the title of Panchen Lama, but that still has to be approved by the Central Government.

"The reason that I mention all these stories is that an outsider might be quite ignorant. He might feel that the successors to the Panchen Lama need to be confirmed by the Dalai Lama (Laugh)! Even for Dalai Lama himself, the final title needs to be confirmed and approved by the Central Government. That is not something that has started from today; this system has been for 200 years. The Chinese government has acted strict in accordance with the religious rituals and conventions.

"If you are interested in this, we have a documentary film concerning the Panchen Lama. The identification of the soul-boy 10th Panchen Lama who passed away on the 10th January, 1989, was carried out exactly in accordance with the above conventions and rituals shortly afterwards. With the approval of the State Council, a search team made up of Living Buddhas, Khenpos and senior monks was set up in Tashilhunpo. By 1995, it had made remarkable progress. Precisely at this moment, the Dalai Lama illegally declared a boy as the reincarnated soul-boy of the Panchen Lama, thereby disrupting the normal search process.

"The Central Government thoroughly expelled the scheme of the Dalai Lama and restored the search to its correct path. On 29th November, 1995 State Council sent an official to host the ceremony and official confirmed that the boy chosen, Gyalsten Norbu, should be the 11th Panchen Lama. The installation ceremony was held on the 3rd December, 1995.

On behalf of the Committee members Mr. Hanunarberg (Swedish) commented, "I would like to make brief comment on the best interest of the child. Article 15 of the fundamental rights of children applies to this case. Frankly, I get the feeling that perhaps the full dimension of this article has not been fully appreciated by the Chinese authorities. This is the key principle in the convention. It is particularly relevant when there is a conflict between the interest of the child and other interests in the society."

If ever there were to be a political solution to Tibet, religion and religiosity of Tibetans will always remain a challenge and a threat. Will the religion wither away or the State, only history will answer. At least, none other than Mao was afraid of religion.

II. Escape of the Third Jewel: Jewel of an Escape

Three jewels in the Tibetan flag connote three high lamas, the Dalai Lama, Panchen Lama and Karmapa Lama. The First Karmapa: Dusum Khyenpa (1110-1193) was called "Dusum Khyenpa" — means Knower of the Three Times (Past, Present and Future), referring to the total lucidity he attained at enlightenment, giving him knowledge of three modes of time, and "timeless time" of enlightened awareness.

He was born to a family of devoted Buddhist practitioners in Tesho in East Tibet. Already quite learned by the age of twenty, he became a monk and spent the next twelve years or so engaging in study and meditation practices. His practice produced rapid results and great accomplishments, or *siddhis.* Such accomplishment is often perceived by followers as the ability to perform miraculous activity, and the legends of the Karmapas through the ages speak of their ability to create a great sense of wonder and faith. All the Karmapas have since been known for their ability to inspire this profound sense of wonder and faith.

The first Karmapa, Dusum Khyenpa, made predictions about future Karmapas. In particular, he was the first Karmapa to present a prediction letter, detailing his future incarnation. He gave it to his main disciple, Drogon Rechen, whom he chose to become the next lineage-holder. Successively, fifteen reincarnations were discovered.

The 17th Karmapa was an adolescent boy when he managed to repeat in December 2000 what the Dalai Lama had done in March 1959. How he managed to get off while he was right under the Chinese nose, shall ever remain a mystery. This is what he had to tell us at a specially arranged interview at Sidhbari.

When we approached him in early 2001, the security around him was very tight. One of the attending lamas took our camera. He looked at the snow peaked Dholadhar mountains from the window and, there goes a few exposures! Then we realized, only recently, Iranian Prime Minister was shot dead through the camera of an assassin! The Karmapa Lama said:

"On December 28, 1999, under the cover of a dark night, my senior attendant and I escaped from my monastery in Tibet and fled to India. The decision to leave my homeland, monastery, monks, parents, family, and the Tibetan people was entirely my own: no one told me to go and no one asked me to come.

"I left my country to impart the Buddha's teachings in general and, in particular, to receive the excellent empowerments, transmissions, and instructions of my own Karma Kagyu tradition. These I could only receive from the main disciples of the previous Karmapa, Situ Rinpoche and Gyaltsap Rinpoche, who were predicted to be my teachers and who reside in India.

"There have been various reports about my escape, and, so I will simply and briefly tell the truth. In great secrecy, my companions and I made our plans, using various stories to cover our true activities. For example, when the preparations were complete, I announced that I was entering a traditional, strict retreat and would not come out for some days. This story worked and prevented us from being pursued right away.

"On December 28, around 10:30 at night, my attendant and I slowly climbed down from my room and jumped on to the roof of the Protector Mahakala's shrine room. From this building, we leapt to the ground where a jeep was waiting nearby, with Lama Tsultrim and a driver. We left immediately. It was said that Lama Tsultrim and his companions were going on a journey. As if preparing for this, they had driven in and out of the monastery several times during the day; and therefore, everyone knew about this trip and we could easily leave. Usually, the monastery was strictly guarded and, we left through a side road.

"After a while, Lama Tsewang and another driver joined us at a designated place. We decided to head directly towards Western Tibet since few travellers used this road and the check posts were not so strictly guarded. Driving day and night, we stopped only to change drivers. By taking back roads through the hills and valleys, we avoided check posts and two army camps.

"I think it is through the power of my prayers to the Buddha and through his compassion, we were not discovered and arrived in Mustang, Nepal, on the morning of December 30,1999. Continuing the journey on foot and horseback, we crossed over several passes and finally reached Manang. This part was extremely difficult and exhausting due to the poor and often dangerous condition of the paths and the freezing cold weather. During this time, I was tired and not very well physically, yet despite the difficulties, I was completely determined to reach my goal.

"Once in Manang, a close friend of Lama Tsewang Tashi helped us hire a helicopter. We landed in Nepal at a place known as Nagarkot and then went by car to Rauxal. From there, we travelled by train to Lucknow and continued with a rented car to Delhi, arriving at last in Dharmashala early on the morning of January 5, 2001. I went straight to meet His Holiness the Dalai Lama, and he received me with his great love and affection. My joy knew no bounds.

"Ever since my arrival, the Dalai Lama has given his continual and generous assistance. Following his wishes, the Office of Religion and Culture from the Tibetan Government in Exile has made arrangements for my temporary stay at Gyuto Ramoche Tantric University. This was a source of great happiness for me.

"Pursuing my aim in fleeing Tibet, I am now receiving from Situ Rinpoche and Gyaltsap Rinpoche all the empowerments and transmissions of the Kagyu lineage. In this way, I am preparing for my life's work: to teach and study Buddhism and to encourage compassion and wisdom within the hearts of all beings.

"In 1959, my previous incarnation, H.H. the 16th Karmapa Rangjung Rigpe Dorje, was also forced to flee Tibet and come to India as a refugee. He settled in Sikkim and, with the assistance of the Central Government and the State Government of Sikkim, he was able to build the Dharmachakra Centre, Rumtek Monastery.

"I am fully confident that I will be able to go there since Sikkim is a state of India. I am also confident that just as my predecessor did, I will be able to travel abroad to meet my numerous disciples and fulfil their spiritual needs. With this end in mind, I have submitted an application to the proper authorities.

"In the past, the Gyalwa Karmapas did not engage in political activity and I can do nothing but follow in their footsteps. Concerning the future path of Tibet and the Tibetan people, I endorse and fully support everything that His Holiness the XIVth Dalai Lama stands for.

"The Indian Government has decided to grant us refugee status. With this new status, I was able to go on pilgrimage for five weeks, visiting major sites of Buddhism in the sacred land of India. In these places, I gave blessings and initiations according to the wishes of numerous disciples who came from near and far."

It is more than five years since then[1]. The Chinese dubbed it as motivated to grab the crown and enormous wealth that stays at the monastery in Sikkim. Karmapa has insisted that he is in India only for propagating Buddha *dharma.* He cannot have a political ambition as per the tradition. While the media were agog with the sensational news of the escape, it has not made any important contribution to the cause of Tibet so far on the political scene. A few years after, he will be the sole surviving high lama in exile. Who can foretell what his calling can be then!

III. Vajrayana: The Secret of Self Transformation

About 2500 years ago, Lord Buddha sat under the Bodhi tree practising severe penance. After 42 days of fasting, he pondered over the nature of ultimate reality. He attained enlightenment. But this pondering was not dialectical discursive play of thought. Instead, it was in the nature of inner reflection and contemplation. This process which begins in the mind and leads one to go beyond mind is what we call meditation today.

Through the meditative process Buddha came to understand the Four Noble Truths[2]. He also came to know the real nature of suffering. The Ultimate Nature of Reality manifested to him as *sunyata* (Void). While the universe has a beginning and end in the very nature of *sunyata*, all the phenomena come to be derived from it. That way, all the occurrences are interconnected and therefore, interdependent. An individual is also a natural phenomenon, therefore, all such occurrences all over the globe, are connected wholistically. This deductive logic, though easily understood by ordinarily intelligent persons, is not easily realized so that one can derive virtues from it. One has to change the paradigm from the discursive logic to an experience that can be generated only after an initiation. The initiation leads to the gateways of *Vajrayana.* The *Vajrayana* practice has pacified innumerable minds, drawn numerous pupils to Buddhism and generated controversies!

For every Buddhist, a logical understanding of the philosophical precepts is not enough. Buddhists are trained in dialectics so as to intelligently appreciate philosophy. However, the discursive thought bifurcated into two main streams. Hinyana Buddhism advocated *sadhana* towards the attainment of *nirvana* for oneself, so as to be liberated from the cyclic existence. Mahayana postulated that there are several layers of attainment. The one who has progressed higher should revert back so that he takes along the less enlightened with him. One should, therefore, of necessity strive to lessen the suffering of all fellow beings.

Vajrayana is full of techniques—*tantra*–that can lead to the attainment of above goals. Its practice generates *Bodhichitta,* a pure state of consciousness. Further it leads one to a state of *Bodhisattva.* A *Bodhisattva* reincarnates at will. This is for the betterment of the fellow beings. The Dalai Lama is one such *Bodhisattva*. It is, therefore, that he repeatedly sings,

> "As long as suffering lasts,
> And misery exists in this world;
> I shall be born again and again,
> To alleviate the suffering of my fellow beings."

Being the Dalai Lama, it is his duty to look after the temporal affairs of Tibetan people. But he is a reluctant politician. Spirituality and its practical dispensation to as many as possible, is his primary motivation. In the historic month of March 2005, he spent about three weeks in conducting *Vajrayana* initiations of different kinds. In January 2006, he spent nearly a fortnight at Amravati for *kalachakra initiation. Kalachakra initiation* is the ultimate instrument in *Sadhana.* There used to be total secrecy about it. Only a few were lucky to be so initiated. Till 1987, there were barely five Indians. The Dalai Lama, committed to openness and de-mystification, got the entire initiation published[3]. Now in December 2011-January 2012,. *Kalachakra initiation* is being offered *ad libidum* to all aspirants at Bodh Gaya. Last year it was offered in USA.

The motivation is to strive to accumulate good deeds. Freudians would call it a neurotic compensation for the subjugation that the Dalai Lama has to put up. For the Buddhists, motivation is paramount. We may reflect on a few *Vajrayana* practices.

As such, these meditative practices entailed a lot of secrecy. This caused a myth and mystique about them. The Dalai Lama believes in the spirit of openness, demystification and inquiry. Even the highest of v*ajra tantra, kalachakra* initiation is now available in printed form!

For all kinds of initiations, one has to leave one's ego. Interconnectedness and interdependence are appreciated only through a realization that no man is an island. So he has to take help from the enlightened ones, from recourse to *dharma,* and by seeking refuge in the collective consciousness/wisdom of the group. In *Guhyasamaja sadhana,* this is the first step. It is recited as an experience in the inner mind as:

"I go for refuge continually to the Buddhas in whose mind abides a mental play (realization of void) actualized in stages like the waxing of the stainless moon and infinite methods of pure compassion,

"I go for refuge continually to the holy *Dharma* which (as the Noble Truth of the Path) is the basis for total freedom from all misconceptions and, the foundation for the excellence of the holy beings, and which (as the Noble Truth of Cessation) the very nature (of void) is, the single test of all phenomena,

"I go for refuge to the hosts, Bodhisattvas, who are masters of discipline, who abide on the stages of progress. The masters are endowed with a glory of *Bodhichitta.* This is incited by supreme compassion. They became freed from the fetters as they progressed."

And following such a surrendering of will, there is a resolve that,

"I shall generate my mind into a pure *Bodhichitta*, adorned with a pure selfless wish, by application of which the instincts of all the obstacles can be removed."

Having arrived at a state of complete relaxation and having thrown all the worries to the wind, there is intense creative visualization[4, 5]. This is visualizing various forms of Buddha as well the feminine deity Tara. And one has to imbibe the qualitative virtues of these deities[6]. Further empowerment is derived by chanting of HUM and various other *sutras.* Before concluding, one takes refuge into Buddhas, such as *Akshobhya vajra, Vairochana, Ratnasambhava, Vajra Amitabha* and *Amoghasiddhi-vajra.*

The visualization ends by a resolve when one sees that 'by virtue of meditation, may I swiftly attain the state of *Vajradhara*, the nature of all the Buddhas, and may all beings attain it as well. May I practice both kinds of activities[7], those actions that are for becoming enlightened, as well as those being of a fully Enlightened Buddha. May there be no interference to my proper attainment of this marvelous path. And by spreading and causing it to flourish in all directions and times, may I free all beings by this skilful means.

The Dalai Lama is eager to scientifically explore the mechanism by which *Vajrayana* practices bring about a transformation. When we do not understand the psycho-cybernetics, we either call it a myth and discard it or call it a mystery and worship it. Science is a tool for the exploration of such phenomena. For the first time in the history of *Vajrayana* Buddhism, the Dalai Lama has made the entire gamut open to scientific scrutiny.

Relaxation techniques in general are stress alleviating. Several variants of relaxation technique include autogenic training, biofeedback, reflexology, self-hypnosis and transcendental meditation (TM) or meditation by any other name. These techniques convert the fight or flight response of stress to flow. The benefits accruing out of all the above techniques are both psychological and physiological. Spiritual is not mentioned specifically since it is not quantifiable. However, some psychologists claim to have evolved a method to gauge spiritual quotient too.

The benefits start accruing from the very beginning but get more potent over a period of time. At the psychological level, changes like acceptance of self, spontaneity, self regard, acceptance of aggression and capacity for intimate contact occur. The anxiety is decreased. Not only perceptual ability is enhanced but there is potent self actualization. At the physiological level, there is a marked decrease in oxygen consumption and elimination of carbon dioxide, indicating a lowering of metabolic rate. There is significant decrease in the rate of respiration and heart rate. There is a sharp increase in skin resistance. The blood pressure levels decline. The blood level of lactate, a parameter indicating the efficiency of metabolic process is also reduced.

There are changes in the electrical potentials of the brain too. At the beginning of the meditative process and just before coming out of it, there is a consistent production of alpha waves. It is so consistent that some think the generation of alpha activity as synonymous with meditation!

The physiological parameters of the meditative state were studied by a Harvard professor of medicine, Herbert Benson[8]. The Dalai Lama permitted him to carry out the experiments on long time practitioners of *Vajrayana* meditation. The results documented by Benson were almost identical with what has been seen with the adepts in TM technique. The physiological effects were generally the reverse of the effects seen with the stress syndrome. Benson therefore called it a relaxation response. He also came across a specific accomplishment amongst the practitioners of *g-tummo-yoga.* Those who were practicing this modality over the years were able to control their body temperature. This was scientifically tested and it was noted that they could raise it at will. This gave them the ability to withstand cold temperatures. The ability amongst the beginners was, Benson observed, a matter of friendly competition. It was tested by the number of wet sheets dried over the body in a given time by the competitors.

Recently, physiologists have detected the secretion by the brain of several neurotransmitters directly into the blood stream[9]. The first to be detected was a substance which counters pain. It is common experience that following an injury, one does not notice pain immediately. This is on account of secretion by the brain of a morphine-like substance which is named endorphin. We have known the production of internal secretions by the endocrine glands in response to stress. Secretion of endorphins by the brain brought a new dimension to its function. And in less than three decades, we have now known about two hundred such substances which the brain secretes directly in the blood stream!

Is meditative experience brought about by secretions of the brain in response to the meditative process? Though the experience in holistic paradigm extends much more into the realm of consciousness, in biochemical terms the answer is, yes. That is, how the drugs like marijuana trigger the experience.

This possibility has almost wiped out the interphase between the thoughts and feelings on one hand and the neural tissue on the other. There is secretion of one or more neuro-transmitters for each and every thought that one experiences with emotions. In that case for the experience of compassion and love too, the secretions of such internal biochemical modalities are operative!

In the light of the above research, the Buddhist understanding of the mind turns out to be scientific. After arriving at the concept of *sunyata* through a scholarly dialectical argument, Buddhism describes all phenomena as "dependent(ly) arising (from)", even though the emptiness is empty of inherent existence! For those with inclination to be rational at all times, such Buddhist precepts and dialectics are fruitful ways to understand the concept of *sunyata.* For its experience, one need not follow any particular methodology. There is unlimited choice to select a method as a modality for meditation.

The classical *Vajrayana* practices not only indicate several ways to meditate, but the *siddhis* (beneficial values, the nearest inaccurate translation) accrue according to a particular method.

Vipassyana meditation is a reflection on *kayanupassana,* where the flow of the breath and the memory of the body are the objects of contemplation in two different forms called *anapana sati* and *kayagati sati* respectively. *Vedana anupassana* observes the flow of the feelings leading to subtle sharp mind. *Chitta anupassana* passively reflects on the contents of the mind. *Dhammanupassana,* contemplation on the philosophical aspects of religious experience like nature, inherent quality, void, merit, and *samadhi* is the final stage of *vipassyanna* meditation.

The classical *mantra* in Buddhist meditation, *Om Mani Padme Hum* has a specific meaning for each word of the *mantra* and regardless of the cultural origin of the meditator and his knowledge or ignorance of the meaning of the *mantra,* it is supposed to be producing beneficial effects. *Om,* is composed of three letters *a, u* and *m.* They symbolize the impure and pure, body, speech and mind of the meditator and Buddha: *Mani* literally means jewel, but symbolizes the altruistic intention towards enlightenment, compassion and love. *Padme* stands for wisdom. *Hum* connotes indivisibility of method and wisdom which can lead to a state where one is not perturbed by anything.

The Tibetan Buddhist meditative practice has a profoundly rich repertoire to choose from. But the individual choice is limited to the choice of an initiator. It is he, who will decide whether to offer *mantra, sutra* or *deity-yan* meditation. Each one of them signifies a specific aspect in the realm of consciousness. The highest initiation in *Vajrayana* is *kalachakra.* The meditation here is on a *mandala* where 928 deities are inscribed. While meditating, one extracts the essential qualities of each of the deities and incorporates within.

The utilitarian would ask how much time it is likely to take. Meditative practices have a specific software as per the aspiration. The software will discharge functions according to the design. Many have wondered about the inexhaustible recourse to energy, spontaneous laughter and persistently positive attitude of the Dalai Lama. How can a person be so free from anxiety, depression, learnt helplessness and such other signs of post-traumatic stress syndrome which he has experienced at a young age and, is subjected constantly while stoically facing the brutalities upon the Tibetans inside Tibet and, striving relentlessly to solve the insurmountable problems of the refugees? The answer to this remarkable trait lies in the practice of *kalachakra* meditation.

Paul Brunton, after a life time pursuit in fathoming the mysteries of Eastern mysticism, recommends the meditation as follows: "of all day's activity, this non-activity provides a glimpse of vistas beyond the religious, whose nonchalant faith alone is not enough to do so. For the moralist, his morals and ethics are only preliminary to fulfilment of purpose of life. Once he knows the credo of contemplation, his aim will automatically be achieved. To the artist, it will provide an inexhaustible stream of inspiration constantly swelling within. To the idealist, it is a blessed sanctuary of aspirations. For the overworked, it provides a secret sacred place and thus for everyone it is an easily accessible pathway to reclaim the divine status and the estate."

It is said that when the practice of meditation went to Japan, *dhyana* became Zen. Its parables are mystic poetry like "the clapping of one hand." Many Tibetan discourses too are beautiful poetical expressions. For example,

> "When Bodhisattva meditates on Buddhas[10] with singleness of thought, he sees them; having appeared to him they stay with him; staying with him they explain things to him he wishes to understand. Being thus enlightened by them, he is delighted; he now reflects: whence do these Buddhas come from? And whither does this body of mind vanish? When he thus reflects, he sees that all the *Tathagats* come from nowhere and go out to nowhere. So it is with my own body, it has no definite path by which it comes, and how can there be any returning to anywhere?"
>
> Alternatively,
>
> "Misery only doth exist, none miserable,
> Nor doer is there; naught save the deed is found,
> *Nirvana* is, but not the man who seeks it.
> The path exists, but not the traveller on it!"

Philosophically,

> "There is no *time,* but there is only all abiding *timelessness,* there is no *space* but there is all pervasive *void which is full* (of energy). In this enormous limitless expanse of timelessness, there exists void space, surcharged with energy. A little undulation in the energy field brings forth the birth of Universe[11]. The consciousness too originates from the void but in the universe it is[12]. In the sphere of emptiness, even the consciousness may cease to be. When it will revert back to the eternal *void,* that is the stage of *nirvana."*

Poetically, it is said, "a bird does not turn back because it has reached the limits of the sky."

This is the apt description of the experience. But how is it brought about? So far we are advancing on the path of logical positivism. Do we have any empirical proofs? How do we validate the metaphysical data? What is the physical basis of consciousness and physiologically how one would define various parameters and explain them? This is the pursuit of scientists today. During one of his audiences with an American businessman, R. Adam Engle, the Dalai Lama was asked whether there is any possibility of a dialogue between him and the scientists so as to arrive at a synthesis or convergence. The Dalai Lama readily agreed.

We met R. Adam Engle following first such dialogue in 1991. He said apart from service of science and Buddhism, the interaction has brought about a radical change in his life. Thereafter he founded Mind-Life foundation. That is now conducting a biennial workshop which is alternately held in Dharmashala and USA. The proceedings have been published which provide a large base for knowledge of the mind and consciousness from Buddhist view as well as modern science.[13]

The scientific exploration of the mind has now reached stupendous proportions. Neuroplasticity, a subject discussed at the last Mind-Life Workshop at Dharmashala explored the scientific data so far uncovered as to how the transformation of mind may change the brain. Neuroplasticity refers to structural and functional changes in the brain that are brought about by training and experience. The brain is the organ that is designed to change in response to experience. Neuroscience and psychological research is leading to new insights about many ways in which brain, behaviour and experience change in response to experience. All the work invariably leads to the conclusion that the brain is not static but, rather is dynamically changing and undergoes such changes throughout one's life. Research on structural plasticity has revealed how the literal composition of the adult brain is constantly changing.

Other studies at the molecular level reveal how the chemistry of DNA can be changed by experience in ways that affect the expression of our genes. Moreover, such effects on the chemistry of DNA can be produced by social experience, which in turn modifies gene expression in ways that can persist for the duration of a lifetime. These findings have radical implications for conceptualizing the dynamic interplay between nature and nurture. The neural systems that underlie complex behaviours are transformed through experiential alterations.

The participants at 2004 workshop were drawn from several universities in USA, Japan, Canada, Nepal and France. While they explored the advances that science has made in understanding the physical structure of brain and, its plasticity as well as in the nature of the mind, did their perceptivity stop at the limits of their scientific discipline? The air at Dharmashala is permeated with the poignancy and relevance of Tibet Question! Most of them return as friends for the cause of Tibet.

Let us just see how the esoteric mysticism of *Vajrayana* and *Tantra* can become a tragic controversy. When the Dalai Lama visited Britain in 1995 and USA in 1998, there were demonstrations against him! And the demonstrators were Buddhist monks and nuns from Tibet! It was for the first time that the Dalai Lama has been faced with a protest from his own followers while visiting the United States.

Time Magazine on 11th May, 1998, writing under the caption Monks *versus* Monks, wrote that 'the devotees of a ferocious Buddhist deity are seeking to put a dent in the Dalai Lama's aura of sainthood.... the icon of enlightened harmony was met by demonstrators'.

"On 30th April, 1998, the Dalai Lama faced protest from a section of Buddhist in New York. Their grievance was that he has imposed a ban on worshipping Dorje Shugden. He is depicted as a lightening-breathing terror with three bloodshot eyes, wreathed in the smoke of burning human flesh, in fact, however, as one of the pantheon of "protector deities". While Dorje is considered to be a deity by this section, the Dalai Lama considers him a malevolent spirit. This was counterpoised against the purpose for his visit to New York where he was to give Wisdom teachings. He was also to discuss the physiological benefits of meditation with scientists at Beth Israel Medical Center. Later at Boston he was to be awarded honorary degrees by a couple of Universities."

"The Dalai Lama reportedly stopped worshipping Dorje Shugden as a protector deity in 1976 after an oracle told him, 'the deity was a malevolent spirit harmful to the leader's well-being'. Over the last 20 years, worship of Shugden, a traditionally worshipped deity of historical origin, has decreased considerably in the Tibetan communities and in Tibet itself. The current controversy is being engineered by a small group of Tibetans and Westerners whose rhetoric is extreme in attacking the Dalai Lama. Protests have been staged in England, Germany and the United States."

At the surface it may appear that the tradition verges on superstition and is in contradiction to the modernity. Samdong Rinpoche, argues in the defence of the tradition, taking recourse to modern thinkers like Ananda Coomaraswamy, Rene Guenon, Marco Pallis and Frithjof Schuon, that 'the deceptive power of modern ways of thinking could be insidiously dangerous'. The tradition may be so integrated with spiritual life so as to have a symbolic meaning within an impartible universe.[14]

Robert Thurman, a professor of Indo-Tibetan studies at Colombia University, defended the Dalai Lama. The Dalai Lama has meant that the followers of Dorje will not be allowed to the teachings and initiations given by him. However, the Western press highlighted the controversy since it is only such items that make juicy news.

The Dalai Lama told *Time Magazine* that he was worried about people's seeking "external help", while neglecting Buddha's teaching of compassion and wisdom: Shugden activists denounce that they receive funds from the Chinese government. But the Chinese, happy at any Exile strife, are restoring Shugden temples in occupied Tibet!

American Tibetan-style Buddhists, however, will have to digest the occultism, interschool feuding and occasional violence that have long marked the culture they thought was their model.[15]

Says the fracas will help Americans realize they "have a bowdlerized version of Tibetan Buddhism."

Time editor Tworkov goes further: "This allows us Westerners to ask, 'How do we bring this tradition into our society and our lives, and what is best left behind in Tibet or Japan?' Every Buddhist culture has elements we'd rather not import. Those of us who come from non-Buddhist backgrounds to admire and acquire Buddhist virtues, did not lay down one set of cultural baggage to pick up another." How much baggage can you jettison without calling off the whole trip?

Lodi Gyari, aware that China is bent upon calling the practice *abracadabra* – superstition, so that the discussive, discursive, dialectical, logical Westerners see the practice as diabolical warned, that the squabble should not obscure the fact that "a culture and people are being destroyed." Let us hope so.

References on *Vajrayana*

- The Dalai Lama, *Freedom in Exile*, London, 1990, p. 297.
- Suzuki, D.T., *Essays in Zen Buddhism*, First Series, London, 1980, p. 48.
- *Ibid.* Second Series, London, 1985, p. 274.
- Huntington, C.W. Jr. and Geshe Namgyal Wangichen, *The Emptiness of Emptiness*, Honolulu, 1989, p. 190.
- *Ibid.*, First Series, London, 1980, p. 129.
- The Dalai Lama, *The World of Tibetan Buddhism*, Boston, 1995, p. 34.
- The Dalai Lama, *Consciousness at Cross Roads*, New York, 1999, pp. 37-55.
- Suzuki, D.T., *Essays in Zen Buddhism*, First Series, London, 1980, pp. 57-58.
- The Dalai Lama, *The World of Tibetan Buddhism*, Boston, 1985, pp. 18-35.
- *Ibid.*, *Path to Bliss, A Practical Guide to Stages of Meditation*, New York, 1991, pp. 207-215.
- Mehta, Rohit, *Yoga, The Art of Integration*, Madras, 1990, pp. 105-115.
- The Dalai Lama, *The Four Noble Truths*, New Delhi, 1998.
- The Dalai Lama, *Ethics for the New Millennium*, London, 2000.
- Maharshi Mahesh Yogi, *Creating an Ideal Society*, Seelisberg, 1977.
- Wallace Robert Keith, *The Physiological Effects of Transcendental Meditation, A Proposed Fourth Major State of Consciousness*, Los Angeles, 1970.
- Orme-Johnson, D.W. and Farrow, J.T., *Scientific Research on the Transcendental Meditation Programme*: Collected papers. Meru, Switzerland, 1976.
- Huxley, Aldous, *The Doors of Perception*, London, 1956.
- Ratanakul, P., *The Buddhist Ethics of Metta*, Paper given at the Sion Conference on Ethical Reflections, Netherlands, October 1991.
- The Dalai Lama, *The Four Noble Truths*, New Delhi, 1997, pp. 120-121.
- *Ibid.*, *The Way to Freedom. Core Teachings of Tibetan Buddhism*, Dharmashala, 2000, p. 133.
- Anil Kumar Sarkar, *The Mysteries of Vajrayana Buddhism from Atisha to Dalai Lama*, New Delhi, 1993, pp. 157-173, 205.
- Geshe Kelsang Gyatso, *Essence of Vajrayana, The Highest Yoga Tantra Practice of Heruka Body Mandala*, London 1997, pp. x-xii.

- Geshe Nyawang Dhargyey, *Kalchakara Tantra*, Dharmashala, 1985.
- Geshe, Lhumdub Sopa, Jackson, R. and Newman, J., *The Wheel of Time: The Kalachakra in Context*, New York, 1991.
- John Blofeld, *The Way of Power, A Practical Guide to the Tantric Mysticism of Tibet*, London, 1970, pp. 190-218.
- The Dalai Lama, *Path to Bliss, A Practical Guide to Stages of Meditation*, New York, 1991, p. 194.
- Lama, Thupten Yeshe, *Transference of Consciousness at the Time of Death*, Boston, 1991, pp. 1-42.
- Hayward, J.W. and Franscisco, Varela, Gentle, Bridges, *Conversation with the Dalai Lama on the Science of Mind*, Boston, 1992, pp. 106-125.
- Walsh and Roche, Caution: *Am. J. Psychiatry*, 136; 1085, 1979.
- Suzuki, D.T., *Essays in Zen Buddhism*, First Series, London, 1980, p. 49.
- *Ibid*., p. 121.

REFERENCES

1. An ugly situation developed in 2011. At Karmapa's monastery, large amount of currency was found in foreign denominations. The Dalai Lama came at his rescue.
2. There is truth of suffering, that there is origin of suffering, that there is truth of cessation of suffering and that there is truth of the path.
3. Tenzin Gyatso, The Dalai Lama, *The Kalchakra Tantra: rite of initition*, London, 1985.
   This was published following the first initiation in Madison, USA.
4. Ranjan Panda, Creative Visualization, in *The Indian Hand Book of Clinical Hypnosis*, eds. Bhaskar Vyas and Rajni Vyas, Calcutta, 2006.
5. Shakti Gowain, *Creative Visualization*, New York, 1990.
6. At the crown of my head is *Virochana*, at the throat *Amitabha*, at my heart *Akshobhya*, at my navel *Ratnasambhava* and at the energy-channel where my thighs join is *Amoghasiddhi*. At my navel is Lochana, at my heart, *Mamaki*, at my throat, *Padmaravasin* and at the crown of my head, Tara. At my eyes are, *Kshitigarbhas*, at my ears, *Vajrapanis*, at my nose, *Khagarbha*, at my tongue *Lokeshvara*, at my heart, *Manjushri*, at my secret organ, *Sarvanivarana-viskambhini*, at my joints, *Samantabhadra* and, at the crown of my head is *Maitreya*. At the gateways of my eyes are, *Rupavajra*, at the gateways of my ears, *Shabdavajra*, at the gateway of my nose, *Gandhavajra*, at

the gateway of my mouth, *Rasavajra* and at the gateway of my *vajra* organ, *Sparshavajra*. At my right hand is, *Yamantakrit*, at my left hand, *Aparajita*, at my mouth, *Hayagriva*, at my *vajra*-organ, *Vignantakrit*, at the energy-channel of my right shoulder, *Achala*, at the energy-channel of my left shoulder, *Takkiraja*, at my right knee, *Niladanda*, at my left knee, *Mahabala*, at the crown of my head, *Ushnisha-chakravartin* and, at the soles of my two feet are, *Sumbharajas*.

7. This has a reference to action without and action within, see, Bhaskar Vyas and D.V. Nene, *Changing Course of Brahmaputra, the Dalai Lama, the Change Initiator*, Bombay, 1992.
8. Herbert Benson, *The Relaxation Response*, Boston, 1980.
9. Bhaskar Vyas and Rajni Vyas, *The Indian Book of Clinical Hypnosis*, Kolkata, 2006.
10. It is a common mistake to think of only one Buddha. Siddhartha Gautama became a Buddha on attaining enlightenment. But there can be countless number of Buddhas and all of us have the potentiality to become one.
11. Bhaskar Vyas and Rajni Vyas, *Space-Time-Consciousness: The Fifth Dimension*, New Delhi, 2004.
12. But it transmigrates and may even reverberate anywhere in the animal kingdom. So the Buddhist view is that there is consciousness at the conception. It was either in *bardo* (astral plane) or, even in some higher realms, before it incarnates in the womb. Therefore, immediately after the physical event of fertilization, the embryo is conscious.
13. www.mindandlife.org/pastconf.html
14. S. Rinpoche, *Calls From a Far, Introduction to Collected Works of A.K. Saran*, Sarnath, Varanasi, 1998. pp. 3-6.
15. Donald S. Lopez Jr., *Prisoners of Shangri La: Tibetan Buddhism and the West*.

13
Bending of the Bamboo: Diplomacy of Desperation

A fateful morning to mourn: 10th March, 2005; God has failed; Tibetan fight forty-five years old; That may be too early to derive any conclusion.

The sky was overcast on the morning of 10th March, 2005. It had rained the previous evening as a downpour. And there was unprecedented snow in the Himalayan ranges this winter. The entire Dhauladhar range of mountains surrounding the McLeod Gunj was layered with a thick coat of snow that gave the atmosphere an eerie feeling of still life. And when the Dalai Lama arrived at 8:30 a.m. to deliver his customary statement on the National Uprising Day, it appeared that it may rain anytime.

On the previous evening, Kalon Tripa, Prime Minister of Tibet, Samdong Rinpoche had briefed the press. He had described the fight for freedom as a perpetual one. Describing India's struggle for freedom as a fight for four hundred years, he had said the Tibetan fight is barely forty-five years old. That may be too early to derive any conclusion and the judgement could be precarious.

The rectangle in front of the temple was crowded to the brim, as usual. There were a few foreign guests in the guest enclosure and, the press gallery was crowded with national and international media persons. The school band beat a ceremonial welcome. Probably for the Head of a State this school band might be the most rudimentary, and yet, the boys and the girls from the local Tibetan school were exuding their best of patriotic fervour. There was singing of the Tibetan National Anthem followed by prayer to the Lord Avalokiteswar, the Buddha of compassion.

Before the speeches, Zamira Chenn, a famous singer from Israel sang a couple of freedom songs. She sang a symbolic message, "The answer, my friend, is blowing in the wind". She exhorted the audience to join. Except for a very few, hardly anybody joined. Was it because that the Tibetans did not know enough English? Or, was it because that audience had a premonition of what was to come?

Kalon Tripa Samdong Rinpoche read out the statement of the Kashag. It was almost an apology for the upcoming 10th March, 2005 statement. He said that the Dalai Lama's Middle Way approach is not a new policy formulated during his time of prime ministership. Since 1979, it has been a policy adopted by the Kashag, the Assembly and Tibetan public through a democratic process. So long as this policy does not change through the same process, the non-implementation would amount to a lack of responsibility by the 12th Kashag. He also took note of a possibility of criticism and differing opinions from a section of Tibetan organizations. But he went on to say that the Kashag is determined to move forward, so that they themselves do not become the cause for the failure of negotiations as it has happened in the past.

The Dalai Lama began by offering greetings to the Tibetans in Tibet as well as in Exile. And at the onset by extending the greetings to all the friends around the world, he acknowledged the significant contribution to the Tibetan cause by sympathizers across the globe.

But thereafter, this statement on the 46th anniversary of Tibetan People's Uprising was different than any other of the preceding years. The Dalai Lama acknowledged the tremendous economic progress not only in China but in Tibet. This even included the praise of Golmud Lhasa railway link! The Government in Exile has consistently been critical of laying of this railway line connecting Lhasa to the Chinese mainland. Previously the argument was that it will open the floodgates of Hans' migrants from the mainland China to Tibet as well as transportation of mineral wealth out to China. And here it was that the railway link was mentioned as a landmark of economic progress[1]! One wondered as to what was coming next.

There seemed to be a counterbalance by quoting independent journalists and tourists to Tibet. The Dalai Lama said that they portrayed a very different picture than the claims of the Chinese government. According to these reports, the Dalai Lama said that there was a clear lack of human rights, religious freedom and autonomy in Tibet. The Tibetans had no access to authority and, the power really vested with the Chinese leaders. The Dalai Lama defined the problem as, "the lack of true ethnic equality and harmony and, the absence of genuine stability." The problem has persisted ever since Tibet was occupied. Even though there may be an official show of jubilation and fun fair, most Tibetans in their hearts are extremely unhappy.

With this preamble, the Dalai Lama embarked on making significant announcements. When the Tibetans returned to Tibet, he shall not hold any official political position. He shall not head the Tibetan government.

The Tibetan Administration in Exile will be dissolved. Then he further extended the Middle Way approach. He categorically said that Tibetans are not seeking independence and, are willing to remain within the People's Republic of China. The Dalai Lama said that it was in the benefit of the Tibetan people to do so. The age old comparison of Chinese being a cat and the minorities/other nationalities being like mice is well known. It was repeated only a few years back by Deng. "Whatever may be the colour of the cat, as long as the cat is catching mice it was alright." Now it appeared that the Dalai Lama's perception has changed.

Referring to the recent round of talks, he allayed the Chinese apprehensions and assured that in the further round of negotiations the Tibetans will refrain from raising sundry issues!

While profusely thanking Government of India for the steadfast support there was an evident Freudian slip when he said that he feels very much a part of Indian nation. Two decades back, while explaining the Strasbourg proposals to us he had unequivocally told us that he would rather wish Tibet to be a part of India than China. The same statesman had now swallowed his words. Samdong Rinpoche has said that the Tibetans should strive more for merit accumulating meditation and prayers. One cannot but remain without feeling that any amount of prayers that one may offer for the brave Tibetan men and women who gave their blood and laid down their lives in the cause of Tibetan freedom, shall not be able to redeem the damage to the cause of Tibetan freedom that was done on this day!

TYC was not visible at all. It could not have escaped the notice of anyone connected to the Tibetan cause that there were no pamphlets demanding Rangzen this time. The officials of the Central Tibetan Administration had quietly but effectively persuaded the audience not to shout the slogans for Rangzen.

Phil Void, a musician from United States has been singing Rangzen song ever since 1977, on the occasion of National Uprising Day celebrations. Following a Buddhist initiation, he came to a spiritual realization of emptiness as all abounding infinite principle in the universe. So he dropped his American name, Philip Hemley, to become Phil Void. At the same time, spiritual experience also made him realize the immensity of Tibetan suffering. Phil felt drawn to the cause of Tibetan freedom. So ever since then he had sung the Rangzen songs after the conclusion of the ceremony on 10th March. He called his musical band, Dharma Bums from then on. This time Phil wanted to sing but could not, because he was told that this will embarrass the Government in Exile. There were hardly any young people, we looked for the members of Tibetan Youth Congress and could hardly find any.

No sooner the ceremony ended the members of the Kashag silently and swiftly left with ashen faces. There was no customary exchange of courtesies with the guests and friends. It was noticed that even while listening to the Dalai Lama's speech most of them were praying, some quite visibly with rosary moving in their hands and, their lips whispering *mantras*. Within a couple of minutes the rectangle wore a deserted look. The celebrated Israeli singer wondered, and asked us as to why no Tibetans joined her. We asked the ABC correspondent about the previous scoop. Hurriedly winding up his equipment, he said, he was unaware about any previous scoops by the ABC Television[2] but was satisfied with this one.

We were left bewildered. Not even the recourse to the dialectics of impermanence of all the objective phenomena and such other esoteric Buddhists speculations could set our hearts to rest. We were reminded of the historic times on the eve of partition of India. At that time, Frontier Gandhi, Khan Abdul Gaffar Khan had wept and told Mahatma Gandhi that he was throwing his people to the wolves. Here was the Dalai Lama doing the same. Throughout history, Tibetans and the Chinese were never the same people and, all the interactions between them have been at the peril of the Tibetans. Is it likely that Dalai Lama will succeed in reversing this historical trend?

All the national media carried the news on front page. Several of them wrote editorials. There was some praise: *Hindustan Times*, praising the conciliatory attitude, commended the Dalai Lama's gesture and said that the ball was now in China's court. However, the critical appraisal percolated after a few days. The gist of what was the critique may be summarized as:

> "The most analysts said that this was a total surrender. The Dalai Lama was criticized as the God that failed. What did the Tibetans get by worshipping him? Cataloguing the various summersaults he has made, he was labelled as an opportunist. The Dalai Lama earned for himself an altruistic stature and heads of the States as well as celebrities across the globe felt themselves expiated, when they touched his feet. It is said that a meeting with him inspires peace. All this has been turned into hocus-pocus. Even when there is an ever increasing queue of devotees, the Dalai Lama has failed for the Tibetans.
>
> "The bubble of the spiritual power burst when on 10th March, 2005, the Dalai Lama prostrated himself at the feet of the Chinese and,

surrendered the cause of Tibetan freedom. As the Head of the State, it was his duty to further the movement in the cause of freedom and, when he somersaulted this time, it was no mistake. There was nothing in between the lines. He said, he was convinced that the material benefit of the Tibetans lie in remaining within the People's Republic of China.

"In 1980s the Dalai Lama formulated Strasbourg proposals. They centre on the principle of Tibetan autonomy. However, it appeared that there was further softening of his stand in the last few years. But nobody could have ever thought that he will give in this way, this is total surrender.

"The same Dalai Lama had nurtured the dreams of a democratic independent Tibetan Nation for the Tibetans. He had promised them so and, exhorted them to never give up. Now that he has buckled himself, the Tibetans feel betrayed and do not hesitate to abuse him publicly. Their anger is justified because they had blindly trusted this God and worshipped him. He was the undisputed leader in the fight for the freedom of Tibet. They appreciated his disguise as a spiritual leader. This was a help to the cause so much so that people started to believe that he has spiritual power/wisdom that shall deliver Tibetan independence. Now it is clear that he has the feet of clay and is getting old and jittery. The Dalai Lama has waged a cold war against the Chinese for 45 years but now, he has got cold feet.

"Instead of independence, the Dalai Lama now talks of negotiating a kind of autonomy for Tibetans while remaining within the clutches of the Chinese. Most of the Tibetans believe that such autonomy is just a façade. Tibetans have never been able to co-exist with the Chinese and, it is impossible to do so now.

"There is a bitter pragmatic side to the story. Did the Dalai Lama have any other alternative? The Chinese Dragon had long before swallowed the Tibetan Snow Lion. With the impressive show of economic and political power, China has succeeded now in blinding the Dalai Lama's eyes. When he succeeded a bit by making the Chinese to talk, he was again deluded. Under the pressure from the Western powers, the Chinese invited the representatives of the Dalai Lama to talks three times in last three years. True to the Chinese tradition, they treated them lavishly as tourists and, just conveyed that there is nothing to negotiate! On the other hand, the Dalai Lama has failed to even get any single nation to arbitrate.

"Samdong Rinpoche, the Prime Minister of Tibet says that the cause for independence is close to the hearts of all Tibetans. 'However we got to understand the ground realities. We have exhausted the means at our disposal to counter Chinese.' He says, he is well aware of the dissent within the Tibetans but is helpless. So the Prime Minister of Tibet has publicly expressed his limitation to voice the Tibetan feelings!

"It is worthwhile understanding the deceit in the usage of the word Tibetan Autonomous Region. Original Tibet was spread out into three provinces of Kham, Amdo and U-tsang. They covered an area of 2.5 million sq. km. TAR as carved by the Chinese today is barely half the size. Even if there was autonomy for Tibetans, where would it be located?

"The gist of the matter is that the Dalai Lama has only enhanced his personal image internationally at the expense of Tibetan independence. He is sold out in the service of his self-image as a messiah of non-violence. This has only served the Chinese. Jagdish Vyas, a political scientist from United States said that he failed to understand the spirituality of this ever smiling Lama with folded hands. What is he smiling at, after betraying the cause of freedom and, leaving the Tibetans to suffer under the Chinese rule?

"The fact of the matter is that the Dalai Lama has totally failed. He had no daring to talk to the Chinese eye to eye. He could provide no impetus to the freedom movement. He had no diplomatic strategy. Many Tibetans ask now as to what have they got by following the advice of the Dalai Lama? Why did we follow peace? Could we not have resorted to the terrorist way? The dictates of the Dalai Lama even cut off the debate of such dialectics. The ghost of non-violence had so overpowered the Dalai Lama's sensibilities that the Tibetans were made to forget that violence is one of the means in the cause of freedom. Violence attracts the attention widely and makes the opponent suffer uncomfortably. The Dalai Lama has brought the Tibetans to such a pass that even if the Tibetans were to disavow him now, the new beginning appears to be implausible."

We approached Mr. Tenzing Geyche, the Personal Secretary to the Dalai Lama a day before our audience that was scheduled on March 16th. We requested him to cancel our appointment since it appeared to be meaningless to discuss the efficacy and relevance of non-violent means. Moreover it would be painful for us to say so to the Dalai Lama whom we have revered personally. Mr. Geyche assuaged our hurt and assured that we should speak frankly without hesitation and, the Dalai Lama welcomes all voices of dissent.

At the interview, with chagrin in our hearts, we told the Dalai Lama that when small people make big mistakes nothing much seems to be lost. But a single small mistake of a big person does tremendous harm. He seems to be making such a mistake. The diplomacy is an art of bartering and he has gained nothing by way of abject surrender. He said that the new policy meant only a little elaboration of the Middle Way approach. Our response was that the Middle Way has extended all the way to the Chinese feet. They have not walked a single step from their well articulated stand. We reminded him that he had said to us in that very room, twenty years ago, that Tibet would rather be a part of India than that of China. He was now following the footsteps of Mahatma Gandhi indeed: since he is also breaking his promise to the Tibetans, as Mahatma Gandhi did, for the Indians. Mahatma Gandhi had promised Indians that the partition can only happen over his dead body. Had Mahatma Gandhi kept that promise, immense suffering that goes on even now after fifty-five years, may not have occurred. We asserted that the Dalai Lama was emulating the Mahatma Gandhi once again by throwing Tibetans to the wolves and, the Chinese cat, whatever its colour, shall always eat the mice.

His last statement, we pointed out mentioned nothing about the population transfer, nuclear policy and Tibet as the zone of demilitarization. It did not spell out what is exactly meant by Tibet and TAR. If there was no alternative, waiting patiently for an alternative to emerge is also an alternative. If the Indian leaders with their advancing age would have been a little less impatient, the scenario would have radically changed with the death of Jinnah. The freedom is the primary instinctual need of all people and, some day the break up of the present dictatorship as well as hegemony in Chinese geography is bound to give way. The break up of China cannot be ruled out. On the contrary, it is certain at some time or other.

We asked the Dalai Lama whether he had noticed the fallen faces of Kashag members after his address. The Dalai Lama indicated that every member of the Kashag had given their consent. We said that the Dalai Lama is a benevolent dictator for the Tibetans. When the Resolution 14 was carried by 21 *versus* 9, by the Kashag, with 14 deputies walking out before voting, it only meant that they were doing so in accordance with the wishes of the Dalai Lama.

In his statement there was a reference that the shift in the Tibetan stance has pleased the friends in India as well as in the West. He clarified that friends in India meant mainly the Government of India. While the Indian

Government is taciturn about the matter, it has probably come to realize the law of diminishing returns from its Tibetan involvement. The friends in the West meant, once again the Western Governments. They have been primarily involved in the cause of Tibet at the insistence of their electorate. The amount of effort and persistence that they have put is immense. They had experienced the stress in their relationship with China. If Tibet were now to abdicate, they will, of course, heave a sigh of relief.

The Dalai Lama winded up the interview by concluding that the outcome of the forthcoming fourth round of the talks between his representatives and the Chinese will be deterministic as to what happens next.

During our stay at Dharmashala we had met a young Korean American lady, Oceana (name changed), of about 30 years. She had undergone several teachings and initiations from the Dalai Lama. Per chance, we had asked her if she would want to come along with us for the audience. Oceana was so delighted that she was in the seventh heaven. After presenting her to the Dalai Lama, she was asked to wait in the anti-chamber. When we came out, we found her crying silently with tears constantly rolling down her eyes! Alarmed, we inquired as to what is the matter with her? Her reply was that she is overflowing with joy! Not even in her dreams she had ever thought that she would be holding the Dalai Lama's hand and, she even now, feels electrified! She had nothing to do with the political context!

However, amid such wide ranging criticism, a gentle voice of impolite dissent was finding expression. When we contacted the leaders of the Tibetan Youth Congress, they led us to their ramshackle office. They quietly led us to an inside room. On a large table was laid out a white cloth. It carried a map of Tibet, with Rangzen marked over it. And there were many signatures in blood! They said whatever may be the official policy or the dictates of His Holiness, they shall not rest without achieving freedom from the Chinese rule. Independence of Tibet is there goal.

And one of their members, Mr. Tenzin Tsundue, was quick to dart off his dissent immediately in the form of a Letter to the Editor of *Hindustan Times*. He said that the Editorial, "*The ball is in China's court,* (But who wants to play?)" has misread the statement of the Dalai Lama. When he said that we are willing to remain a part of China, it was meant only an acceptance of the *status quo* and not that Tibet was part of China historically. Tsundue went a step further. He was categorical to say that no one can do so, not even the 14th Dalai Lama. The Dalai Lama may be making a practical compromise but most Tibetans, Tsundue asserted, think that the Middle Way policy is not practicable in dealing with Beijing.

How shall they do it? This time let their reason and the youthful bash be the guide. Hope lies eternal in human breast. Firmly rooted in the belief of interconnectedness that causes all the phenomena in the nature to unfold, the Dalai Lama had told us at an earlier audience, whether China goes the Soviet Union way or not — and he would rather not wish a sudden collapse that shall cause great hardship for the common masses — freedom is the basic appetite of the soul. Exposure to democratic ways through trade and commerce shall ultimately bring about the real democratization of China when the Tibetans shall govern Tibet.

Let us review various options available to the Tibetans at this bifurcation point.

Thus, in the year 2005, the world focus has shifted to a realignment of interests between USA, China, India, Japan and the rest of the world. USA with its historical commitment would certainly wish to neutralize communism in China. It is evidently clear that it is not going to fight any war anywhere on the issue of containment or elimination of communism anymore. In its foreign policy US has defined the policy of free trade and human rights as the future equalizers for democracy.

On the other hand, China has a compulsive need to better the living conditions for its burgeoning masses and, since the land is limited, would not want to agree to voluntarily give up any land that it has managed to grab. It has come under increasing pressure from the Western nations to make amends for its human rights records as well as to come to terms with Tibet. However, it does not see any threat from the Dalai Lama or even Tibetans inside Tibet. It believes it can counter the Dalai Lama by mere procrastination and the wheel of the time will see that the Dalai Lama disappears. It is convinced that Tibetans inside Tibet will eventually be assimilated through (1) hard repressive measures, (2) by better standards of living, and (3) by massive population transfer. For them to have the Dalai Lama outside Tibet is safer than having him in.

The traditional rivalry between Japan and China does not seem to provide any corridor for Tibet. This is in spite of the fact that Japan is Buddhist. The Watershed event can be the future of Taiwan. United States has committed to protect Taiwan. On the other hand, China has publicly declared its intention for military action against Taiwan. Five years have passed since. There is gross similarity between Tibet and Taiwan except that the former has been digested long ago.

When the Dalai Lama has reconciled to the stark reality of no hope for independent Tibet, will the Chinese have any need or magnanimity to resolve a recurring irritant, is a matter of astute statesmanship. Till 2011, the Chinese have yielded no further ground. They maintain that to return or not, is up to the Dalai Lama. The conditions laid down by Deng remain as they are. There is hardly any hope of genuine autonomy as the Dalai Lama demands. The Dalai Lama says, "We both are repeating the mantra. We say we want genuine autonomy. They say Tibet is part of China."

For the emergence of collative mindsets, there have to be imperatives that motivate. As a child hankers for the mother's lap, the Dalai Lama is frantically wishing to return. Are the Chinese willing to buy peace in return of the natural dues of Tibetans? Imperialism is dead and gone and, colonialism was outdated even earlier. Accepting that Tibet remains within the mainland China, the Chinese have only to change their mindset and, it should be governed by Tibetans; Chinese citizens as they will be. That will be a change to modernity and, may augur well for both, so that a win-win situation emerges. Given the fact that even within the totalitarian Chinese regime, the leadership is changing for the younger generation, this may indeed be a possibility. However, the Chinese will have to trust Tibetans first. If they wish to enforce unity through guns, it has never happened before and, will not happen ever.

REFERENCES

1. This indeed is debatable as was the case of British laying railways before 1857.
2. In 1990, ABC Television had brought out a stunning scoop. They sent two correspondents who disguised themselves as tourists and, carried hidden cameras. They succeeded in carrying out a sting mission. Back home, ABC invited the Chinese Ambassador to the studio. He projected various pictures of tremendous progress in Tibet. These consisted of new buildings, sport stadiums and race courses. Everything appeared to be rosy for Tibetans. Thereafter ABC showed their film, which depicted abjectly poor conditions of the Tibetans. Within minutes, the face of Chinese Ambassador fell to ashen gray. He could not comment beyond a few words, muttered as, "I am sure there must be some mistake. This is not true."

14
How to Win a Battle and Lose the War

Psychodynamics of Challenge; Reluctant politician; Spiritual dimensions of combat; Defiance in defeat; Peace itself is the path; Means are the ends.

At the crossroads of history, weary of the fact that time is fast running out (the Dalai Lama is born on 6th July, 1935), he has now taken refuge into the Buddhist precept of *Madhyam Prati-pada.* The Sanskrit word literally translates as the middle way. The practice of the Middle Way lies in acceptance of middle position between the opposites and, such equilibrium is supposed to be generative of peace. So, the Dalai Lama has unequivocally stated that he is giving up the stand for Tibetan independence and shall be reconciled to be an autonomous part of China. And, he has been waiting for the Chinese to walk the rest of the half towards him. Chinese have not moved an inch till 2011. What the Chinese have so far responded is nothing beyond the Five-Point Proposals that they have enunciated in 1981.

It cannot be said that the Chinese mind-set is unknown to him. Yet, he again walks half the way by proclaiming that he wants to build trust and mutual respect. Relying on the Buddhist precept of *karma,* he bears no ill-will and, is even advocating that one should love ones enemy.

Mao tse-Tung had exclained, when he heard of the Dalai Lama's escape in 1959, "We have lost Tibet". The perception of Chou En-lai and the subsequent functionaries ruling Tibet has been that China is not going to collapse without him. And indeed, it has not. For them, exiled Dalai Lama has been a "good riddance of bad rubbish."

Dynamics of negotiations require that the resolution has to be win-win situation. A meeting point may be arrived by both the parties walking half the distance. This is not the case nor, it is likely to be. What happens when only one party continues to make moves to walk half the distance. Zeno, a Greek philosopher has reflected on this. He argues metaphysically that for an object to move from one place to another, it first must move, say, half the distance. That would be the middle position and let us say the Dalai Lama has done so.

Now to move the rest of the half, the Dalai Lama will have to move half of the half once again. The opposite party stays where it was. The Dalai Lama will then have to move half the distance infinite number of times, since the opposite half has not been covered at all. The opposite side has been maintained *status quo* on the initial position. Every step in the motion takes some time, how so ever small. Thus, the Dalai Lama will not only go through an infinite number of the half distances, it will take infinite time. Unless the other party has agreed to move forward, in no finite time shall they ever meet.

Though Buddha encouraged dialectics and dwelt in metaphysics, he also advised to be pragmatic and act according to the contingency of a given situation. The action then would be guided by the clear perception of the reality and application of wisdom. Wisdom lies in masterful administration of future in the present.

The Dalai Lama has charismatic personality. He has(d) two roles, one as a sovereign in guiding the destiny of Tibet and, the other role as the Protective Deity, reincarnated *Avalokiteshwara*. He has undertaken enormous toil. The results of such persistence perseverance will also be the yard sticks that the worldly-wise will use to judge.

Tibet is now at the cross roads with her destiny. A bifurcation point is arrived, that has never been before. The Protector Divinity whom they have installed as their sovereign, at the age of three, has been shaping their destiny for last 56 years (DOB, 6th July, 1935, sovereign in 1950). He has been considered to be an *Ocean of Wisdom*. And, most Tibetans have abdicated their will to his dictates. Even though he is a sovereign without a throne and a king without any territory, his word is the last word for most Tibetans.

The refined entwining of the Buddhist precepts and modern political science[1, 2] has brought about a situation that is full of contradictions. The Dalai Lama quotes Buddha as well as the fundamental dictates of democracy, when he says that everybody must exercise his/her wisdom and, has a basic, fundamental right to a choice. The choice has to be played within the social contract since no man is an island; more so in the present day world. So when he is shaping the destiny of Tibet, his choice has primarily be moulded by the aspirations of his people. *The destiny has to be given a destination*. He has been repeatedly saying that, finally, the happiness of the Tibetans should be the sole criterion for deciding the future of Tibet.

The improvement in the material conditions do make up for the comfort. The physical conditions in Tibet have changed and so have they, for most of the regions of the world. It is elementary that if material progress was the sole decipher of happiness, the people of United States or other Western Nations would be the happiest. Most social studies have revealed the situation to the contrary[3, 4, 5]. It is elementary that man does not live by bread alone. Even Colin Powell, a pragmatic politician, has said so to the Chinese. Freedom, equality and justice are not confined to the West only, they are universal aspirations. A large section of the Tibetan Society is restless and would want to say the same to the Dalai Lama.

The Dalai Lama has relentlessly pursued the Tibetan cause. He has persisted when there was no hope and Tibet seemed to be a lost nation. Most of the diplomacy of the present political system seems to be woven around banquets and dinners. He is a refugee and had no platform. Deriving his sustenance and strength by sheer patience and perseverance, he has provided a classic illustration of survival of the weakest. The official life is so formal that most statesmen were shying away from him since he had materially nothing to give. He built the entire edifice of Tibetan diplomacy on the social, cultural, religious and spiritual values in life, so that a mechanism for the exercise of immeasurable intangibles evolved.

The conscience of the civilized people of the world was aroused. With refined sensibilities, he not only touched the hearts of his audiences but made them understand the nuances of the Tibet situation. Moods of the politicians changed. The relationships were created.

In the meanwhile, West evolved a strategy where by Russian monolith disintegrated[6]. When Henry Kissinger made his trip to Beijing that finally led to the lifting of the Bamboo curtain, the obvious motivation may have appeared as trade and commerce. It was a bifurcation point in the ways of diplomacy. During the cold war years, it was thought that military superiority and sophisticated weapons will contain and combat communism. Proliferation of the weapons of mass destructions changed it all.

There is no virus more powerful than the ideas. With modern means of communications, there are no impenetrable curtains. In dealing with the free nations of modern world, it was evident that China will make itself vulnerable. Tiananmen Square bears an invisible testimony.

The patience pays, but the tryst with the destiny needs infinite, inexhaustible patience. The Dalai Lama has practiced it so far. But like any statesman, he is a prisoner of necessity. Interactions with the Western statesmen have imposed a compensatory rationalization to his Buddhist spiritual values. And, it appears that he has started to think that the diplomacy is the art of possible. He has yielded to pressure and bent. As bamboo would better bend than break. He is confronted with an environment he did not create and is shaped by an impersonal history he can no longer change.

Though *Avalokiteshwara* he is, he is in human form. It may be argued that he is prone to everyday occurrence of human emotions: pleasure and pain, hope and despair are human. Regular practice and teachings of meditation and *tantra* has immunised him from insults to the ego so that he may not need any recourse to its defence. Announcing his decision to devolve power he said, "I have received repeated and earnest requests both from within Tibet and outside, to continue to provide political leadership. My desire to devolve authority has nothing to do with a wish to shirk responsibility. It is to benefit Tibetans in the long run. It is not because I feel disheartened. Tibetans have placed such faith and trust in me that as one among them I am committed to playing my part in the just cause of Tibet. I trust that gradually people will come to understand my intention, will support my decision and accordingly let it take effect."

Vajrayana practice is a royal road to a state of "egolessness". Freudian psychoanalysis knows nothing about this psychological state: even then, if psychoanalysed, there is only mature defence in asceticism. And, the practice of *Kalachakra* meditation empowers him with essence of 928 deities — archetypal virtuous forces.

However, he is born to a mother and a nation has mothered him too. Cultivation of the virtues have kept him childlike; that innocence does make him to regress to the mother(s) that he was separated from, at the tender age of three and twenty-four. The autumn has already approached, with only a few roses in December 2011. At the root of his being, a clear longing to return to the lap of the mother and to the motherland has become a powerful urge.

The pressure of circumstances is great indeed. His choices are limited to the extent of exhaustion. But, the public life is a continual struggle to rescue an element of choice. As a spiritual statesman, he has witnessed the working of subtle forces and he has derived/provided succor through his beliefs. He has seen collapse of the Berlin Wall, unification of Germany(ies), crumbling of the Russian Union and emergence of capitalistic order, even in Communist China. Of late, popular upsurge in Greece and Arab countries have brought radical transformation. The dissent within China and the dare to publicly voice[7] it are phenomena that gives evidence to him of the actual operation of the principle of interconnectedness.

Therefore, let history be not taken as just a chance[8]. The forces of history are intangible but they are on display on wide screen on the arena of civilizations. And, the political scientists[9] of the modern age define them succinctly. The historians view personalities as only forces of history and review them ruthlessly. Did not Eric Erickson attribute Gandhi's spirituality to Freudian neurosis? Strange were the ways of sons of great personages,[10] Raj Mohan Gandhi and Gopal Radhakrishan[11] when they reviewed their fathers historically from a distance. There will be no surprise if the Dalai Lama is psychoanalysed critically the same way. Psychoanalytic truths are always true since they can never be proved wrong!

The Dalai Lama's struggle has been a fight between David and Goliath. Diplomacy is the art of bartering. When negotiating, equilibrium is essential between the parties. China is awesomely powerful and is bereft of rationality even in dealing with its own Tibetan citizens. It knows no restraint when its power is challenged by any of its citizens (there were at least 74,000 challenges as per BBC report during the year 2005, and, the number has doubled by 2011. This is in spite of the possible detention for three years without trial.) Without restraint by the mighty and superior, there can be no justice.

So, the moral compass is limited for a diplomat. That is the difference between the academicians and a politician. He does not have the luxury of absolute good and bad. For the politician any partial step may be the art of possible. Therefore, his actions are inherently morally imperfect and morality cannot be approximated to it.

The Dalai Lama calls himself a reluctant politician. He is the only statesman who will see beyond the expediency of the situation. Statesmen do not dream; but they have visions of distant future. While a philosopher's test is the reasoning behind his maxims, the statesman's test is not only the exaltation of his goals but the catastrophe he averts. Once thwarted, the consequences can never be proved. Alternatively some argue that without philosophy, policy will have no standards; but without the willingness to peer into darkness and, risk some faltering steps, humanity will never know peace. It is said, history knows no resting place. But the statesman by perseverance and intuition must choose and, thereby control the speed of historical forces. History is the foe of permanence, but no leader is entitled to resignation with an unfinished task. To ignore objective realities may amount to inviting peril but to modify the objectives of a struggle in the name of historical inevitability is accepting moral abdication; it amounts to negation of strength, hope and inspiration which have sustained Tibetans so far. He owes to his people to strive, to create and to resist the decay that besets all human institutions. The statesman has to struggle against transitory tendencies; and, paradoxically he cannot insist on the eternity. This is how the Dalai Lama's handing over the reins to a democratically elected leader should be viewed; it has provided for a smooth transition.

Tibetan perspective as of now is piquantly poised. Immanuel Kant in Perpetual Peace said that world peace was inevitable; it would come about either because all nations shared the same sense of justice or because of a cycle of wars of ever increasing violence that would teach men the futility of conflict. Cycle of wars of ever increasing violence has already occurred. But humane treatment of the adversary, even when accepted for war criminals, is missing in Chinese context. The fear of oppression has become a weapon in the hands of the ruthless. Instead of sharing the values of justice with the developed Western world, China has its own distorted standards about human rights, that are based on dictatorship, expansionist nationalism and communist ideology. For the Dalai Lama, peace is a moral responsibility. But, can the quest of peace turn into *sole* objective of the policy?

Probably increasing might of Chinese is causing a nervousness that makes for the compromise. The management of balance of power (Tibet has none accept its moral and just ground) without a foreseeable end is arduous task. But balance is a psychological phenomenon. In the face of British Empire, what power did Gandhi have? If the balance is perceived, then it will not be tested; no sooner a weakness is spotted it will be dented. Estimation of power must include potential which is intangible. Calculation is based on pragmatic reasons. But then, they reflect less of a principle and more of a judgement. Tibet having had visions of intangible potential cannot just be content to have arrived thus far; now there has to be a will to bear with perseverance, subtlety, lots of courage and, the management of unforeseen.

Apart from the historical traits in the Chinese mindset, communist ideology transforms relations into confrontation. It is a doctrine that rests on history and the motivating forces in class consciousness. The communists claim to have self-proclaimed insights into the forces of history. Convinced that their cause is the cause of historic inevitability, at one time, they predicted that class conflict will finally make the entire world a single communist nation. Such ultimate goal does not come through compromise but by victory of one side. And they see it as historical inevitability; so they are destined to win over Tibet.

Summarising, Tibet has nothing more to lose. By a compromise, they have tightened the shackles around themselves. Intention to wage a permanent struggle for independence is the only choice, since there is no other choice but accepting subjugation. The forces of history finally function through the minds of men. These engines are powered by the fundamental aspirations. Historical trends, therefore, are immune from tactical, transient compromise. To aspire so is not just wishful thinking. From the sordid controversies of adversaries, great and shining truths do take shape. The accidental and transitory will yield to the essential and permanent. After co-operating with British for long many years, Gandhi had to give an ultimatum, Quit India. It is not a somersault: consistency is a virtue of stale minds. The matrix of a situation changes constantly. A vibrant mind with clear perception notices the change and, so does it change its response. This satisfies an intellectual craving of symmetry of form and substance[12]. Logic, history and custom have their place; but up to this limit that they will not override values rooted in fundamental aspirations. Tilak said, 'freedom is my birth right and I shall have it'. Freedom is the birth right of Tibetans and, not even the Dalai Lama will be able to deny it![13]

With the change in the format of governance, it is an opportunity now for the New Government to take a U-turn; as even Mahatma Gandhi did in 1942. Let the New Government proclaim all commitments made during nine rounds of negotiations null and void; let the New Government proclaim 17-Point Agreement made under duress and deceit null and void. Let there be a clarion call for Rangzen — independence. Chinese will not be able to bombard Dharmashala. Instead of more repression in side Tibet, this may even soften the lives of Tibetans inside. At least, it will make their sacrifices meaningful.

Now there is no path to peace; yet, peace itself is the path. Not the goal but motivation only is important. Aldous Huxley will say, "Means are the Ends."

REFERENCES

1. Henry Kissinger, *The Anatomy of Power*, New York, 1970.
2. Henry Kissinger: *The White House Years*, London, 1979.
3. Eric Fromm, *The Sane Society*, New York, 1951.
4. John Gailbraith, *The Affluent Society*, New York, 1966.
5. Amartya Sen, London, 2003.
6. Bhaskar Vyas and Damodar Nene, *The Changing Course of Brahmaputra, Dalai Lama the Change Initiator*, Bombay, 1992.
7. In December 2011, a rare event in China, of Government accepting the villagers demands at a peaceful protest may be the harbinger of more.
8. Warren Smith, *Tibet's last Chance*, 2008.
9. Henry Kissinger, *The White House Years*, New York, 1979.
10. Raj Mohan Gandhi, *Gandji. The Boatman*, 1991.
11. Gopal Radhakrishan, *S. Radhakrishnan, A Biography*, 1990.
12. Benjamin Cardozo, *The Nature of the Judicial Process*, New Delhi, 1995.

13. When we said this at the book release function of the First Edition, little did we realize that we may have upset the apple cart. We were summoned to Dharmashala. With profound reverence, tears rolling down, we explained that

the Nation is Bigger than any individual: once it was said in India. "India is Indira and Indira is India." It can never be true.

Reverberations did not stop. Next year a referendum was called again. More than 85 per cent of Tibetans voted for being An Autonomous Region in the People's Republic of China. *New York Times* in the Editorial asked, Were not the Tibetans voting for their time honoured protector? A TYC president told us, "only one Tibetan will be happy to be a Chinese citizen; viz. His Holiness."

15
Survival of the Weakest

Charles Darwin is wrong: even the Weakest survives.

The forces of history point to a multitudinous possibilities for Tibet. Past is absolute. Its repercussions resonate in the present and shape the future. However, the interpretation of an event undergoes changes with the additional dimensions that emerge with the passage of time. The Dalai Lama, though rooted in Buddhism and in fundamental belief of karmic connection, believes that the future can be changed through the present *karma*. With this view in mind, let us examine the various possibilities that are likely to emerge now. So long as the Dalai Lama is the undisputed leader of the Tibetan people, the future is likely to be decided by him. So let us reflect initially on his mindset.

In usual dealings in business and trade, as well as in interpersonal relationships usually honesty and goodness of the people is taken for granted. However, when it comes to any kind of deal where one is involved in exchange of any kind of goods or value, of necessity, caution comes in. Since Plato ruse, greed, cheating, treachery, deceit and such other craft to beguile the adversary is as common in the world as the air.

It is elementary that there can be no peaceful resolution to conflict without negotiations. Discussion, dialogue, debut, dialectics, diametrical divisions, non-cooperation, nonchalance, chance and rarely but surely, even bluff are the necessary components to an ongoing process in dealings with adversaries. In such a tug of war, if the powerful were to win all the times, there will only be survival of the fittest. Charles Darwin philosophized to articulate the theory of the evolution on this basis. That envisaged even wiping off many species and only those survived that evolved to a better order.

The weak may remain apparently weak in tangible ways that are ordinarily seen. But the survival instinct is encoded in the genes; and in

Nature itself. From the gut feelings that may be called faith, the weak come to synthesize elaborate systems of survival strategy. Strategy is imperceptible till it is exercised. And it is through the strategic application of a different kind of combat that the weak overpowers the strength of mighty. Guerilla warfare is one such illustration. To fight violence with non-violence is the software system of Twentieth century. The survival of even weakest can be seen operational in Nature. That is being exercised by the Dalai Lama in his struggle. It is neither implied that he may not have succeeded had he carried forward the violent struggle masterminded by his elder brother. Sun Tzu, a contemporary of Confucius whom Mao tse-Tung considered to be his teacher has written, "To fight and conquer in all your battles is not supreme excellence, supreme excellence consists in breaking the enemy's resistance without fighting. Also know the enemy and yourself, and in a hundred battles, you will suffer no defeat". The secret of Mao's success in overrunning Koumintang forces (they had backing of CIA as well as open support of USA) is attributed to this kind of indoctrination. Chinese "success" in negotiation so far is based on attrition of the opposite.

Good people see no evil. Therefore, the Dalai Lama, ignoring the lessons from history says, Tibetans must trust Chinese in negotiations. Tibetans have now a third cheek to offer.

Madhyam pratipada amounts to walking on a razors' edge. Sincerity of implementation becomes visible with passage of time. The pause between a statement and its implementation gives opportunity for cybernetic interplay. And the process may eventually culminate in further steps towards conflict resolution or stagnation or mere procrastination or retaliation while the interlude is utilized for fortification.

A diplomat is one who *lies* in the interest of his country abroad. The communications in the Twenty-first century have come to a stage where it has become virtually impossible to say a lie. Nobody will be able to fool all people all the times. Simultaneously as the freedom to choose has emerged as one of the most cherished values in the present century, a change in diplomatic stance is no longer seen as treachery.

From the dialectics and diversity in mending and minding the ways a certain possibility may emerge. Generally the Survival of the Fittest prevails. It is more than a century and a half since Charles Darwin postulated the principle. There was a mistake in the axiom; the definition of the fitness was wrong. Solid, hard, rigid and sturdy objects and systems also collapse or can be cut down with the fine edge of a diamond. A software consisting a small file of a virus can crash giant computers. Refined Tibetan culture has such a capacity so that eventually it will prevail over the communist hegemony. That will be the Survival of the Weakest.

With this backdrop the following scenario is likely to emerge. Talks having a stalemate now.

If any further negotiations are conducted, they will have to be as per the dictates of the Chinese. That implies that there is no point. The Dalai Lama shall not return; if he were to return, he would then be not returning to Tibet but he shall be going to China. Though the ministers and the administrators might be offered jobs within Tibet and would be persuaded to return, most of the refugees and certainly all of Tibetan youth would not return. In that case, the international support for Tibet shall at least dwindle if not disappear. Tibetan refugees are amongst the best cared for internationally today. They would be left in the lurch.

The Dalai Lama will have much more loyalty now, following his abdication of sovereignty. His role in terms of religious/spiritual teachings will assume dominance. Thus, apart from the Tibetans, his charisma will pervade even larger masses.

In desperation to return, the New Government may make further concessions. This may generate a kind of desperation amongst young Tibetans. A Tibetan Godse may be born! Heavens forbid!

Nothing of any consequence may come out. The Chinese will carry on the procrastination. Wait till the Dalai Lama dies. They will then install a baby Dalai Lama of Chinese choice so that the Chinese versions of the Dalai Lama as well as Panchen Lama will speak the Chinese language.

A section of Tibetan community in exile will dissociate itself from the official Tibetan line. They shall continue to pursue the road to Rangzen. This may also take a violent turn and a terrorist outfit may emerge. Falun Gong, a world-wide religious network which has connotations of freedom movement is already operating. The secret activity is widespread in Chinese mainland. This may align with Tibetan freedom movement as well as such other movements from three stars of the Chinese flag, Mongolians, Manchurians and the people of East Turkistan. This may erupt into a widespread violent network. This road is a route similar to Ireland and Palestine. Whether it will lead to any resolution is a matter of doubt but the world will take notice.

China will use force to unify Taiwan with the mainland. This will arouse the Japanese sensitivity and the region will become a hotbed of politics based on apprehension and suspicion. A possibility of US-Japan-India axis *vis-à-vis* China is likely to emerge by 2020 that shall upset the present power equations.

Based on its intrinsic contradiction, there may be a collapse of the Chinese communist government on a model similar to USSR. China survives as a single hegemony because of its highly repressive laws. It is already under severe pressure from Western democracies to make room for liberal human rights. Though it enjoys the status of being the third largest economy in the world today, the contradictions in the working conditions of labour class are many.

Political scientists base their arguments mainly on the basis of social and economic weakness inherent in the present Chinese system. There is contradiction in the maxim, "one country two systems" by itself. When two systems interact, they may compliment but they may as well contradict and confuse. The merger of Hong Kong was supposed to highlight this contradiction. It is not apparent as of today.

The high level of corruption in the Chinese system as well as the chasm between the elite in the leadership, administrators and the common man are said to be a major weakness. China observers are uniform that the major creed in China is the greed to make as much money as soon as possible and not communist ideology. However, this is the case with most developing nations and unless the people do not find a fulfilment in consumerism but aspire and struggle, the sacrifice needed for a revolution is hard to come by.

Collapse of the banking system and the financial structure are again emphasized as the cracks that shall widen. Even if the deposits in the State banking system become valueless, and thus cause a great amount of hardship and the run by the people, most nations in the world today have a stake in the survival of the Chinese economy. The financial crisis may therefore be sorted out with international help. And on the performance front there is enormous success in the growth of exports. It appears that the state owned enterprises in China have suitably adjusted themselves to the competition generated through the World Trade Agreements.

The revolutions may be born out of the discontent of the masses because of economic hardships. But they are nurtured by the yearnings of the cross-sections of the people to breathe the free air. The only argument in favour of collapse of China is that freedom is the basic appetite of the soul.

And there is a clear double bind here. Coupled with economic progress, if China were to exercise moderation in utilizing the coercive power of the State, this will provide a hiatus for the ethnic minorities to assert their identity. Can the State shall wither away? In such withering of the oppression, archetypal symbols hiding in the deep unconscious mind find expression in the strivings of the herd and masses. This can be one of the ways and possibly the only intangible way that China may collapse.

Tiananmen Square happenings are now about 25 years old. It only earned a further period of martial law. And thereafter, hardly any large demonstration has occurred. The Chinese now boast of decreasing number of political detainees every year. But all these cannot mean that the people under the Chinese communist system have given up the basic appetite of the soul, i.e. freedom. The ethnicity is imprinted into the genes. The dynamic demiurgic forces of the herd are constantly on interplay to find expression into open from the hidden recesses of the unconscious.

The alternative to the withering of the State could be continued oppression for an indefinite time. Needless to say, this cannot last for ever. China is bound by its international commitments about human rights, world trade agreement and opening up of the system as a whole. If it was to ignore the international sensibilities and if the other countries were to keep on dealing with China only in terms of trade and commerce, then also at some stage, more likely to be sooner than later, the patience of the people will get worn out and hitherto unknown subversive forces (we now know the role of Pope Paul and Richard Nixon in breaking up of Soviet Russia) will just provide a spark to ignite.

So either way, the breakdown of mainland China into its five nationalities is a foregone conclusion, though, it cannot be predicted how soon. The Dalai Lama and the Tibetans were calculating on such a possibility in 1995, 1997 and 1999. This was even prophesied. Nothing of the sort has happened and China is more powerful than ever. This is one of the major factors driving the Tibetans to desperation apart from the advancing age of the Dalai Lama.

The Peoples' Congress, i.e. the Communist party voted by 2896 *versus* zero to use force against Taiwan.

Taiwan is really threatened now. It will have to rally the public sentiments in the island, as it did through a massive public rally on March 14, 2005. It may as well as seek US intervention. President Hu Jintao said that he will try to prevent wars but if they were to occur he would make every effort to win. There is no indication as to when Taiwan would be attacked but now the way to attack is evidently clear.

Chinese methodology of subverting the Tibetan culture, civilization and the Buddhist religion is the slow method of poison, Comunists believe that religion is opium of the masses. They are not to succeed in this strategy.

The legacy of the philosophers Lao-tse and Confucius tell them to rather flow than fight. Therefore, their principle target is the upcoming young generation, be it in Mongolia, Manchuria or Tibet. If the impressionable young mind of the new generation can be indoctrinated, why worry about aging and old who would be their only for a few more years. With this perspective, the Chinese were absolutely alert about the reincarnation of the Panchen Lama and they played ruse when they pretended to let the lamas decide this "religious matter". They just abducted the child and the parents.

Should it surprise anybody that such a child is abducted and after a lapse of several years nothing is heard about his whereabouts? However, in spite of all the brain washing that he may receive, archetypal symbols are encoded in genes. Before his death, 10th Panchen Lama had unfurled a thanka of the Dalai Lama and wished him long life. If there is Buddhism in his veins, it is most likely that this new incarnation will finally owe his allegiance to the Tibetan race and its independence.

So did Karmapa Lama as of now.

It is frequently asked to the Dalai Lama as to what will happen to the institution of the Dalai Lama after him. His answer is that as long as there is misery on this earth and there is suffering to be elevated, he shall be borne again and again. But not in China.

With the constitution of the government in exile and a democratic parliament – Kashag, the Tibetans have already decided on the form of future governance if ever there were a Tibetan rule in Tibet. They have also sorted out decision of sovereignty. However, the Dalai Lama will remain the only benevolent dictator in the modern world today. The Dalai Lama's word is a last word and nobody even dreams to disrespect him. Not only Tibet but all-over in the world history, the time to the succession of the supreme authority has always been a period of turbulence and turmoil with tragic consequences. Even China is no exception. In consonance with political wisdom and astute statesmanship, the Dalai Lama has assured a smooth transition.

And there is Karmapa Lama, an adolescent bright, intelligent, promising reincarnation already in India. Why should he not foot the bill and take to politics when he matures?

What will be the future of the exiled community in India and elsewhere? History records show that the refugees do not return. In the event of any kind of settlement with Chinese, exiled community shall remain a tricky issue. They may keep the Tibetan issue alive.

There is a scope for somersault. With the change in the structure of governance, it is possible to annul all the commitments, from 17-Point Agreement to the Ninth round of negotiation and argue that they were not of the people, by the people and, for the people of Tibet. Let us reflect on this.

There are about 1,30,000 Tibetan refugees in India. The history of refugees world over reflects that they seldom return. How many of the

Tibetans are likely to return to Tibet that will be permanently a part of China? Our surmise is, barely a handful. There may be a possibility of finding jobs, probably more lucrative than that they occupy in India, for the ministers and secretaries in Tibetan Central Administration. Even though unwilling, they may be persuaded to follow the leader (China will accept the Dalai Lama: would they Lobsang Sangay?). An average Tibetan who has opened a restaurant in some far away city, like Tempa Tsering, would still have the fire burning within him of his Tibetan Youth Congress days and would rather cater for the Indian palate and fund whatever TYC activity he possibly could. The ordinary Tibetans have learnt to live the common place life of Indian street vendor selling woollens on the pavements. Why would they barter their political and economic freedom for the unreliable uncertain Chinese citizenship?

In the year 2000[1], UN statistics for refugees world over show that Tibetan refugees are highest in the cared for category. The funding comes to about $ 2000 p.a. per refugee. With ever increasing awareness about the plight of Tibetans and exposure to the Buddhist teachings of the Dalai Lama, the number of sympathizers is on increase and so would be donations.

The teachings about Buddhism have suffered a decline in Tibet. Lamas still trickle down to Dharmashala in search of genuine initiation. Their grievance is that Buddhism that is preached in Tibet now is Chinese brand of Buddhism[2].

None of the cadres of Tibetan Youth Congress will return. Now they are hamstrung by the Dalai Lama. Once they are free from his reins, the future of these mavericks will have a distinct bifurcation point. If they find funds, nothing would stop them from turning into suicidal terrorists. Given to this remote possibility their fate is likely to be like that of Palestinians. Their biggest constraint may be the want of a launching pad.

There is a real possibility that apart from the saber rattling, there shall not be war. Taiwan will continue to be as it is for last half a century. Tibet shall continue the same way. The Yellow River will continue to flow as unquiet and turbulent as it has done hither to before. Meanwhile Brahmaputra would continue to change its course regardless of the Dalai Lama's absence.

Buddhism is emerging as a pacifist religion of the Twenty-first century. The echoes of the meditative silence from innumerable monasteries across the world would reverberate to shake the pillars of Chinese hegemony since it is a classic software for transformation of self, society and civilization.

REFERENCES

1. Tsering Shakya, *The Dragon in the Land of Snow Lion*, London, 1994.
2. Some time in nineties, it was thought, at the instance of Pope Paul, that Dharmashala should export about 1500 erudite lamas to Tibet. China cannot refuse entry to Tibetans to their own land. But once again, Chinese were simply clever. They are welcome provided they have proper travel documents. The refugees today travel on Indian Government papers with refugee status. Instead, they will apply for Chinese passport and as Chinese citizens they may travel to China. All the selected lamas refused to do so.

16
Happenings Happen: No Echos of Nothingness

2008 critical year, Riots in Lhasa; Olympics; China challenged; only the challenge survives; Nobel Peace Prize, 2008; Chinese dissidents; Internet twitting; Forces of history; collective Consciousness of people – Marx; Universal collective consciousness; Carl Jung; Law of karma; Quantum physics; Sambhavami yuge yuge.

On a global scale, nearly 7 billion human minds are at work; each one deciphering their primary needs and, the ways to satisfy them. As the hierarchy of the needs ascend to tertiary needs, such as love, sense of belonging, acceptance further transcending to esteem, complex conceptualizations generate in the psyche. The intangible prevails, so that creative upsurge arises. Creativity needs 359 degrees of freedom; since it knows no direction. And, the essential difference for humans is that they can create new ideas, novel forms, innovative designs and marvelous structures in hardware and software too. Thereby, a thesis is undergoing constant construction; simultaneously an antithesis is born. There will surely be a contest. Yet, opposites accommodate by synthesis. In the process, adaptation to the others in psychological, social and cultural matters is a must. The interaction not only can nurture creativity; it even stimulates it by arousing genes. That is biological essence. Software scientists call it human essence. It is like a perfume in the air: so are the happenings that are reverberating at the local and global scale predicting the changing course of Brahmaputra in Tibet. Let us have an overview.

1. Riots in Lhasa and Tibet

It almost appeared at the onset of the year 2008 that crucial events are to happen. Negotiations have yielded nothing for the Tibetans; Chinese have been implementing the programmes as announced in Tibet Work Forums.

Anger has been building for years in response to Chinese policies. It was feared that the last remnant of Tibetan nationalism would be wiped out. There was no hope within China. But the world was watching now and it gave rise to hopes. Focus of the world was on Beijing Olympics. Statesmen across the globe were invited. Their responses drew much publicity. Everyone was convinced about the deplorable state of human rights in China. Most were trying to articulate their response. March 10th is observed as the National Uprising Day by the Tibetan community. Buddhist lamas have only their lives to lose. They dare. And, they take out a procession from the monastery[1]. On March 10, 2008, the 49th anniversary of the 1959 National Uprising that led to the exile of the Dalai Lama into India, some 200 monks of Drepung monastery, located a few miles northwest of Lhasa, attempted to march into the centre of the city. They were soon stopped by Chinese security police; some were arrested and beaten and the rest were confined to their monastery, which was surrounded by police.

China had to hold Olympics for sure. They were ruthless. Only one fact is evidently clear thereafter. Lhasa and several places in various locations were on fire. Tibetans in some of the most developed areas of Tibet in close proximity to urbanizing centres in mainland China, such as Kanlho Tibetan Autonomous Prefecture in Gansu province and eastern Qinghai were at the forefront of the protests. Urban Lhasa in particular, which is a showcase of China's development Tibet, was the scene of protests and violence. This was an unequivocal rejection of China's rule altogether. The coming of the railway from Golmud in Qinghai to Lhasa resulted in a major influx of Chinese migrants that some analysts had predicted.

Before the quiet was restored, several innocent Chinese and Tibetans had lost their life. The demonstrations and riots were the largest since March 1959. They spread to all parts of the Tibet, including areas outside the Tibet Autonomous Region (TAR). The popular Tibetan reaction has had an air of desperation. It was an opportunity to act if Tibetans have to preserve their national and cultural identity.

The Chinese leadership is close to its goal of extinguishing the Tibetan spirit. The response of the Chinese government was ruthless suppression that may be compared to Tiananmen Square. Here was one more opportunity to blame the Dalai Lama and "terrorists" in exile. There was apprehension not only about public image before Olympics but spread to other People's Republic—the Uighurs of East Turkestan and Taiwan.

When asked, why did many monks and lay Tibetans raise their hands against the ordinary Chinese citizens? The Dalai Lama warned about mistaking ordinary Chinese citizens for Chinese Government. Tibetans cannot raise their hands; least against innocent citizens.

On 8th August, there was a detailed clarification from Tibetan side. "The first protest of 2008 in Tibet occurred in the afternoon of 10 March. This was then followed by more protest demonstrations on 11, 12 and 13 March. The Chinese security people blocked the road. On 14 March, the incident of setting shops on fire, hurling stones and destroying properties occurred. The Chinese government hired some mischievous people on the morning of 14 March to indulge in rioting, which they video-shot for later use in shifting the blame on the Tibetans.

In the monasteries of the Kham and Amdo regions, there is an ancient custom of keeping old swords, spears and rifles in the shrines of the guardian deities. These weapons were forcefully taken out in order to blame the monasteries. A few people in their fits of anger may have caused some harm to the Chinese people. Tibetans cannot be blamed for airing their grievances against the Chinese government policies. The Chinese government strikes hard upon the Tibetans."

One foreign journalist reported, "Apart from video-taping the entire happening, the Chinese security personnel at the scene did nothing to stop them."

Now, Tibetans visiting the Chinese cities and towns seem to be facing problems.

The Dalai Lama issued a condolence statement, addressing Chinese as "brothers and sisters":

> In the light of the recent developments in Tibet, I am deeply saddened by the loss of life. I am aware that some Chinese have also died. I feel for the victims and their families and pray for them. The recent unrest has clearly demonstrated the gravity of the situation in Tibet and the urgent need to seek a solution. Even at this juncture I express my willingness to the Chinese authorities to work together to bring about peace and stability.
>
> I assure you I have no desire to seek Tibet's separation. Nor do I have any wish to drive a wedge between the Tibetan and Chinese peoples. My commitment has been to find a solution to the problem of Tibet that ensures the interests of both Chinese and Tibetans. My primary concern is to ensure the survival of the Tibetan people's distinctive culture, language and identity. As a simple monk who strives to live his daily life according to Buddhist precepts, I assure you of the sincerity of my personal motivation.
>
> I have appealed to the leadership of the PRC to understand problems by "seeking truth from facts". The state media using deceit and

> distorted images could sow the seeds of racial tension with long-term consequences.
>
> Despite my repeated support for the Beijing Olympics, with the intention of creating a rift between the Chinese people and me, the Chinese authorities assert that I am trying to sabotage the games."

There is little doubt that the inspiration for March 2008 uprising was the importance of Olympics. This was, of course, an inspiration, as was there in 1988. That time, seeing the pictures/video images of the Dalai Lama being warmly facilitated in US Congress after making his seminal proposals, naïve Tibetans felt that the end is just insight. If they felt that on the eve of Olympics, a blow up will precipitate some solution, it is but a reasonable aspiration. Sad as it is, it happened at a very heavy price and some unwarranted blemish for the Dalai Lama.

On the other hand, the Dalai Lama had supported the Olympics in Beijing from the time that it was awarded in 2004.

Chinese agreed to another round of talk in May 8, 2008 – obviously to keep a lid on Tibet issue. Lodi Gyari was beguiled by a comment by Chinese President Hu Jintao. He had said, "our attitude towards contacts and consultation with the Dalai Lama is serious". Lodi Gyari said: "It is welcome that the leader of such an important nation stands in front of the world and says that China is serious about the relationship at the highest level. Not only was it a direct comment about the recent meeting that took place, but it was also in the context of a historic press conference with Japanese PM Yasuo Fukuda."

Have the Chinese ever cared to keep their promises, leave aside prouncements at Press Conferences?

2. Olympics

The torch relay was protested by advocates of Tibetan independence and people protesting against China's human rights record, resulting in confrontations at a few of the relay locations. These protests, which ranged from hundreds of people in San Francisco, to effectively none in Pyongyang, have forced the path of the torch relay to be changed or shortened on a number of occasions. The torch was extinguished by Chinese security officials several times during the Paris leg for security reasons.

The questions were being voiced loudly. What do you have in mind for the Olympics? A torch-holder surrounded by Chinese 'flame attendants' who in turn are being helped by police while protestors noisily voice their opposition to Chinese policies and try and get to the torch. In London, the event was intended to hold 3000 people at the end of the procession. It was attended by only 300.

China was concerned, worried. One point of their soft line propaganda was: political protesters agitating about China are violating the spirit and charter of the Games. It did not work.

In Paris, an ugly incident occurred. There was an attack on a handicapped lady. The "Tibetan" who attacked a handicapped lady during the Beijing Olympics Torch relay was found to be a fake! Apparently, the Chinese Communist Party paid for someone to act as a Tibetan to attack. The attacker was later found walking with pro-Beijing protesters, instead of pro-Tibetan protesters.

French President Nicolas Sarkozy considered boycotting the opening ceremony. He was snubbed by Chinese media; he is not welcome. After a meeting with Chinese counterpart Hu Jintao at the G8 conference in Japan, he decided to attend. Prime Minister Gordon Brown demured but finally went to the closing ceremony.

Asked on NBC "Nightly News", The Dalai Lama said that he did not support a boycott of the Beijing Olympic Games. He wanted the world also not to boycott the Olympics.

When the network asked whether he wanted the leaders of the U.S. and other nations to boycott the opening ceremony in support of Tibet and as a statement against China's recent crackdown there, the Dalai Lama replied, "That's up to them."

There were protests in Olympia, Istanbul, London and Paris. In San Francisco – Seven Tibet independence activists were detained this afternoon after three of them scaled the Golden Gate Bridge and unfurled a large protest banner reading "One World, One Dream, Free Tibet 2008." The three climbers remained on the bridge for about 2 hours before coming down voluntarily.

Tibet Protesters unfurled a banner in Paris at Pont Au Change on April 7. Two Tibet independence activists were detained this morning along the torch route after two SFTers descended off Pont Au Change, unfurling a banner reading "Pas de Flame au Tibet." More than 60 pro-Tibet marchers spontaneously gathered round the team on surrounding bridges and streets, chanting free Tibet slogans.

A similar event was planned in UK too on April 6th. Four members of Students For Free Tibet were detained after two activists abseiled off Westminster Bridge and unfurled a 74 square metre protest banner reading, "One World, One Dream: Free Tibet 2008." This brave action took place on the eve of the passing of the Olympic Torch through London.

There was a group known as "Boycott the 2008 Genocide Olympics" with over 6700 members. Mia Farrow led the group and wrote extensively in media.

In India, a total of five intended torchbearers — Kiran Bedi, Soha Ali Khan, Sachin Tendulkar, Bhaichung Bhutia and Sunil Gavaskar — withdrew from the event, citing "personal reasons", Indian national football captain, Baichung Bhutia refused to take part in the Indian leg of the torch relay, citing concerns over Tibet. Bhutia said, he explicitly wished to "standby the people of Tibet and their struggle" and protest against the PRC "crackdown" in Tibet. Bhutia, who is Sikkimese, is the first athlete to refuse to run with the torch. Aamir Khan stated that the "Olympic Games do not belong to China" and confirms taking part in the torch relay, but "with a prayer in his heart for the people of Tibet, and for all people across the world who are victims of human rights violations". Rahul Gandhi, son of the Congress President Sonia Gandhi, also refused to carry the torch.

Activists of Students for Free Tibet, Kate Woznow and Tsering Lama, and Free Tibet Campaign Matt Whitticase were barred from entering Hong Kong on the eve of China's torch relay there. But they went ahead with the planned press conference at 2 p.m. Hong Kong time today. Their deportation underscores China's failure to uphold their promise of ensuring 'openness' before the Summer Games.

While the Chinese side finally seems to have realized that their allegations against the Dalai Lama for instigating the events in Tibet and in sabotaging the Olympic Games have become untenable, they demanded that the Dalai Lama not to support violence, terrorism, and sabotaging the Olympics. The Tibetan retorted that no one needs to urge this. They have consistently rejected and opposed such acts.

There could have been an Olympics that can accelerate political liberalization and create more tolerance for dissent: There could have been loosening of the grip of the authoritarian state eager for validation rather than wobbling under the heat of international criticism.

3. Nobel Prize

Liu Xiaobo was jailed mainly for drafting Charter 08. There were 10,000 visionaries who signed. It almost demanded democratic rule, if not the dissolution dictatorship. He won the Nobel Peace Prize 2008 Liu for his "long and non-violent struggle for fundamental human rights in China. This was an announcement that Chinese had anticipated. They bitterly criticized it now and say it would damage ties between China and Norway. Beijing also strongly criticised Oslo after the 1989 prize went to Tibet's exiled spiritual leader, the Dalai Lama.

Jailed Chinese Liu Xiaobo wins Nobel for Peace

Liu was jailed for 11 years from last December for subversion of state power. He participated during protests on "Tiananmen Square" in 1989. He was later jailed for 20 months and then spent three years in a "labour re-education" camp during the 1990s and, was under virtual house arrest too.

Liu's name is now joined with Soviet dissidents Andrei Sakharov and Aleksander Solzhenitsyn, Polish leader Lech Walesa and Myanmar leader Aung San Suu Kyi and, of course, the Dalai Lama.

Chinese Premier Wen Jiabao sprang a surprise. China had opposed Nobel award vehemently. Yet he said that freedom of speech is indispensable for any country and people's wish for democracy and freedom are irresistible. The Dalai Lama said they are a reflection of the growing understanding for yearning for a more open China. He said such reforms can only lead to a harmonious, stable and prosperous China, which can contribute greatly to a more peaceful world. However, Wen Jiabao insisted that political pluralism must wait. "China will go backwards, split and fall into chaos" if the party cedes control. Millions of Chinese accept that view as real politik, and are content with new homes and cars.

But the Charter 08 signatories dream bigger. They believe that China has proved itself ready to "join the mainstream of civilized nations" by embracing democracy. They are the future.

4. Chinese Dissidents

There are also a large number of Chinese who claim to be dissidents and seek to defect, usually to USA, Canada, UK, Australia or New Zealand. To support their application to migrate, it is quite common for these dissidents to cite their participation in Tiananmen Square protests, their strong religious belief in Falun Gong or that they are being pursued by a network of spies (Chen Yonglin). They are too numerous to name here. Many Chinese political activists have been detained or jailed or exiled for their pro-democracy activities.

Charter 08 is a manifesto initially signed by over 350 Chinese intellectuals and human rights activists. It was published on 10 December, 2008, the 60th anniversary of the Universal Declaration of Human Rights, adopting name and style from the anti-Soviet Charter 77 issued by dissidents in Czechoslovakia. Since its release, more than 10,000 people inside and outside of China have signed the charter.

One of the authors of Charter 08, Liu Xiaobo, was awarded the Nobel Peace Prize in 2010.

Many of the original signatories were prominent citizens inside and outside the government, including lawyers; a Tibetan poet and essayist, Woeser; and Bao Tong, a former senior Communist Party official, who all faced a risk of arrest and jail. The Charter calls for 19 changes including an independent legal system, freedom of association and the elimination of one-party rule. "All kinds of social conflicts have constantly accumulated and feelings of discontent have risen consistently," it reads. "The current system has become backward to the point that change cannot be avoided." China remains the only large world power to still retain an authoritarian system that so infringes on human rights, it states. "This situation must change! Political democratic reforms cannot be delayed any longer!"

Specific demands are:

1. Amending the Constitution.
2. Separation of powers.
3. Legislative democracy.
4. An independent judiciary.
5. Public control of public servants.
6. Guarantee of human rights.
7. Election of public officials.
8. Abolition of Hukou system.
9. Freedom of association.
10. Freedom of assembly.
11. Freedom of expression.
12. Freedom of religion.
13. Civic education.
14. Free markets and protection of private property, including privitizing state enterprises and land.
15. Financial and tax reform.

16. Social security.
17. Protection of the environment.
18. A federated republic.
19. Truth in reconciliation.

There were 10,000 signatories to Charter 08.

On October 8th, 2010, the Dalai Lama said:

> This is the international community's recognition of the increasing voices among the Chinese people in pushing China towards political, legal and constitutional reforms, encouraged by the efforts of hundreds of Chinese intellectuals and concerned citizens, including Mr. Liu Xiaobo in signing the Charter 08.

Ai Wei Wei is one of the most celebrated controversial artist in China. True to the visions of artists of great stature, his works are not supposed to depict beauty only. Of course, he was commissioned to paint the Great Wall. He had State awards inside and outside China. He is offered a guest professorial post for Ai Wei Wei at the Berlin University. But an artist has a calling beyond that. His role is to arouse the conscience of the people through an intangible connection with their consciousness. He has a design firm. The government has put up a huge tax bill of some $US1.85 millions. It is politically motivated to curb him. Challenging a in unpaid taxes and fines required that he should pay up some money upfront. He sat in Tiananmen Square to paint and instantly raised $1.37 Million. He is now further taxed on this money.

- Lu Qing is the legal representative for his design company Beijing Fake Cultural Development Limited!

There are several detained and jailed people. A few amongst them are:

Name	*Occupation*	*Detained*	*Charges or Reason for detention*	*Sentence*	*Notes*
Bao Tong	Government official	1989	Revealing state secrets and counter-revolutionary propagandizing	7 years	Sentenced 1992. Prison: 1989-1996 as of 2009, under surveillance.
Tang Baiqiao	Activist	1989	Spreading counter-revolutionary propaganda; inciting counter-revolutionary activities; defection to the enemy; treason.	3 years	Released under international pressure 1991. Fled to Hong Kong, then U.S. 1992.
Bao Zunxin	Historian	1989	Counter-revolutionary propaganda and incitement	5 years	Sentenced, 1991. released 1992, died 2007
Cai Lujun	Businessman, writer	2003	Incitement to subversion	3 years	Released 2006, sought political asylum in Taiwan in 2007
Gao Xingjian	Writer, painter, director				Recipient of the 2000 Nobel Prize in Literature
Gao Zhisheng	Lawyer	~2006	Disturbing public order	5 yrs suspended	Illegally detained and tortured in 2007; forcibly removed from family home in Shaanxi in 2009. 'Disappeared' by government in 2009, reappeared in 2010. The Chinese Foreign Minister claimed

Name	Occupation	Detained	Charges or Reason for detention	Sentence	Notes
					a prison sentence was for 'subversion'.
Guo Quan	Professor	2008	Subversion of state power	10 years	Sentenced 2009. Awaiting appeal.
He Depu	Writer	2002	"Incited subversion" on the Internet	8 years	Sentenced 2003. Expected release 2010.
Hu Jia	Activist	2007	Inciting subversion of state power	3.5 years	Arrested, imprisoned, and sentenced in 2008. Expec-ted release 2011.
Huang Qi	Webmaster, anti-human trafficking activist	2000	Inciting subversion	5 years	Sentenced 2003. Accused of violating articles 103, 105, 55 and 56. Released 2005.
" "		2008	Illegal possession of state secrets	3 years	Sentenced 2009. Arrested after essay regarding the Sichuan Earthquake.
Jiang Lijun	Writer	2002	Inciting subversion of the state power	4 years	Sentenced 2003. Arrested for "Internet writing and publishing dissident arti-cles". Also sentenced to 'deprivation of political rights' for 1 year..

Name	*Occupation*	*Detained*	*Charges or Reason for detention*	*Sentence*	*Notes*
Jiang Yanyong	Doctor	2004			Detained and released in 2004. Broke story on SARS epidemic. Wrote critical letter regarding Tiananmen.
Li Hai (de:Li Hai)		1994		9 years	Sentenced in 1995. Relea-sed 2004.
Li Zhi	Civil Servant	2003	inciting subversion	8 years	Sentenced 2003. Yahoo! helped the government against him. Expected release in 2011.
Liu Di	Student	2002			Released in 2003.
Liu Xiaobo	Professor of Literature	2008	Inciting subversion of state power	11 years	Sentenced 2009. Expected release 2020. Recipient of the 2010 *Nobel Peace Prize*.
Lü Jiamin	Writer	1989			Released 1991.
Shi Tao	Journalist, writer, poet	2004	Illegally supplying state secrets to overseas organizations	10 years.	Sentenced 2005. Yahoo! helped the government against him. Expected release 2014.
Tan Zuoren	Writer	2008		3 years	Sentenced 2009.
" "		2010	Subversion of state power	5 years	Sentenced 2010

Name	Occupation	Detained	Charges or Reason for detention	Sentence	Notes
Wang Dan	Professor of History	1989	Tiananmen activities	4 years	Sentenced 1991. Released on parole in 1993.
" "		1995		11 years	Sentenced 1996. Released on medical parole to U.S. in 1998; currently in Taiwan.
Wang Xiaoning	Engineer	2002	Incitement to subvert state power	10 years	Sentenced 2003. Yahoo! Helped the government against him. Expected release 2012.
Wang Bingzhang	Doctor	2002	Spying, terrorism	life	Sentenced 2003.
Wang Youcai		1989			
" "		~1998	Subversion	11 years	Released and exiled in 2004; currently in the United States
Wei Jingsheng	Electrician	1979	Passing military secrets	15 years	Released and jailed again in 1993; released for "medical reasons" and deported to the US in 1997.
Yuan Hongbing	Jurist, writer	1994			Detained and forced to leave Beijing in 1994; travelled to and sought

Name	*Occupation*	*Detained*	*Charges or Reason for detention*	*Sentence*	*Notes*
					political asylum in Australia in 2004.
Zhao Changqing	Teacher of History	1989	Tiananmen activities		Released after about 1/2 year.
" "		1998	Workers rights activity	3 years	
" "		2002	Attempted subversion of state power	5 years	Sentenced 2003.
Zeng Jinyan	Blogger	2006	Suspected of harming state security		Under *house arrest* with husband *Hu Jia* from August 2006 — March 2007; currently under house arrest again, since May 2007.

Chinese Government Blacklist

The Chinese government has many blacklists. One of them was reported in the *South China Morning Post* on January 8, 1995 and forms the basis of this list:

To be Arrested on Entry to China

- *Yan Jiaqi* (born 1942). Former aide to ousted party chief Zhao Ziyang. Escaped from China after June 1989. In New York (as of 1995).
- *Chen Yizi* (born 1940). Former director of the Chinese Research Institute for Reform of the Economic Structure in Beijing. Escaped after June 1989. In Princeton, New Jersey (as of 1995).
- *Wan Runnan* (born 1946). Former chief executive officer of the Stone Computer Corp in Beijing. Escaped after June 1989. In France (as of 1995).
- *Su Xiaokang* (born 1949). Writer, author of controversial TV series *River Elegy*. Escaped after June 1989. In Princeton, New Jersey (as of 1995).
- *Chai Ling* (born 1966). Former student leader who escaped to the US after June 1989. She studied for an MBA at *Harvard University*, worked at *Bain* and started a software company. On June 4, 2009 she announced a one-million-dollar humanitarian effort to help the victims of the Tiananmen massacre.
- *Liang Qingtun* (born 1969). Former student leader who escaped after June 1989. In San Francisco (as of 1995).
- *Feng Congde* (born 1967). Former student leader who escaped after June 1989. In France (as of 1995).
- *Wang Chaohua* (born 1952). Former student leader who escaped after June 1989. Studying in Los Angeles (as of 1995).
- *Zhang Zhiqing* (born 1964). Former student leader, still on Beijing's most wanted list. Whereabouts unknown since June 1989 (as of 1995).
- *Zhang Boli* (born 1959). Former student leader who escaped after June 1989. He is currently (2008) a pastor in the *Washington DC* area and leads a church called "Harvest Chinese Christian Church" in Fairfax, Virginia.
- *Li Lu* (born 1966). Former student leader who escaped after June 1989. Studying at *Columbia University* and became an investment banker and venture capitalist.

- *Yue Wu* (born 1946). Former factory director in Shanxi, China. Involved with organising workers during the 1989 movement. In France (as of 1995).
- *Zhang Gang* (born 1949). Former deputy director of public relations at the Chinese Research Institute for Reform of the Economic Structure. Escaped after June 1989. In New York (as of 1995).
- *Yuan Zhiming* (born 1955). Writer. Escaped after June 1989. In Mississippi (as of 1995).
- *Wang Runsheng* (born 1955). Former researcher with the Institute of Politics at the Chinese Academy of Social Sciences. Escaped after June 1989. In France (as of 1995).
- *Chen Xuanliang* (born 1947). Former teacher of philosophy at the Chinese College of Politics. Escaped after June 1989. In France (as of 1995).
- *Zheng Yi* (born 1949). Writer. In hiding for three years after June 1989. Escaped in 1992. In Princeton, New Jersey (as of 1995).
- *Lu Jinghua* (born 1962). Former merchant who became involved in the Beijing Workers' Autonomous Federation in 1989. In New York (as of 1995). Attempted to return to Beijing in June 1993 but was refused entry and sent back to US (as of 1995).
- *Robert Wu* (born 1986). Law student at *Monash University*, Melbourne, Australia, who wrote a letter to the Chinese president demanding more human rights for Chinese citizens. Wu was named in the 2008 list of Beijing's Dissident *Blacklist* by the *Central Committee of the Communist Party of China* and is liable to 12 years imprisonment under *Chinese law*.

To be Refused Re-entry to China

- *Wang Bingzhang* (born 1947). Studied medicine in Canada from 1981, where he established *China Spring*, the first overseas pro-democracy Chinese magazine. Founded the Chinese Alliance for Democracy in 1984. In 2002, he was abducted by Chinese secret agents in *Vietnam* and is currently in prison in *Guangdong*, China (as of 2009).
- *Hu Ping* (born 1947). Activist in the Beijing Democracy Wall Movement in 1979, former president of the Chinese Alliance for Democracy. Went to the USA in 1986. In New York (as of 1995).
- *Xu Bangtai* (born 1949). Former Shanghai student. Went to the USA in 1984 to study journalism. Chair of the Alliance for a Democratic China. In San Francisco (as of 1995).

- *Han Lianchao* (born 1951). Former officer of the Chinese Foreign Ministry. Was a congressional assistant in Washington as of 1995.
- *Cao Changqing* (born 1953). Former deputy editor-in-chief of Shenzhen Youth News. Lost his job in 1987 after publishing an article calling on Deng Xiaoping to retire. In New York (as of 1995).
- *Liu Yongchuan*, Alex (born 1959). Went to the USA in 1986. Founding president of the *Independent Federation of Chinese Students and Scholars* in USA. Became a well-known measurement expert based in Los Angeles, and a known thinker of *spiritual capital.*
- *Liu Binyan* (1925-2005). Author and journalist for the People's Daily. Later, published monthly newsletter China Forum, from the USA.
- *Han Dongfang* (born 1963). Former leader of the Beijing Workers' Autonomous Federation. Imprisoned for two years following the 1989 crackdown. Went to the US for medical treatment in 1992. Returned to China in August 1993 but was deported to Hong Kong. Founded *China Labour Bulletin* in 1994. Now residing in Hong Kong.
- *Tang Baiqiao* (born 1967). Former leader of the Hunan Students' Autonomous Federation. Imprisoned for two years following the 1989 crackdown. He fled to Hong Kong in 1992, and then the U.S. Now residing in New York City where he has been active in the overseas China democracy movement. He has tried to return to China several times, but the government will not grant him a visa.
- *Xiong Yan* (born 1964). Former student leader. Arrested in Beijing and served two years in jail before leaving China in 1992. Joined US Army. Chair of the Chinese Freedom and Democracy Party. Still active in overseas China democracy movement (as of 2005). He successfully re-entered Hong Kong in 2009.
- *Wu'er Kaixi* (born 1968). Former student leader who escaped to *France* after June 1989. He then studied at *Harvard University* and now lives in *Taiwan* (as of 2009). He has been refused entry visas into China in June 2009 (Macau) and June 2010 (Tokyo).
- *Zhao Pinlu* (born 1956). Involved in Beijing Workers' Autonomous Federation in 1989. Escaped and was based in New York in 1995. Chair of the International Chinese Workers Union.
- *Cheng Kai* (born 1946). Former editor-in-chief of Hainan Daily. Left China in 1989. In 1995 was doing business in Hong Kong and had made several trips to China over the previous two years. Blacklisted on August 21, 1993.
- *Feng Zhenghu* (born 1954). Economist and scholar based in *Shanghai.* Refused entry to China eight times in 2009 and remains at *Narita International Airport* in *Japan.*

To bc Dealt with "According to Circumstances of the Situation"

- *Fang Lizhi* (born 1936). Former vice-president of University of Science and Technology of China. Arrived in the US after a year-long refuge in the US Embassy in Beijing. He is now a professor of physics at the *University of Arizona* (as of 2009).
- *Li Shuxian* (born 1935). Wife of Fang Lizhi and former professor of physics at Beijing University (as of 1995).
- *Yu Dahai* (born 1961). Went to the USA in 1982 to study physics at Princeton. Was acting editor-in-chief of the journal Beijing Spring in New Jersey (as of 1995).
- *Wu Fan* (born 1938). Former teacher in Anhui University. Was working in San Francisco (as of 1995). Chairman of the Board of the Alliance for a Democratic China.
- *Ni Yuxian* (born 1945). Democracy Wall activist. Secretary general of the Chinese Freedom and Democracy Party. Attempted to return to China in 1992 but was refused entry. In New York (as of 1995).
- *Yao Yueqian* (born 1938). Lives in Tokyo (as of 1995).
- *Tang Guangzhong* (born 1949). Teacher in US (as of 1995).
- *Guo Luoji* (born 1932), professor of Beijing University, punished for criticising the conviction of Wei Jingsheng in 1979, protested closing of the Democracy Wall, afterwards sent to Nanjing University with no permission to teach. Became a scholar at Columbia University (as of 1995)
- *Harry Wu* (born 1937). Went to US in 1985 as a visiting scholar at Stanford University. Became executive director of the *Laogai Foundation* in California and a US citizen. In November 2008, Wu opened the *Laogai Museum* in *Washington, DC*, calling it the first ever United States museum to directly address human rights in China.
- *Shen Tong* (born 1968). Former student leader who went to US after June 1989. Returned to China in August 1992, arrested in Beijing and deported to the US. Studied at *Boston University* and founded software company *VFinity*. Chair of the China Democracy Fund.
- *Wang Ruowang* (1918-2001). Writer and human rights activist from Shanghai. Imprisoned for a year after June 1989. Moved to the US in 1992. Was Convenor-general of the Co-ordinating Committee of the Chinese Democratic Movement.
- *Feng Suying* (also known as *Yang Zi*) (born 1938). Engineer and human rights activist. In New York (as of 1995).
- *Liu Qing* (born 1948). Imprisoned for almost 11 years after the

Democracy Wall Movement of 1979. Arrived in the US in July 1992. Chair of New York-based Human Rights in China (as of 1995).

- *Xue Wei* (born 1943). Went to the US in 1980. Was a business manager for Beijing Spring (as of 1995).
- *Chen Jun* (born 1958). Former democracy activist in Beijing. Deported in April 1989.
- *Yang Jianli* (born 1950 or 1963). Went to the US as a student in 1982. At Harvard University; Vice-chair of the Alliance for a Democratic China (as of 1995) and/or founder of the *Foundation for China in the 21st Century.*
- *Zhao Haiqing* (born 1956). Went to the US in 1982 to study at the University of Pennsylvania. Former president of IFCSS. Working in Washington; Chair of the National Council of Chinese Affairs (as of 1995).
- *Zhu Jiaming* (born 1950). Economist. Former deputy director of the International Policy Institute of the Zhongxing Investment Company. Became a visiting scholar at Massachusetts Institute of Technology (as of 1995).
- *Xu Jiatun* (born 1916). Former director of the Hong Kong Bureau of Xinhua. Defected to the US after the 1989 crackdown. In Los Angeles (as of 1995).

The Dalai Lama has now established an Internet link to tweet with the Chinese inside Tibet. He invites them to Dharmashala too. The show as well as the answers are on the Net.

5. Devolution of Power

The weakest link in Tibetan hierarchy was that the sovereign was to be born. He has to be located. By the time he achieved maturity, administrators ruled. This was the main reason behind uncertainty of Tibetan course.

The Dalai Lama, without derailing the Institution of the Dalai Lamas, has provided stability to the governance by devolving power to the democratic head. The Spiritual and Temporal are now separate. No ruler in the living history has abdicated power without compulsion. The Dalai Lama having set an example has provided a permanent solution.

> "As early as the 1960s, I have repeatedly stressed that Tibetans need a leader, elected freely by the Tibetan people, to whom I can devolve power. Now, we have clearly reached the time to put this into effect. During the forthcoming eleventh session of the fourteenth Tibetan Parliament in Exile, which begins on 14th March, I will formally propose that the necessary amendments be made to the Charter for Tibetans in Exile, reflecting my decision to devolve my formal authority to the elected leader.
> My desire to devolve authority has nothing to do with a wish to shirk responsibility. It is to benefit Tibetans in the long run. It is not because I feel disheartened. Tibetans have placed such faith and trust in me that as one among them I am committed to playing my part in the just cause of Tibet."

Damodar Nene, Lobsang Sanjay, Nirupa Vyas, Bhaskar Vyas, Sonam, Rajni Vyas

Dr. Sangay said "I will be more forthright and active in speaking about the situation in Tibet. I will also be maintaining the basic principles of non-violence and democracy as I do so."

6. Self-immolations in Tibet: Till December 15, 2011

This heart-rending trend is not new to Buddhist as a form of protest. But now they are doing it so often and yet, they are amongst the least reported important news in media. This is not a suicide; it is surely meant to convey that life is difficult to bear, harder to live than burning alive.

- Thirteen Tibetans, namely *Tenzin Phuntsog*, *Palden Choetso*, *Dawa Tsering*, *Tenzin Wangmo*, *Norbu Damdrul*. *Choepel*, *Kayang*, *Kelsang Wangchuk*, *Lobsang Kelsang*, *Lobsang Kunchok*, *Tsewang Norbu*, *Phuntsog* and *Tapey* have self-immolated since February 27, 2009; 24 by March 2012
- 11 men, two women
- Six of the 13 are known to have died following their protest
- Nine of the 13 are from Ngaba Tibetan and Qiang Autonomous Prefecture, Sichuan province
- Three are from Kardze Tibetan Autonomous Prefecture, Sichuan province (One monk from Nyitso monastery, one monk from Kardze monastery and one nun from Tawu)
- Five of the 13 were monks at Kirti monastery in Ngaba

(*Contd.*)

- Three of the 13 are former monks at Kirti monastery in Ngaba (It is currently not known whether the three chose to disrobe, or were expelled from the monastery by government authorities)
- One of the 13 was a nun from Mame Dechen Chokorling nunnery in Ngaba
- 12 of the self-immolations have occurred since March 16, 2011

Chinese response can be imagined. In a population of 1.3 billion, 13 does not mean any count at all. The human torches will be burning in all compassionate hearts for ever/Let us pray that this is enough!

7. Human Rights

Issue of fundamental human rights is like having free air. When deprived, then only suffocation is evident. And, while the tourists see the gross development on the surface, little do they have access to the hearts of masses.

A review of Human Rights abuses was given at the United Nations Council by Mr. Tenzin Samphel Kayta. He represented the Society for Threatened Peoples. Mr. Kayta urged the Communist regime to put an "end to harassment against human rights defenders and Tibetan intellectuals in Tibet" and to implement the recommendation put forward by the UNHRC High Commissioner, Special Rapporteur on Human Rights Defenders and the Committee Against Torture.

Mr. Kayta talked about the Tibetan environmentalist and philanthropist

Karma Samdup who is serving 15 years of imprisonment on a charge that was dropped more than a decade ago.

The Tibetan environmentalist is the latest victim of what many Tibet activists and analysts say is China's recent stepping up of control against influential Tibetans like artistes, writers, singers and intellectuals.

Citing one instance, "Karma Samdup is severely tortured by the police during several months of interrogation and the court's dismissal of his testimony as irrelevant," Mr. Kayta said. The Council was also informed of the arrest and sentences awarded to six of his family members within a span of one year.

8. Collective Consciousness: Marxist and Jungian

Karl Marx based communist ideology on *Consciousness* refers to the idea of a being who is self-aware. It is a distinction often reserved for human beings. A line of political and philosophical inquiry opened up which explores consciousness in terms of one's political state of mind. For Marx, consciousness describes a person's political sense of self. While Hegel placed God behind the workings of consciousness in people, Marx saw the *political economy* as the engine of mind. In Marx's view, consciousness was always political, for it was always the outcome of politic-economic circumstances. What one thinks of life, power, and self is always a product of ideological forces.

Karl Jung's concept of universal collective consciousness has a play in all human affairs; particularly when there are happenings in the deep unconscious minds of a large mass of humanity[2].

Buddhist and Scientific Views as well as parallel realities in the quantum world and the quantum concept of consciousness are now pointing to the postulates that Karl Marx and Carl Jung conceptualized. Regardless of the social and political repercussions of thesis, a single fact emerges about consciousness. It is radiant. It may or may not be unitary, it reflects on the other. Quantum physicists established, even to the astonishment of Einstein who said that he found it impossible to believe that a mouse looking at the stars can affect the Universe. In the (w)holistic nature of Universe, no man is an island.

Chinese intransigence to the fundamental aspirations of its own people cannot last for ever. Samdong Rimpoche said: India's fight for independence took some 200–400 years. Tibetans have fought only for 50-60 years as yet. But, they shall overcome.

Every time in the history of struggles for independence, the freedom fighters are treading a path where he is on the edge of violating law everyday.

It is the plain and simple fact that freedom is not won by law suits in a court of law. In India, Gopal Krishan Gokhale and Bal Gangadhar Tilak had fought legal battles in a court of law. Gandhi had realized the futility of this course. He relied on mass support.

What triggers off the mass upsurge in the collective consciousness of a people is very unpredictable and difficult to decipher. What were the psychodynamics of masses to 10th March, 1959, or the German people gathered to breakdown the Berlin wall or all the Polish people who veered around Lech Varela or Russian people who pulled down the statue of Lenin, causing the collapse of the communist rule? What were the forces that created mass upheavals in Greece and Middle East, Africa and India with Anna Hazare in 2011? The Dalai Lama said these events have shown once again that determined non-violent action can indeed bring about positive change. These inspiring changes lead to genuine freedom, happiness and prosperity for the peoples in these countries.

They may not have a written recipe for a future revolution. But these are most memorable, noble examples of how revolutions happen.

But when there is a wave of upsurge a leader is needed to ride over. When the party bosses rolled the tanks in the streets of Moscow it required a courageous leader like Yeltsin to mount over an armored tank. Nelson Mandela spent more than two decades in South African prison. Valecha, Havell and Yeltsin, could have been killed. They decided to take the risk and plunged.

At the risk of repetition, when it comes to any kind of deal where one is involved in exchange of any kind of goods or value, caution of necessity comes in. It was told by Plato a long time back that ruse, greed, cheating, treachery, deceit and such other craft to beguile the adversary is as common in the world as the air that surrounds us.

The Chinese communists were making the same mistake that Marks did. In *des capitol* Karl Marks had postulated that the initial strengthening of the state will eventually result into a gradual weathering away of the State. Once there was economic party leading to cessation of class struggle. In the process of liberalization, the Chinese attempted to corrupt the high Lamas by granting thcm perks and privileges. It is now well known that another privileged class gets created. That class then, wants to preserve its advantages.

Chinese had thought that once the high Lamas can be made to toe the official line, their faith in religion will wither away. Nothing can be more erroneous than this. There are varieties of religious experiences. But the uniqueness of a religious experience is common to all the kinds of religious experiences[3].

The year 2011 has seen unprecedented military preparedness on Indo-China borders with stock piling of nuclear missiles at the striking distance to the major cities on both sides. War should not happen; but any unstable element, maybe even Taiwan, Japan or Tibet, can trigger a Third World War. Let us pray!

In conclusion, the Dalai Lama's world view, his special bond with the Tibetan people and the respect he enjoys in the international community all make the personage of the Dalai Lama key to achieving a negotiated solution to the Tibetan issue. This is why, far from being the problem, the Dalai Lama is the solution.

REFERENCES

1. Warren W. Smith, *Tibet's Last Stand?* New York, 2008.
2. Bhaskar Vyas and Rajni Vyas, *Space, Time and Consciousness*, New Delhi, 2002.
3. William James, *Varieties of religious experiences*, Edinburgh, 1892.

APPENDIX I

Sardar Vallabhbhai Patel's Letter to Prime Minister Jawaharlal Nehru New Delhi, 7 November, 1950

My Dear Jawaharlal,

Ever since my return from Ahmedabad and after the cabinet meeting the same day which I had to attend at practically 15 minutes' notice and for which I regret I was not able to read all the papers, I have been anxiously thinking over the problem of Tibet and I thought I should share with you what is passing through my mind.

2. I have carefully gone through the correspondence between the External Affairs Ministry and our Ambassador in Peking and through him the Chinese Government. I have tried to peruse this correspondence as favourably to our Ambassador and the Chinese Government as possible, but I regret to say that neither of them comes out well as a result of this study. The Chinese Government has tried to delude us by professions of peaceful intention. My own feeling is that at a crucial period they manage to instill into our Ambassador a false sense of confidence in their so-called desire to settle the Tibetan problem by peaceful means. There can be no doubt that during the period covered by this correspondence the Chinese must have been concentrating for an onslaught on Tibet. The final action of the Chinese, in my judgement, is little short of perfidy. The tragedy of it is that the Tibetans put faith in us; they choose to be guided by us; and we have been unable to get them out of the meshes of Chinese diplomacy or Chinese malevolence. From the latest position, it appears that we shall not be able to rescue the Dalai Lama. Our Ambassador has been at great pains to find an explanation or justification for Chinese policy and actions. As the External Affairs Ministry remarked in one of their telegrams, there was a lack of firmness and unnecessary apology in one or two representations that he made to the Chinese Government on our behalf. It is impossible to imagine any sensible person believing in the so-called threat to China from Anglo-American machinations in Tibet. Therefore, if the Chinese put faith in this, they must have distrusted us so completely as to have taken us as tools or stooges of Anglo-American diplomacy or strategy. This feeling, if genuinely entertained by the Chinese in spite of your direct approaches to them, indicates that even though we regard ourselves as

friends of China, the Chinese do not regard us as their friends. With the Communist mentality of "whoever is not with them being against them," this is a significant pointer, of which we have to take due note. During the last several months, outside the Russian camp, we have practically been alone in championing the cause of Chinese entry into UN and in securing from the Americans assurances on the question of Formosa. We have done everything we could to assuage Chinese feelings, to allay its apprehensions and to defend its legitimate claims in our discussions and correspondence with America and Britain and in the UN. In spite of this, China is not convinced about our disinterestedness; it continues to regard us with suspicion and the whole psychology is one, at least outwardly, of skepticism perhaps mixed with a little hostility. I doubt if we can go any further that we have done already to convince China of our good intentions, friendliness and goodwill. In Peking we have an Ambassador who is eminently suitable for putting across the friendly point of view. Even he seems to have failed to convert the Chinese. Their last telegram to us is an act of gross discourtesy not only in the summary way it disposes of our protest against the entry of Chinese forces into Tibet but also in the wild insinuation that our attitude is determined by foreign influences. It looks as though it is not a friend speaking in that language but a potential enemy.

3. In the background of this, we have to consider what new situation now faces us as a result of the disappearance of Tibet, as we knew it and the expansion of China almost up to our gates. Throughout history we have seldom been worried about our north-east frontier. The Himalayas have been regarded as an impenetrable barrier against any threat from the north. We had friendly Tibet which gave us no trouble. The Chinese were divided. They had their own domestic problems and never bothered about frontiers. In 1914, we entered into a convention with Tibet which was not endorsed by the Chinese. We seem to have regarded Tibetan autonomy as extending to independent treaty relationship. Presumably, all that we required was Chinese counter-signature. The Chinese interpretation of suzerainty seems to be different. We can, therefore, safely assume that very soon they will disown all the stipulations which Tibet has entered into with us in the past. That throws into the melting pot all frontier and commercial settlements with Tibet on which we have been functioning and acting during the last half a century. China is no longer divided. It is united and strong. All along the Himalayas in the north and north-east, we have on our side of the frontier a population ethnologically and culturally not different from Tibetans and Mongoloids. The undefined states of the frontier and the existence on our side of a population with its affinities to the Tibetans or Chinese have all the elements of the potential trouble

between China and ourselves. Recent and bitter history also tells us that communism is no shield against imperialism and that the communist are as good or as bad imperialist as any other. Chinese ambitions in this respect not only covered the Himalayan slopes on our side but also include the important part of Assam. They have their ambitions in Burma also. Burma has the added difficulty that it has no McMohan line round which to build up even the semblance of an agreement. Chinese irredentism and communist imperialism are different from the expansionism or imperialism of the western powers. The former has a cloak of ideology which makes it ten times more dangerous. In the guise of ideological expansion lie concealed racial, national or historical claims. The danger from the north and north-east, therefore, becomes both communist and imperialist. While our western and non-western threat to security is still as prominent as before, a new threat has developed from the north and north-east. Thus, for the first time, after centuries, India's defence has to concentrate itself on two fronts simultaneously. Our defence measures have so far been based on the calculations of superiority over Pakistan. In our calculations we shall now have to reckon with communist China in the north and in the north-east, a communist China which has definite ambitions and aims and which does not, in anyway, seem friendly disposed towards us.

4. Let us also consider the political conditions on this potentially troublesome frontier. Our northern and north-eastern approaches consist of Nepal, Bhutan, Sikkim, the Darjeeling (area) and tribal areas in Assam. From the point of view of communication, there are weak spots. Continuous defensive lines do not exist. There is almost an unlimited scope for infiltration. Police protection is limited to a very small number of passes. There, too, our outposts do not seem to be fully manned. The contact of these areas with us is by no means close and intimate. The people inhabiting these portions have no established loyalty or devotion to India even the Darjeeling and Kalimpong areas are not free from pro-Mongoloid prejudices. During the last three years we have not been able to make any appreciable approaches to the Nagas and other hill tribes in Assam. European missionaries and other visitors had been in touch with them, but their influence was in no way friendly to India/Indians. In Sikkim, there was political ferment some time ago. It is quite possible that discontent is smoldering there. Bhutan is comparatively quiet, but its affinity with Tibetans would be a handicap. Nepal has a weak oligarchic regime based almost entirely on force; it is in conflict with a turbulent element of the population as well as with enlightened ideas of modern age. In these circumstances, to make people alive to the new danger or to make them defensively strong is a very difficult task indeed and that difficulty can be

got over only by enlightened firmness, strength and a clear line of policy. I am sure the Chinese and their source of inspiration, Soviet Union would not miss any opportunity of exploiting these weak spots, partly in support of their ideology and partly in support of their ambitions. In my judgement, the situation is one which we cannot afford either to be complacent or to be vacillating. We must have a clear idea of what we wish to achieve and also of the methods by which we should achieve it. Any faltering or lack of decisiveness in formulating our objectives or in pursuing our policies to attain those objectives is bound to weaken us and increase the threats which are so evident.

5. Side by side with these external dangers, we shall now have to face serious internal problems as well. I have already asked (H.V.R.) Iyengar to send to the E.A. Ministry a copy of the Intelligence Bureau's appreciation of these matters. Hitherto, the Communist party of India has found some difficulty in contacting communists abroad, or in getting supplies of arms, literature, etc., from them. They had to contend with the difficult Burmese and Pakistan frontiers on the east with the long sea board. They shall now have a comparatively easy means of access to Chinese communists and through them to other foreign communists. Infiltration of spies, fifth columnists and communists would now be easier. Instead of having to deal with isolated communist pockets and Telengana and Warangal we may have to deal with communist threats to our security along our northern and north-eastern frontiers, where, for supplies of arms and ammunition, they can safely depend on communist arsenals in China. The whole situation thus raises a number of problems on which we must come to early decision so that we can, as I said earlier, formulate the objectives of our policy and decide the method by which those objectives are to be attained. It is also clear that the action will have to be fairly comprehensive, involving not only our defence strategy and state of preparations but also problem of internal security to deal with which we have not a moment to lose. We shall also have to deal with administrative and political problems in the weak spots along the frontier to which I have already referred.

6. It is, of course, impossible to be exhaustive in setting out all these problems. I am, however, giving below some of the problems which in my opinion, require early solution and round which we have to build our administrative or military policies and measures to implement them.

(a) A military and intelligence appreciation of the Chinese threat to India both on the frontier and internal security.
(b) An examination of military position and such re-disposition of our forces as might be necessary, particularly with the idea of

guarding important routes or areas which are likely to be the subject of dispute.

(c) An appraisement of strength of our forces and, if necessary, reconsideration of our retrenchment plans to the Army in the light of the new threat. A long-term consideration of our defence needs. My own feeling is that, unless we assure our supplies of arms, ammunition and armour, we should be making a defence position perpetually weak and we would not be able to stand unto the double threat of difficulties both from the west and north and north-east,

(d) The question of Chinese entry into UN. In view of rebuff which China has given us and the method which it has followed in dealing with Tibet, I am doubtful whether we can advocate its claims any longer. There would probably be a threat in the UN virtually to outlaw China in view of its active participation in Korean War. We must determine our attitude on this question also.

(e) The political and administrative steps which we should take to strengthen our northern and north-eastern frontier. This would include whole of border, i.e. Nepal, Bhutan, Sikkim, Darjeeling and tribal territory of Assam.

(f) Measures of internal security in the border areas as well as the states flanking those areas such as U.P., Bihar, Bengal and Assam.

(g) Improvement of our communication, road, rail, air and wireless, in these areas and with the frontier outposts.

(h) The future of our mission at Lhasa and the trade post of Gyangtse and Yatung and the forces which we have in operation in Tibet to guard the trade routes.

(i) The policies in regards to McMohan line.

7. These are some of the questions which occur to my mind. It is possible that a consideration of these matters may lead us into wider question of our relationship with China, Russia, America, Britain and Burma. This however would be of a general nature, though some might be basically very important, i.e. we might have to consider whether we should not enter into closer association with Burma in order to strengthen the latter in its dealings with China. I do not rule out the possibility that, before applying pressure on us, China might apply pressure on Burma. With Burma, the frontier is entirely undefined and the Chinese territorial claims are more substantial. In its present position, Burma might offer an easier problem to China, and, therefore, might claim its first attention.

8. I suggest that we meet early to have a general discussion on these problems and decide on such steps as we might think to be immediately

necessary and direct, quick examination of other problems with a view to taking early measure to deal with them.

Yours,
Vallabhbhai Patel
To
The Hon'ble Shri Jawaharlal Nehru, New Delhi

· Goleman Daniel, Healing Emotions, Conversations with the Dalai Lama on Mindfulness, Emotions and Health, Boston, 1997, p. 217.

APPENDIX II

Correspondence between the Dalai Lama and General Tan, March 1959

On 10th March, 1959, after hearing from his Ministers that the Dalai Lama could not leave the Norbulingka to attend the theatrical performance in the Chinese camp, the Chinese commander wrote:

Respected Dalai Lama,

It is very good indeed that you wanted to come to the Military Area Command. You are heartily welcome. But since the intrigues and provocations of the reactionaries have caused you very great difficulties, it may be advisable that for the time being you do not come.

Salutations and best regards,
Tan Kuan-san

The Dalai Lama replied on 11th March:

Dear Comrade Political Commissar Tan,

I intended to go to the Military Area Command to see the theatrical performance yesterday, but I was unable to do so, because of obstruction by people, lamas and laymen, who were instigated by a few evil elements and who did not know the facts; this has put me to indescribable shame. I am greatly upset and worried and at a loss what to do. I was immediately greatly delighted when your letter appeared before me—you do not mind at all.

Reactionary, evil elements are carrying out activities endangering me under the pretext of ensuring my safety. I am taking measures to calm things down. In a few days, when the situation becomes stable, I will certainly meet you. If you have any internal directives for me, please communicate them to me frankly through this messenger.

The Dalai Lama,
written by my own hand

On the same day General Tan wrote to the Dalai Lama:

To Dalai Lama,

The reactionaries have now become so audacious that they have openly and arrogantly engaged in military provocations. They have erected fortifications and posted large numbers of machine guns and armed reactionaries along the national defense highway (the highway north of the Norbulingka) thereby very seriously disrupting the security of national defense communications.

On many occasions in the past, we told the Kashag that the People's Liberation Army is in duty bound to defend the country and to ensure the protection of communications related to national defense; it cannot remain indifferent to this serious net of military provocation. The Tibet Military Area Command has sent letters therefore, to Surkong, Shasu and Pala asking them to tell the reactionaries to remove all the fortifications they have set up and to withdraw from the highway immediately. Otherwise, they will have to take full responsibility themselves for the evil consequences. I want to inform you of this. Please let me know what your views are at your earliest convenience.

Salutations and best regards
Tan Kuan-san

The Dalai Lama replied on 12th March:

Dear Comrade Political Commissar Tan,

I suppose you have received my letter of yesterday forwarded to you by Ngapo (Apei). I have received the letter you sent me this morning. The unlawful activities of the reactionary clique cause me endless worry and sorrow. Yesterday I told the Kashag to order the immediate dissolution of the illegal conference and the immediate withdrawal of the reactionaries who arrogantly moved into the Norbulingka under the pretext of protecting me. As to the incidents of yesterday and the day before, which were brought about under the pretext of ensuring my safety and have seriously estranged relations between the Central People's Government and the local government, I am making every possible effort to deal with them. At eight thirty Peking time this morning, a few Tibetan army men suddenly fired several shots near the Chinghai-Tibet Highway. Fortunately, no serious disturbance occurred. I am planning to persuade a few subordinates and give them instructions. Please communicate to me frankly any instructive opinions you have for me.

The Dalai

General Tan answered on 15th March:

Respected Dalai Lama,

I have the honour to acknowledge receipt of your two letters dated March 11 and March 12. The traitorous activities of some reactionary elements among the upper social strata in Tibet have grown to intolerable proportions. These individuals, in collusion with foreigners, have engaged in reactionary, traitorous activities for quite some time. The Central People's Government has all along maintained a magnanimous attitude and enjoined the local government of Tibet to deal with them in all earnestness, but the local government of Tibet has all along adopted an attitude of feigning compliance while actually helping them in their activities, with the result that things have now come to such a grave pass. The Central People's Government still hopes that the local government of Tibet will change its wrong attitude and immediately assume responsibility for putting down the rebellion and mete out severe punishment to the traitors. Otherwise the Central People's Government will have to act itself to safeguard the solidarity and unification of the motherland.

In your letter, you said: "As to the incidents... which were brought about under the pretext of ensuring my safety and have seriously estranged relations between the Central People's Government and the local government, I am making every possible effort to deal with them." We warmly welcome this correct attitude on your part.

We are very much concerned about your present situation and safety. If you think it necessary and possible to extricate yourself from your present dangerous position of being held by the traitors, we cordially welcome you and your entourage to come and stay for a short time in the Military Area Command. We are willing to assume full responsibility for your safety. As to what is the best course to follow, it is entirely up to you to decide.

In addition, I have much pleasure in informing you that it has been decided that the Second National People's Congress will open its first session on April 17.

Salutations and best regards,
Tan Kuan-san

The third and last letter of the Dalai Lama to General Tan was written on 16th March.

Dear Comrade Political Commissar Tan,

Your letter dated the 15th has just been received at three o'clock. I am very glad that you are so concerned about my safety and hereby express my thanks.

The day before yesterday, the fifth day of the second month according to the Tibetan calendar, I made a speech to more than seventy representatives of the government officials, instructing them from various angles, calling on them to consider seriously present and long-term interests and to calm down, otherwise my life would be in danger. After these severe reproaches, things took a slight turn for the better. Though the conditions here and outside are still very difficult to handle at present, I am trying tactfully to draw a line separating the progressive people among the government officials from those opposing the revolution. In a few days from now, when there are enough forces I can trust, I shall make my way to the Military Area Command. When that time comes, I shall first send you a letter. I request you to adopt reliable measures. What are your views? Please write me often.

The Dalai

APPENDIX III

United Nations General Assembly Resolutions

UNITED NATIONS GENERAL ASSEMBLY RESOLUTION 1353 (XIV) 21 OCTOBER 1959

The General Assembly,

Recalling the principles regarding fundamental human rights and freedoms set out in the Charter of the United Nations and in the Universal Declaration of Human Rights adopted by the General Assembly on 10 December 1948.

Considering that the fundamental human rights and freedoms to which the Tibetan people, like all others, are entitled include the right to civil and religious liberty for all without distinction,

Mindful also of the distinctive cultural and religious heritage of the people of Tibet and of the autonomy which they have traditionally enjoyed,

Gravely concerned at reports, including the official statements of His Holiness the Dalai Lama, to the effect that the fundamental human rights and freedoms of the people of Tibet have been forcibly denied them,

Deploring the effect of these events in increasing international tension and embittering the relations between peoples at a time been earnest and positive efforts are being made by responsible leaders to reduce tension and improve international relations,

Affirms its belief that respect for the principles of the Charter of the United Nations and of the Universal Declaration of Human Rights is essential for the evolution of a peaceful world order based on the rule of law;

Calls for respect for the fundamental human rights of the Tibetan people and for their distinctive cultural and religious life.

UNITED NATIONS GENERAL ASSEMBLY RESOLUTION 123 (XVI) 20 DECEMBER 1961

The General Assembly,

Recalling its resolution 1353(XIV) of 21 October 1959 on the question of Tibet,

Gravely concerned at the continuation of events in Tibet, including the violations of the fundamental human rights of the Tibetan people and the suppression of the distinctive cultural and religious life which they have traditionally enjoyed,

Noting with deep anxiety the severe hardships which these events have inflicted on the Tibetan people, as evidenced by the large scale exodus of Tibetan refugees to the neighbouring countries,

Considering that these events violate fundamental human rights and freedoms set out in the Charter of the United Nations and the Universal Declaration of Human Rights, including the principle of self-determination of peoples and nations, and have the deplorable effect of increasing international tension and embittering relations between peoples,

Reaffirms its conviction that respect for the principles of the Charter of the United Nations and of the Universal Declaration of Human Rights is essential for the evolution of a peaceful world order based on the rule of law,

Solemnly renews its call for the cessation of practices which deprive the Tibetan people of their fundamental human rights and freedoms, including their right to self-determination,

Expresses the hope that Member States will make all possible efforts, as appropriate, towards achieving the purposes of the present resolution.

UNITED NATIONS GENERAL ASSEMBLY RESOLUTION 209 (XX) 18 DECEMBER 1965

The General Assembly

Bearing in mind the principles relating to human rights and fundamental freedoms set forth in the Charter of the United Nations and proclaimed in the Universal Declaration of Human Rights,

Reaffirming its resolutions 1353 (XVI) of 21 October 1959 and 123 (XVI) of 20 December 1961 on the question of Tibet,

Gravely concerned at the continued violation of the fundamental rights and freedoms of the people of Tibet and the continued suppression of their distinctive cultural and religious life as evidenced by the exodus of refugees to the neighbouring countries,

Deplores the continued violation of the fundamental rights and freedoms of the peoples of Tibet,

Reaffirms that respect for the principles of the Charter of the United

Nations and of the Universal Declaration of Human Rights is essential for the evolution of a peaceful world order based on the rule of law;

Declares its conviction that the violation of human rights and fundamental freedoms in Tibet and the suppression of the distinctive cultural and religious life of its people increase international tension and embitter relations between peoples;

Solemnly renews its call for the cessation of all practices which deprive the Tibetan people of the human rights and fundamental freedoms which they have always enjoyed;

Appeals to all States to use their best endeavours to achieve the purposes of the present resolution;

Whereas the three UN General Assembly resolutions passed in 1959, 1961 and 1965 acknowledged Tibet's right to self-determination, reiterates its condemnation of the continuing human rights violations by the Chinese authorities in Tibet;

Supports the Dalai Lama's proposal on negotiations on the future of Tibet and invites the Chinese Government to react in an official and positive way to this proposal;

Asks the Council, the Member States and the Commission to do everything possible in the framework of the relations between the Union and the Republic of China and the United Nations in order to bring the two sides together with a view to reaching an agreement which satisfies the legitimate requests of the Tibetan people;

Calls on the governments of the Member States to have the question of Tibet's occupation and decolonization placed on the agenda of the United Nations General Assembly;

Instruct its President to forward this resolution to the Council, the Commission, the governments of the Member States, the Government of the People's Republic of China, H.H. the Dalai Lama, the Tibetan Government in exile and the United Nations.

APPENDIX IV

Strasbourg Proposal and Subsequent Resolutions at Parliaments

Strasbourg Proposal

The Dalai Lama made a visit to the European parliament, and said, on June 16, 1988, said:

"We are living today in a very interdependent world. One nation's problems can no longer be solved by itself.... I always believed in the need for better understanding, closer cooperation and greater respect among the various nations of the world. The European Parliament is an inspiring example. Out of chaos of war, those who were once enemies have, in a single generation, learned to co-exist and to cooperate.

The Tibetans, particularly those who live under Chinese occupation, yearn for freedom and justice and a self-determined future, so that they are able to fully preserve their unique identity and live in peace with their neighbours.

For over a thousand years we Tibetans have adhered to spiritual and environmental values.... Inspired by the Buddhist teachings, we sought to respect every form of life and to abandon war as an instrument of national policy.

Our history, dating back more than two thousand years, has been one of independence. At no time, since the founding of our nation in 127 BC, have we Tibetans conceded our sovereignty to a foreign power....In 1949 the People's Republic of China forcibly invaded Tibet. Since that time, Tibet has endured the darkest period in its history. More than a million of our people have died as a result of the occupation. A generation has grown up deprived of education, economic opportunity and a sense of its own national character. Though the current Chinese leadership has implemented certain reforms, it is also promoting a massive population transfer onto the Tibetan plateau. This policy has already reduced the six million Tibetans to a minority. Our tragedy continues.

I have always urged my people not to resort to violence in their efforts to redress their suffering. All people have the moral right to peacefully protest injustice. The demonstrations in Tibet have been violently suppressed by the Chinese police and military. I will continue to counsel for non-violence, but unless China forsakes the brutal methods it employs, Tibetans cannot be responsible for a further deterioration in the situation.

Every Tibetan hopes and prays for the full restoration of our nation's independence. Thousands of our people have sacrificed their lives and our whole nation has suffered in this struggle. Even in recent months, Tibetans have bravely sacrificed their lives to achieve this precious goal. On the other hand, the Chinese totally fail to recognize the Tibetan people's aspirations and continue to pursue a policy of brutal suppression.

I have thought for a long time on how to achieve a realistic solution to my nation's plight. On September 21, 1987, at the Congressional Human Rights Caucus in Washington, DC, I announced a Five Point Peace Plan for Tibet. In it I called for the conversion of Tibet into a zone of peace, a sanctuary in which humanity and nature can live together in harmony. I also called for respect for human rights and democratic ideals, environmental protection, and a halt of the Chinese population transfer into Tibet.

The fifth point of the Peace Plan called for earnest negotiations between the Tibetans and the Chinese. The goal is defined so as whole of Tibet known as Cholka-Sum (U-tsang, Kham and Amdo) should become a self-governing democratic political entity founded on law by agreement of the people for the common good and the protection of themselves and their environment. This is in association with the People's Republic of China.

The Government of the People's Republic of China could remain responsible for Tibet's foreign policy. The Government of Tibet should, however, develop and maintain relations, through its own Foreign Affairs Bureau, in the fields of religion, commerce, education, culture, tourism, science, sports and other non-political activities.

As individual freedom is the real source and potential of any society's development, the Government of Tibet would seek to ensure this freedom by full adherence to the Universal Declaration of Human Rights, including the rights to speech, assembly, and religion. Because religion constitutes the source of Tibet's rich culture, it would be a special duty of the Government of Tibet to safeguard and develop its practice.

The Government should comprise a popularly elected Chief Executive, bi-cameral legislative branch, and an independent judicial system. Its seat should be in Lhasa.

The Government of Tibet would pass strict laws to protect wildlife and plant life. The exploitation of natural resources would be carefully regulated. The manufacture, testing and stockpiling of nuclear weapons and other armaments must be prohibited, as well as the use of nuclear power and other technologies which produce hazardous waste. It would be the Government of Tibet's goal to transform Tibet into our planet's largest natural reserve.

The Chinese Government should cease its human rights violations in Tibet and abandon its policy of transferring Chinese to Tibet.

I am aware that many Tibetans will be disappointed by the moderate stand they represent. I would like to emphasize, that whatever the outcome of the negotiations with the Chinese may be, the Tibetan people themselves must be the ultimate deciding authority. Therefore, any proposal will contain a comprehensive procedural plan to ascertain the wishes of the Tibetan people in a nationwide referendum.

I do not wish to take any active part in the Government of Tibet.

The Chinese leadership needs to realize that colonial rule over occupied territories is today anachronistic. A genuine union or association can only come about voluntarily, when there is satisfactory benefit to all the parties concerned. The European community is a clear example of this. On the other hand, even one country or community can break into two or more entities when there is a lack of trust or benefit, and when force is used as the principal means of rule.

We are encouraged by the keen interest being shown in our situation by a growing number of governments and political leaders, including former President Jimmy Carter of the United States. We are also encouraged by the recent changes in China which have brought about a new group of leadership, more pragmatic and liberal."

German Bundestag
June 19, 1996

What the Dalai Lama mentioned as keen interest was evident in the form of resolutions by numerous Western Parliaments. German Bundestag had passed a resolution way back in 1987 supporting Tibet. Now they buttressed it with a further move on June 19, 1996, as:

Since the October 15, 1987 resolution of the German Bundestag, which was adopted by all parliamentary groups, the human rights situation in Tibet has not improved, but rather deteriorated.

This is the chief finding of the Foreign Affairs Committee's hearing on Tibet, on June 19, 1995.

Starting with the inhuman military action since the invasion by China in 1950, the violent suppression of Tibet and her aspirations for political, ethnic, cultural and religious self-determination has continued to this day. China's continued policy of repression in Tibet has led to severe human rights violations and destruction of the environment, as well as large-scale economic, social, legal and political discrimination against the Tibetan people and, in the final analysis, the sinification of Tibet. The denial of educational opportunities to Tibetans is one point of this fact.

One example of encroachment on the religious life of Tibetans is the kidnapping of the boy who was nominated by the Dalai Lama as the reincarnation of the Panchen Lama as well as the investiture of a second Panchen Lama by the Chinese authorities.

For years now the Dalai Lama has been attempting to bring about peaceful discussions with the Chinese Government.

The German Bundestag: passed the following resolution:

1. Considering that during its entire history, Tibet has preserved its own ethnic, cultural and religious identity,
2. Expressing its deep concern that this authentic identity is The members of Parliament (22 names from the CDU/CSU, SPD, Greens and FDP) propose a motion to improve the human rights situation in Tibet threatened with destruction by China's brute force of arms since 1950,
3. Considering that during the hearing of the German Bundestag on June 19, 1995 the status of Tibet under international law remained a controversial issue among experts,
4. Taking into consideration that it is the policy of the Federal Republic of Germany to globally support the realization of the right to self-determination, and in view of the historical-legal status of Tibet, her claim to autonomy is obvious,
5. Also taking into consideration that it must be the policy of the Federal Republic of Germany not to tolerate illegal use of violence and major violations of human rights, whereas violation of human rights in Tibet continues unabatedly,
6. deeply worried about reports according to which a six-year-old Tibetan boy, Gedhun Choekyi Nyima, as well as his parents were abducted by the Chinese authorities immediately after the Dalai Lama recognized him to be the latest reincarnation of the second religious leader of Tibet, the Panchen Lama, who had passed away in 1989,
    1. Condemns the policies of the Chinese authorities, which particularly in Tibet result in the destruction of the people's identity, brought about especially by the transfer and resettlement of Chinese in large numbers, forced sterilization of women and forced abortion, political and religious

persecution, as well as the subjection of the country to a Chinese-controlled administration;

2. Therefore, calls on the Federal Government to use increased means and ensure that: the government of the People's Republic of China respects the globally-recognized human rights and stops violation of human rights against Tibetans, the Chinese authorities immediately release Gedhun Choekyi Nyima and his family and allow them to return to their village,

the Chinese government rescind all policies which aim at the destruction of the Tibetan culture, as for example, the organized settlement of Chinese in large numbers in order to restrain the Tibetan population and the persecution of representatives of the Tibetan culture, the government of the People's Republic of China responds positively to the efforts of the Dalai Lama and the Tibetan Government in Exile to initiate a constructive dialogue and enter into negotiations for granting more rights to the Tibetan people, the economic, social, legal and political discriminations against the Tibetan people be abolished, all political prisoners in Tibet be released, the voluntary return of Tibetans living abroad becomes possible, also in future the human rights situation in Tibet be an issue of special attention and critical discussion at the meeting of the UN Human Rights Commission, the development, coordination and resources used in Tibet benefit Tibetans and that the Tibetan population gains access to adequate educational opportunities and facilities, the environmental destruction in Tibet ends, that more attention be paid to the desire of the Tibetan people to preserve their culture and religion, and that the sphere of activity be ascertained where the German people and the Federal Government could give assistance, in consultation with the Refugee Commissioner of the United Nations all possible means of aid be worked out that is feasible, particularly to the preservation of the cultural identity of Tibetan refugees, an effective contribution be made towards the professional training of Tibetan junior specialists, especially by granting an adequate number of scholarship at German educational and professional institutions, the above-mentioned principles and measures also find recognition and implementation within the European Community.

European Parliament
March 13, 1997

The European Parliament, having regard to its previous resolutions on Tibet,

Whereas the Chinese authorities continue their repression in occupied Tibet,

Whereas His Holiness the Dalai Lama proposes to start negotiations on the future of Tibet between the Chinese Government and the Tibetan Government in exile, notably on autonomy and self-government for the Tibetan people,

Whereas the three UN General Assembly resolutions passed in 1959, 1961 and 1965 acknowledged Tibet's right to self-determination, reiterates its condemnation of the continuing human rights violations by the Chinese authorities in Tibet;

Supports the Dalai Lama's proposal on negotiations on the future of Tibet and invites the Chinese Government to react in an official and positive way to this proposal;

Asks the Council, the Member States and the Commission to do everything possible in the framework of the relations between the Union and the Republic of China and the United Nations in order to bring the two sides together with a view to reaching an agreement which satisfies the legitimate requests of the Tibetan people;

Calls on the governments of the Member States to have the question of Tibet's occupation and decolonization placed on the agenda of the United Nations General Assembly;

Instruct its President to forward this resolution to the Council, the Commission, the governments of the Member States, the Government of the People's Republic of China, H.H. the Dalai Lama, the Tibetan Government in exile and the United Nations.

Index